D0952143

Our Daily Bread

DEVOTIONAL COLLECTION

DISCOVERY HOUSE
PUBLISHERS®

Feeding the Soul with the Word of God

Discovery House Publishers is affiliated with RBC Ministries,
Grand Rapids, Michigan.

Requests for permission to quote from this book should be directed to:
Permissions Department, Discovery House Publishers,
P.O. Box 3566, Grand Rapids, MI 49501,
or contact us by e-mail at permissionsdept@dhp.org

ISBN: 978-1-57293-570-9

Printed in Italy

Third printing September 2012

Quiet Time with God

Keeping a daily appointment with God is a vital part of the Christian life. The more time we spend with God—reading His Word, conversing with Him in prayer, meditating on thoughts from His Word—the better we get to know Him and the more our lives begin to reflect His image and His truth. This year's worth of daily readings selected from the popular *Our Daily Bread* devotional encourages this daily discipline with short devotional readings for each day of the year.

Each *Our Daily Bread* reading is based on a Scripture passage and developed around a relevant story or illustration that helps to illuminate the truth of God's Word.

> Many followers of Christ find that a daily time of Bible reading and prayer is essential in their walk of faith. This "quiet time" is a disconnection from external distractions in order to connect with God. The "green pastures" and "still waters" of Psalm 23:2 are more than an idyllic country scene. They speak of our communion with God whereby He restores our souls and leads us in His paths (v. 3). —David C. McCasland

We hope that this yearly devotional will encourage you to keep those daily appointments. And may it give you spiritual guidance along your way as it helps to make the wisdom of the Bible understandable and accessible.

Eat Fast, Pay Less

READ: Psalm 63:1–8

My soul thirsts for You; my flesh longs for You. —PSALM 63:1

A hotel in Singapore introduced an express buffet—eat all you can in thirty minutes and pay just half the price! After that experience, one diner reported: "I lost my decorum, stuffing my mouth with yet more food. I lost my civility . . . and I lost my appetite for the rest of the day, so severe was my heartburn."

Sometimes I think in our devotional reading we treat God's Word like an express buffet. We wolf it down as fast as we can and wonder why we haven't learned very much. Like physical food, spiritual food needs chewing! For those of us who have been Christians for a long time, we may have a tendency to speed-read through the passages we've read many times before. But in doing so, we miss what God is meaning to show us. One sure sign of this is when we learn nothing new from that passage.

David's desire was right when he wrote in Psalm 119:15, "I will meditate on Your precepts, and contemplate Your ways." That's the way to treat God's Word—to take time to mull it over.

Let's not come to the Bible as if we were going to an express buffet. Only by meditating on God's Word will we get the most value for our spiritual well-being.   —CPH

Spending time in meditation,
Hiding Scripture in our heart,
Works in us a transformation
So from sin we can depart. —Sper

Reading the Bible without reflecting is like eating without chewing.

Trouble

READ: 1 Peter 4:12–19

Beloved, do not think it strange concerning the
fiery trial which is to try you. —1 PETER 4:12

Does it surprise you that trouble is a part of life? Probably not. We all know trouble close-up and personal—bad health, empty bank account, blighted love, grief, loss of job, and the list goes on.

It shouldn't surprise us, therefore, that God permits the added trials of being ridiculed and hated because we follow Christ (1 Peter 4:12). But trouble, whether it is common to man or unique to Christians, can reveal to us the moral fiber of our soul.

I have never seen a golf course without hazards. They are part of the game. Golfers speak of the courses with the most hazards as the most challenging, and they will travel a long way to test their skill against the most demanding eighteen holes.

Oliver Wendell Holmes said, "If I had a formula for bypassing trouble, I wouldn't pass it around. I wouldn't be doing anyone a favor. Trouble creates a capacity to handle it . . . Meet it as a friend, for you'll see a lot of it and you had better be on speaking terms with it."

Let's not think it strange when trouble comes, for God is using it to test the stamina of our souls. The best way to handle trouble is to commit our "souls to Him in doing good, as to a faithful Creator" (v. 19). —DD

The troubles that we face each day
Reveal how much we need the Lord;
They test our faith and strength of will
And help us then to trust God's Word. —D. DeHaan

Great triumphs are born out of great troubles.

An Overcoming Faith

READ: 1 Samuel 1:1–18

I cried to the Lord with my voice, and He heard me from His holy hill. —PSALM 3:4

Few things disable new workers on a job like criticism from veterans. Good hiring managers protect new employees by surrounding them with mentors willing to shield them from unnecessary barbs.

Hannah is a mentor to us in dealing with criticism and deep desires of the heart (1 Samuel 1:1–18). Surrounded by a husband who didn't understand, a taunting peer, and an overly judgmental clergyman, Hannah found a way through the fog by confiding in God (v. 10). While we now know God answered the prayer of Hannah's heart by giving her a child, we don't know for sure if Eli's blessing was a wish or a promise from God (v. 17). I think her no-longer-sad face came most of all because she gained peace from confiding in Him.

We were created to be in relationship with God; and when we take that relationship to an intimate level, it bonds us not only to His presence but also to His strength. Prayers that express our hurts and emotions are most assuredly welcomed by God because they demonstrate our trust in Him. We will often find perspective, and nearly always come away comforted, knowing we've entrusted the things that are troubling us—whether criticism or deep desires—to the One who is best able to sort through them.   —RK

> *The kindest Friend I've ever had*
> *Is One I cannot see,*
> *Yet One in whom I can confide,*
> *Who loves and blesses me.* —Shuler

In prayer, it's better to have a heart without words than words without heart.

A Lover of God

READ: Matthew 22:34–40

You shall love the Lord your God with all your heart, with all your soul, and with all your mind. —MATTHEW 22:37

In a brief biography of St. Francis of Assisi, G. K. Chesterton begins with a glimpse into the heart of this unique and compassionate man born in the 12th century. Chesterton writes: "As St. Francis did not love humanity but men, so he did not love Christianity but Christ . . . The reader cannot even begin to see the sense of a story that may well seem to him a very wild one, until he understands that to this great mystic his religion was not a thing like a theory but a thing like a love-affair."

When Jesus was asked to name the greatest command in the Law, He replied, "You shall love the Lord your God with all your heart, with all your soul, and with all your mind. This is the first and great commandment" (Matthew 22:37–38). The questioner wanted to test Jesus, but the Lord answered him with the key element in pleasing God. First and foremost, our relationship with Him is a matter of the heart.

If we see God as a taskmaster and consider obedience to Him as a burden, then we have joined those of whom the Lord said, "I have this against you, that you have left your first love" (Revelation 2:4).

The way of joy is to love the Lord with all our heart, soul, and mind.

—DM

Oh, help me, Lord, to take by grace divine
Yet more and more of that great love of Thine;
That day by day my heart may give to Thee
A deeper love, and grow more constantly. —Mountain

Put Christ first and you'll find a joy that lasts.

Lion of Judah

READ: Isaiah 31:1–5

Do not weep. Behold, the Lion of the tribe of Judah,
the Root of David, has prevailed. —REVELATION 5:5

The lounging lions in Kenya's Masai Mara game reserve looked harmless. They rolled on their backs in low-lying bushes. They rubbed their faces on branches as if trying to comb their magnificent manes. They drank leisurely from a stream. They strode slowly across dry, scrubby terrain as if they had all the time in the world. The only time I saw their teeth was when one of them yawned.

Their serene appearance is deceiving, however. The reason they can be so relaxed is that they have nothing to fear—no shortage of food and no natural predators. The lions look lazy and listless, but they are the strongest and fiercest of all. One roar sends all other animals running for their lives.

Sometimes it seems as if God is lounging. When we don't see Him at work, we conclude that He's not doing anything. We hear people mock God and deny His existence, and we anxiously wonder why He doesn't defend himself. But God "will not be afraid of their voice nor be disturbed by their noise" (Isaiah 31:4). He has nothing to fear. One roar from Him, and His detractors will scatter like rodents.

If you wonder why God isn't anxious when you are, it's because He has everything under control. He knows that Jesus, the Lion of Judah, will triumph. —JAL

> *When fear and worry test your faith*
> *And anxious thoughts assail,*
> *Remember God is in control*
> *And He will never fail.* —Sper

Because God is in control, we have nothing to fear.

Get Involved

READ: John 4:7–26

But [Jesus] needed to go through Samaria. —John 4:4

Norena's South Florida home was severely damaged during Hurricane Andrew in 1992. She received an insurance settlement, and the repair work began. But the contractors left when the money ran out, leaving an unfinished home with no electricity. For fifteen years, Norena got by with a tiny refrigerator and a few lamps connected to extension cords. Surprisingly, her neighbors didn't seem to notice her dilemma. Then, acting on a tip, the mayor got involved and contacted an electrical contractor who restored power to her house within a few hours.

When Jesus encountered the Samaritan woman at the well, He got involved in her life and talked to her about her need for spiritual power (John 4). He established common ground with her (water, v. 7) and piqued her spiritual interest and curiosity (vv. 9–14). He was gracious and sensitive as He confronted her sin (vv. 16–19) and kept the conversation centered on the main issue (vv. 21–24). Then He confronted her directly with who He was as Messiah (v. 26). As a result, she and many other Samaritans believed in Him (vv. 39–42).

Let's get involved in the lives of others and tell them about Jesus. He is the only source of spiritual power and satisfies our deepest longings.
—MW

Help me to see the tragic plight
Of souls far off in sin;
Help me to love, to pray, and go
To bring the wandering in. —Harrison

A faith worth having is a faith worth sharing.

Truly Amazing

READ: Romans 5:6–11

Behold what manner of love the Father has bestowed on us,
that we should be called children of God! —1 JOHN 3:1

I read these words on a young woman's personal Web site: "I just want to be loved—and he has to be amazing!" Isn't that what we all want—to be loved, to feel cared for by someone? And so much the better if he or she is amazing!

The one who fits that description most fully is Jesus Christ. In a display of unprecedented love, He left His Father in heaven and came to earth as the baby we celebrate at Christmas (Luke 2). Then, after living a perfect life, He gave His life as an offering to God on the cross in our behalf (John 19:17–30). He took our place because we needed to be rescued from our sin and its death penalty. "While we were still sinners, Christ died for us" (Romans 5:8). Then three days later, the Father raised Jesus to life again (Matthew 28:1–8).

When we repent and receive Jesus' gift of amazing love, He becomes our Savior (John 1:12; Romans 5:9), Lord (John 13:14), Teacher (Matthew 23:8), and Friend (John 15:14). "Behold what manner of love the Father has bestowed on us, that we should be called children of God!" (1 John 3:1).

Looking for someone to love you? Jesus loves us so much more than anyone else possibly could. And He is truly amazing! —AC

Amazing thought! that God in flesh
Would take my place and bear my sin;
That I, a guilty, death-doomed soul,
Eternal life might win! —Anonymous

The wonder of it all—just to think that Jesus loves me.

A Clear Conscience

READ: 1 John 1

I myself always strive to have a conscience without offense toward God and men. —ACTS 24:16

After Ffyona Campbell became famous as the first woman to walk around the world, her joy was short-lived. Despite the adulation she received, something troubled her. Guilt overtook her and pushed her to the brink of a nervous breakdown.

What was bothering her? "I shouldn't be remembered as the first woman to walk around the world," she finally admitted. "I cheated." During her worldwide trek, she broke the guidelines of the Guinness World Records by riding in a truck part of the way. To clear her conscience, she called her sponsor and confessed her deception.

God has given each of us a conscience that brings guilt when we do wrong. In Romans, Paul describes our conscience as "accusing or else excusing [us]" (2:15). For the obedient follower of Christ, care of the conscience is an important way of maintaining a moral compass despite moral imperfection. Confessing sin, turning from it, and making restitution should be a way of life (1 John 1:9; Leviticus 6:2–5).

Paul modeled a well-maintained conscience, saying, "I strive always to keep my conscience clear before God and man" (Acts 24:16 NIV). Through confession and repentance, he kept short accounts with God. Is sin bothering you? Follow Paul's example. Strive for a clear conscience. —DF

> *There is a treasure you can own*
> *That's greater than a crown or throne:*
> *This treasure is a conscience clear*
> *That brings the sweetest peace and cheer.* —Isenhour

If God's Word guides your conscience, let your conscience be your guide.

The Eye That Never Sleeps

READ: Psalm 121

In my distress I cried to the Lord, and He heard me. —PSALM 120:1

Detective Allan Pinkerton became famous in the mid-1800s by solving a series of train robberies and foiling a plot to assassinate Abraham Lincoln as he traveled to his first inauguration. As one of the first agencies of its kind in the US, the Pinkerton National Detective Agency gained even more prominence because of its logo of a wide-open eye with the caption, "We Never Sleep."

There is no better feeling than knowing you are protected and secure. You feel peaceful when the doors are locked and all is quiet as you drift off to sleep at night. You feel safe. But many lie awake in their beds with fearful thoughts of the present or dread of the future. Some are afraid of commotion outside or of a spouse who has been violent. Some cannot rest because of worry over a rebellious child. Others are anxiously listening to make sure a seriously ill child is still breathing.

These are the times when our loving God encourages us to cry out to Him, to the One who will neither "slumber nor sleep" (Psalm 121:4). Psalm 34:15 reminds us that "the eyes of the Lord are on the righteous, and His ears are open to their cry."

Pinkerton may have been the original "private eye," but the One who really has the eye that never sleeps is listening to the cries of "the righteous" (Psalm 34:17).   —CHK

Before you sleep, just gently lay
Every troubled thought away;
Drop your burden and your care
In the quiet arms of prayer. —Anonymous

We can sleep in peace when we remember that God is awake.

Called From

READ: Genesis 12:1–9

The Lord had said to Abram, "Get out of your country,
from your family and from your father's house,
to a land that I will show you." —GENESIS 12:1

One of the smartest people I know is a college friend who became a Christian while studying at a state university. He graduated with honors and went on to study at a respected seminary. He served a small church as pastor for several years and then accepted a call to another small church far from family and friends. After twelve years at that church, he sensed that the congregation needed new leadership, so he stepped down. He hadn't been offered a job at a bigger church or a teaching position at a college or seminary. In fact, he didn't even have another job. He just knew that God was leading him in a different direction, so he followed.

When we discussed it, my friend said, "A lot of people talk about being called to something, but I don't hear much about being called from something."

In many ways, my friend's obedience was like that of Israel's patriarch Abraham, who went out, not knowing where God was leading (Hebrews 11:8–10). Difficulties like famine (Genesis 12:10), fear (vv. 11–20), and family disputes (13:8) gave reason for doubt, but Abraham persevered and because of his faith God counted him as righteous (Galatians 3:6).

A life of obedience may not be easy, but it will be blessed (Luke 11:28). —JAL

> *As Abraham went out,*
> *Not knowing where he was going;*
> *Now, Lord, keep me from doubt,*
> *To go the way you are showing.* —Hess

You don't need to know where you're going if you know God is leading.

Why Not Now?

READ: John 13:33–38

*David, after he had served his own
generation . . . fell asleep.* —ACTS 13:36

I have a dear friend who served as a missionary in Suriname for many years, but in his final years he was stricken with an illness that paralyzed him. At times he wondered why God allowed him to linger. He longed to depart and to be with his Lord.

Perhaps life is very hard for you or a loved one, and you are wondering why God has allowed you or your loved one to linger. When Jesus said He was going to heaven, Peter asked, "Lord, why can I not follow You now?" (John 13:37). You, like Peter, may wonder why entry into heaven has been postponed: "Why not now?"

God has a wise and loving purpose in leaving us behind. There is work to be done in us that can only be accomplished here on earth. Our afflictions, which are for the moment, are working for us "a far more exceeding and eternal weight of glory" (2 Corinthians 4:17). And there is work to be done for others—if only to love and to pray. Our presence may also be for the purpose of giving others an opportunity to learn love and compassion.

So, though you may desire release for yourself or a loved one, to live on in the flesh can mean fruitfulness (Philippians 1:21). And there is comfort in waiting: Though heaven may be delayed, God has His reasons. No doubt about it!   —DR

Not so in haste, my heart!
Have faith in God, and wait;
Although He seems to linger long
He never comes too late. —Torrey

Our greatest comfort is to know that God is in control.

Behind the Scenes

READ: Matthew 6:1–6, 16–18

Your Father who sees in secret will reward you openly. —MATTHEW 6:6

Recently I attended a memorial service for a gifted musician whose life had touched many people. The tribute to this Christian woman included video and audio clips, photos, instrumentalists, and speakers. After everyone had left the church, I stopped to thank the technicians whose flawless work at the control board had contributed so much to this moving tribute. "No one noticed what you did," I told them. "That's the way we like it," they replied.

In Matthew 6, Jesus told His disciples to give (vv. 1–4), pray (vv. 5–6), and fast (vv. 16–18) in order to please God, not to gain praise from people. "When you pray, go into your room, and when you have shut your door, pray to your Father who is in the secret place" (v. 6). Whether giving, praying, or fasting, Jesus said, "Your Father who sees in secret will reward you openly" (vv. 4, 6, 18).

Something within us makes us want to be seen and recognized for our good deeds. While there's nothing wrong with encouragement and appreciation, a desire for praise can undermine our service because it shifts the focus from others to ourselves. When there is no public "thank you," we may feel slighted. But even when we serve God in secret, He sees it all. —DM

The service that we do for God
May go unpraised by men;
But when we stand before the Lord,
He will reward us then. —Sper

It is better to earn recognition without getting
it than to get recognition without earning it.

A Book for Pilgrims

READ: Leviticus 18:1–5

You shall observe My judgments and keep My ordinances, to walk in them: I am the Lord your God. —LEVITICUS 18:4

Many people who determine to read the Bible through in a year get bogged down and quit about halfway through Leviticus. After the fascinating narrative in Genesis and the dramatic deliverance in Exodus, Leviticus seems to unfold with all the excitement of a technical manual for ancient clergymen. But don't let the priestly details fool you. This is a textbook for pilgrims, a life-guide for people who have been delivered from their past and are on their way toward a glorious, God-planned future.

Near the center of the book we find God's charge to His people. He told them they must not imitate the people of Egypt where they had been, nor the practices of those in Canaan where they were going. In Leviticus 18:4, He said to them, "You shall observe My judgments and keep My ordinances, to walk in them: I am the Lord your God."

Leviticus is also filled with word pictures of God's salvation, painted almost 1,500 years before Jesus was born. Every offering and sacrifice points to the cross of Christ, "the Lamb of God who takes away the sin of the world" (John 1:29).

On your journey from Genesis to Revelation, don't let Leviticus stop you. Instead, let it be a wonderful bridge that takes you from the sacrifices to the Savior. —DM

The offerings of animals,
Were made in days of old,
To point us to the Lamb of God,
His sacrifice foretold. —Fitzhugh

The Old Testament altar points to the New Testament cross.

Call It Good?

READ: Psalm 13

I have trusted in Your mercy. —PSALM 13:5

Can we really know whether to label life's circumstances as good or bad? For instance, your car breaks down right before you are to take a family road trip. But when you take the car to the shop, the mechanic says, "Good thing you didn't take this out on the road. It could have caught fire." Is that bad because of the inconvenience, or good because of God's protection?

Or perhaps your child decides to pursue interests that aren't all that interesting to you. You wanted her to play basketball and run track in high school. But she wanted to sing and play the oboe. You feel frustrated, but she excels and ends up with a music scholarship. Is that bad because your dreams weren't fulfilled, or good because God directed her in ways you could not have predicted?

Sometimes it's hard to see how God is working. His mysteries don't always reveal their secrets to us, and our journey is often redirected by uncontrollable detours. Perhaps God is showing us a better route.

To make sure we benefit from what might seem bad, we must recognize and trust God's "unfailing love" (Psalm 13:5 NIV). In the end, we'll be able to say, "I will sing to the Lord, for he has been good to me" (v. 6 NIV). —DB

> *The circumstances in our lives*
> *Seem random and unplanned;*
> *But someday we will surely see*
> *The order of God's hand. —Sper*

We may not be able to control events, but
we can control our attitude toward them.

Freedom at Alcatraz

READ: Philemon 1:4–16

I appeal to you for my son Onesimus, whom I have begotten while in my chains. —PHILEMON 1:10

A tour of the federal prison on Alcatraz Island in San Francisco Bay left me with some unforgettable images. As our tour boat pulled into the dock, I could see why this now-closed maximum-security federal prison was once known as "The Rock."

Later, inside the legendary Big House, I stared at shafts of light coming through heavily barred windows. Then I saw row after row of cagelike cells that housed well-known inmates such as Al Capone and Robert Stroud, the "Birdman of Alcatraz."

But another image made a deeper impression. Stepping into an empty cell, I saw the name "Jesus" scrawled on a wall. In another, a Bible lay on a shelf. Together they quietly spoke of the greatest of all freedoms.

Paul knew such liberty while waiting to be executed. Regarding himself as a "prisoner of Christ," he used his incarceration to help other inmates discover what it means to be an eternally forgiven, dearly loved member of God's family (Philemon 1:10).

Barred windows and doors represent one kind of confinement. Physical paralysis, inescapable poverty, and prolonged unemployment are others. Perhaps you endure another. None are to be desired—yet who would trade "imprisonment" with Christ for life "on the outside" without Him? —MD

> *My heart and soul imprisoned lay,*
> *Not knowing Christ the Lord;*
> *But since the day He set me free,*
> *We live in one accord.* —Hess

To be under Christ's control is to have true freedom.

A Child's Potential

READ: Proverbs 22:1–6

Train up a child in the way he should go, and when he is old he will not depart from it. —PROVERBS 22:6

L ouis Armstrong was well known for his smiling face, raspy voice, white handkerchief, and virtuoso trumpet playing. Yet his childhood was one of want and pain. He was abandoned by his father as an infant and sent to reform school when he was only twelve. Surprisingly, this became a positive turning point.

Music professor Peter Davis regularly visited the school and provided musical training for the boys. Soon Louis excelled on the cornet and became the leader of the boys' band. His life trajectory seemed to have been reset to become a world-famous trumpet player and entertainer.

Louis's story can be an example for Christian parents. The proverb "Train up a child in the way he should go, and when he is old he will not depart from it" can apply to more than the spiritual and moral aspects of our children's lives. We should also realize that a child's giftedness will often determine his or her area of interest. In the case of Louis, a little training in music resulted in a virtuoso trumpet player.

As we lovingly provide our children with godly instruction from God's Word, we should encourage them in their interests and giftedness so that they might become all that God has planned for them to be.
—DF

Our children are a gift from God
On loan from heaven above,
To train and nourish in the Lord,
And guide them with His love. —Sper

Save a child, save a life.

Driving in the Dark

READ: Psalm 119:105—112

*Your Word is a lamp to my feet and
a light to my path.* —PSALM 119:105

I've always thought that I could get through just about anything if the Lord would tell me what the outcome will be. I believe that "all things work together for good" in the end (Romans 8:28), but I'd do a lot better in dark times if I knew exactly what the "good" will look like.

But God usually doesn't show us where He is taking us. He just asks us to trust Him. It's like driving a car at night. Our headlights never shine all the way to our destination; they illuminate only about 160 feet ahead. But that doesn't deter us from moving forward. We trust our headlights. All we really need is enough light to keep moving forward.

God's Word is like headlights in dark times. It is full of promises we need to keep us from driving our lives into the ditch of bitterness and despair. His Word promises that He will never leave us nor forsake us (Hebrews 13:5). His Word assures us that He knows the plans He has for us, plans for wholeness and not for evil, to give us "a future and a hope" (Jeremiah 29:11). And He tells us that our trials are there to make us better, not bitter (James 1:2–4).

So the next time you feel as if you're driving in the dark, remember to trust your headlights—God's Word will light your way.   —JS

*The Word of God provides the light
We need to see the way;
It shows us what we need to know
So we won't go astray.* —Sper

You won't stumble in the dark if you walk in the light of God's Word.

An Open Book

READ: Jeremiah 31:31–34

You are an epistle of Christ. —2 CORINTHIANS 3:3

Because I'm a writer, occasionally a friend will say to me, "I want to write a book someday."

"That's a worthy goal," I reply, "and I hope you do write a book. But it's better to be one than to write one."

I'm thinking of the apostle Paul's words: "Clearly you are an epistle of Christ . . . written not with ink but by the Spirit of the living God, not on tablets of stone but on tablets of flesh, that is, of the heart" (2 Corinthians 3:3).

In his book *The Practice of Piety*, Lewis Bayly, chaplain to England's King James I, said that "one who hopes to effect any good by his writings" will find that he will "instruct very few . . . The most powerful means, therefore, of promoting what is good is by example . . . One man in a thousand can write a book to instruct his neighbors . . . But every man can be a pattern of living excellence to those around him."

The work that Christ is doing in believers can result in an influence far greater than any book they might write. Through God's Word, written "on their hearts" (Jeremiah 31:33), the Lord is displaying His love and goodness for all to see.

You may never write a book, but by living for God you will be one! You will be an open book, an "epistle of Christ" for all to read. —DR

Oh, we would write our record plain
And come in time to see
Our unsaved neighbors won to Christ
While reading you and me. —Anonymous

If someone were to read your life like a book,
would they find Jesus in its pages?

When Someone Falls

READ: 1 Corinthians 10:1–13

Therefore let him who thinks he stands take heed lest he fall. —1 CORINTHIANS 10:12

It has become so commonplace to hear of the misconduct of a respected public figure that even though we may be deeply disappointed, we are hardly surprised. But how should we respond to the news of a moral failure, whether by a prominent person or a friend? We might begin by looking at ourselves. A century ago, Oswald Chambers told his students at the Bible Training College in London, "Always remain alert to the fact that where one man has gone back is exactly where anyone may go back . . . Unguarded strength is double weakness."

Chambers' words echo Paul's warning to be aware of our own vulnerability when we see the sins of others. After reviewing the disobedience of the Israelites in the wilderness, Paul urged his readers to learn from those sins so they wouldn't repeat them (1 Corinthians 10:1–11). He focused not on past failings but on present pride when he wrote, "Let him who thinks he stands take heed lest he fall" (v. 12).

The head shaken in reproach is a common response to public sin. More helpful is the head that nods, "Yes, I am capable of that," then bows in prayer for the one who has fallen and the one who thinks he stands. —DM

Blessed Savior, make me humble,
Take away my sinful pride;
In myself I'm sure to stumble,
Help me stay close by your side. —D. DeHaan

Pride goes before destruction, and a haughty
spirit before a fall. —Proverbs 16:18

Fear and Love

READ: Deuteronomy 10:12–17

What does the Lord your God require of you, but to fear [Him] . . . and to love Him. —DEUTERONOMY 10:12

Someone shared with me her observation about two bosses. One is loved but not feared by his subordinates. Because they love their boss but don't respect his authority, they don't follow his guidelines. The other boss is both feared and loved by those who serve under him, and their good behavior shows it.

The Lord desires that His people both fear and love Him too. Today's Bible passage, Deuteronomy 10, says that keeping God's guidelines involves both. In verse 12, we are told "to fear the Lord your God" and "to love Him."

To "fear" the Lord God is to give Him the highest respect. For the believer, it is not a matter of feeling intimidated by Him or His character. But out of respect for His person and authority, we walk in all His ways and keep His commandments. Out of "love" we serve Him with all our heart and with all our soul—rather than merely out of duty (v. 12).

Love flows out of our deep gratitude for His love for us, rather than out of our likes and dislikes. "We love Him because He first loved us" (1 John 4:19). Our fear and love for God enable us to walk willingly in obedience to God's law. —AL

Lord, you are holy and your thoughts are much higher than mine. I bow before you. Thank you for salvation in Jesus. I love you and want to obey you with all of my heart, soul, mind, and strength. Amen.

If we fear and love God, we will obey Him.

Nature Abhors a Vacuum

READ: Ephesians 3:14–21

Be filled with all the fullness of God. —EPHESIANS 3:19

According to the ancient philosopher Aristotle, "Nature abhors a vacuum." Aristotle based his conclusion on the observation that nature requires every space to be filled with something, even if that something is colorless, odorless air.

The same principle is at work in our spiritual lives. When the Holy Spirit begins to convict us of sin, the idea of starting a self-improvement plan immediately comes to mind. We put forth our best effort to defeat our worst habits. But every attempt to get rid of unclean thoughts, attitudes, and desires is destined to fail because getting rid of one creates a vacuum in our souls. As soon as we empty ourselves of one vice, others move in to take its place, and we end up just as bad or worse than when we started.

Thinking about vacuums helps us to understand the importance of what Paul was saying to the Ephesians when he prayed that Christ would dwell in their hearts through faith and that they would "know the love of Christ . . . that [they] may be filled with all the fullness of God" (3:19).

The only permanent solution to the problem of sin in our lives is to replace it with the love of Jesus, which fills the vacuum. The more we are filled with His love, the less room there is for any evil thing. —JAL

> *Father, thank you for your Spirit*
> *Fill us with His love and power;*
> *Change us into Christ's own image*
> *Day by day and hour by hour.* —*Anonymous*

We don't need to put our house in order before Jesus
comes in; He puts it in order after we let Him in.

The Outcast

READ: James 2:1–9

If you show partiality, you commit sin. —JAMES 2:9

His face was grimy, his hair long and dirty. Beer stained his clothing and perfumed the air around him. When he stepped into the church building, the Sunday worshipers ignored him. They were stunned when the man approached the pulpit, took off his wig, and began preaching. That's when they realized he was their pastor.

I don't know about you, but I tend to be friendly and shake hands with the people I know and those who present themselves well. James issued a serious warning for people like me. He said, "If you show partiality, you commit sin" (2:9). Favoritism based on appearance or economic status has no place in God's family. In fact, it means we have "become judges with evil thoughts" (v. 4).

Fortunately, we can guard against preferential treatment by loving our neighbor as ourselves—no matter who our neighbor may be. Reaching out to the homeless man, the hungry woman, or the heartbroken teen means we "fulfill the royal law according to the Scripture" (v. 8).

In a world that keeps the outcast at arm's length, let's show the love of Christ and embrace the one who needs our care the most.   —JBS

Forgive me, Lord, for prejudice—
Remove its subtle lie;
Oh, fill my heart with your great love
That sent your Son to die. —D. DeHaan

True Christian love helps those who can't return the favor.

God Is at Work

READ: Exodus 14:26–15:2

He is my God, and I will praise Him. —Exodus 15:2

Jack and Trisha were driving to the hospital late one night for the birth of their second child when the unexpected happened. Trisha began to deliver the baby! Jack called 911 and Cherie White, an emergency dispatcher, was able to talk Jack through the delivery. But the baby wouldn't breathe. So Cherie then instructed Jack how to give emergency breathing, which he had to do for six anxious minutes. Finally the newborn took a breath and cried. When asked later how they all got through the ordeal and remained calm, Cherie responded, "I'm glad God works midnights!"

I love to hear media reports in which God gets the glory He deserves for something good that has happened. In the Bible reading for today, it's obvious that God should get the credit for parting the Red Sea to help His people escape from Pharaoh, even though Moses was the one who "stretched out his hand over the sea" (Exodus 14:26–27). All the Israelites and Moses gathered together and sang the Lord's praises: "Who is like You, O Lord, among the gods? Who is like You, glorious in holiness, fearful in praises, doing wonders?" (15:11).

When something good happens, the Lord deserves the credit, for He is the source of all that is good. Give Him the glory. Aren't you glad He works midnights? —AC

What may seem like coincidence
As we live out our story
Is God at work behind the scenes—
So give Him all the glory. —Sper

Seeing God at work puts a song in our heart.

Still True Today

READ: Acts 17:16–31

While Paul waited for them at Athens, his spirit was provoked within him when he saw that the city was given over to idols. —ACTS 17:16

The Chester Beatty Library in Dublin, Ireland, has an extensive collection of ancient Bible fragments dating back to the second century AD. One fragment on display is a piece of Acts 17:16.

The message that ancient fragment displays, however, is as contemporary as today's newspaper. It reads, "While Paul waited for them at Athens, his spirit was provoked within him when he saw that the city was given over to idols." Paul was angered by the proliferation of idols in ancient Athens, and I am convinced he would be upset with us today.

Some idols that we see in today's world are different than the ones in Paul's day. Whether it's wealth, fame, power, athletes, entertainers, or politicians, contemporary idols abound. As always, our spiritual enemy, Satan, seeks to lure us away from the Savior to the false worship of idols. Christians are not immune, and thus we must guard our hearts against self-righteous anger toward unbelievers who seem to worship everything but God.

We must also be drawn by Christ's love to reach out to those who don't know Him. Then, like the believers at Thessalonica, they may turn "to God from idols to serve the living and true God" (1 Thessalonians 1:9). —BC

> *The dearest idol I have known,*
> *Whate'er that idol be,*
> *Help me to tear it from Thy throne*
> *And worship only Thee.* —Cowper

An idol is anything that takes God's rightful place.

No More Struggles

READ: Revelation 21:1–4

God will wipe away every tear from their eyes. —REVELATION 21:4

Fay Weldon went through what she thought was a near-death experience in 2006 when an allergic reaction stopped her heart. She retold her experience to Elizabeth Grice of the *London Daily Telegraph*. She said that a "terrible creature" tried to pull her through pearly gates, while doctors tried to pull her back. Later, she said, "If that was dying, I don't want to do it again." It's "just more of the same. More struggle."

Often the process of dying is a struggle. But death itself need not be feared by the believer in Christ—for it will bring us to heaven. In Revelation, John gives a wonderful description of what eternity with God will be like (21:1–4). He sees the New Jerusalem coming down out of heaven. The city of Jerusalem was a physical sign of the people of God and was described as the place where God dwells (Psalm 76:2). The New Jerusalem, however, will not be made by human hands. It will be a place where God lives with His people eternally, and it will be a place of "no more"—no more pain, sorrow, and sickness.

We don't know much about eternity, but we do know that for the Christian, whatever our emotional and physical struggles are now, they will cease then. Life with God will be better by far.   —MW

> *Think of a land of no sorrow,*
> *Think of a land of no fears,*
> *Think of no death and no sickness,*
> *Think of a land of no tears.* —*Anonymous*

Heaven's delights will far outweigh earth's difficulties.

Like a Hypocrite

READ: Ephesians 2:1–10

God, who is rich in mercy, because of His great love . . .
made us alive together with Christ. —EPHESIANS 2:4–5

Ray Stedman told about a young man who had stopped attending the church Ray was pastoring. The young man said that when he was at work he would sometimes lose his temper and treat coworkers poorly. Then, when Sunday rolled around, he didn't want to go to church because he felt like a hypocrite.

Stedman told his young friend, "A hypocrite is someone who acts like something he isn't. When you come to church, you are acting like a Christian. You are not a hypocrite at church." Suddenly, the young man realized where he was being a hypocrite. He recognized that the answer was not in avoiding church but in changing the way he was at work.

The term *hypocrite* is from a Greek word that means "play-actor." It means we pretend to be something we aren't. Sometimes we forget our true identity as believers in Jesus. We forget that we are accountable to God. When we do that, we live the way we "once walked" (Ephesians 2:2) and thus are hypocrites.

Let's not let our old ways make us act like someone we're not. Instead, through God's grace, let's live in a way that shows we are "alive together with Christ" (v. 5). That's a sure cure for hypocrisy.   —DB

Consistency! How much we need
To walk a measured pace,
To live the life of which we speak,
Until we see Christ's face. —Anonymous

It is the inconsistent Christian who helps the devil the most.

Upside Down

READ: Matthew 5:38–48

You have heard that it was said, "You shall love your neighbor and hate your enemy." But I say to you, love your enemies. —MATTHEW 5:43–44

If you were to ask me who I am, I'd tell you that I'm a follower of Jesus. But I have to admit, at times following Him is a real challenge. He tells me to do things like rejoice when I'm persecuted (Matthew 5:11–12); to turn the other cheek (vv. 38–39); to give to someone who wants to take from me (vv. 40–42); to love my enemies, bless those who curse me, and do good to those who hate me (vv. 43–44). This kind of lifestyle seems very upside down to me.

But I've come to realize that He's not upside down—I am. We have all been born fallen and broken. Being twisted by sin, our first instincts are often wrong, which inevitably leaves a big mess.

We're like toast slathered with jelly that has fallen upside down on the kitchen floor. Left to ourselves, we can make a pretty big mess of things. Then Jesus comes along, like a divine spatula, scrapes us off the floor of our sinful ways, and turns us right side up. And as we follow His right-side-up ways, we discover that turning the other cheek keeps us from getting caught in a brawl, that it is more blessed to give than to receive, and that dying to self is life at its best.

After all, His ways are not our ways (Isaiah 55:8), and I've come to realize that His ways are always best!　　　　　　　　　　　　　—JS

When we're transformed and made brand-new
We see things differently;
What once seemed right we now abhor,
And wrong we clearly see. —Sper

What may seem upside down to us is right side up to God.

Earthquake City

READ: Acts 16:23–34

Suddenly there was a great earthquake, so that the foundations of the prison were shaken. —ACTS 16:26

In his book *A Crack in the Edge of the World,* Simon Winchester writes of the small earthquake-prone town of Parkfield, California. Seeking to attract tourists, a hotel sign reads: "Sleep Here When It Happens." A local restaurant menu features a large steak called "The Big One," and desserts are called "Aftershocks." But all humor aside, a real earthquake can be a terrifying experience. I know. I've lived through California earthquakes.

In the book of Acts, we read how God used an earthquake to open someone's heart to the gospel. Having been falsely accused, Paul and Silas found themselves in jail at Philippi. Around midnight, an earthquake rumbled through the prison, opening the doors and loosing the prisoners' chains. When the jailer learned that Paul and Silas had not tried to escape, he asked, "What must I do to be saved?" (16:30). Paul responded, "Believe on the Lord Jesus Christ, and you will be saved, you and your household" (v. 31). That night the jailer and his family believed and were baptized. And it all started with an earthquake.

Sometimes life's upsets can make people more open to the gospel. Do you know anyone who is going through a crisis? Prayerfully stay in contact with them, and be ready to share a sensitive word of witness. —DF

Lord, use us as your instruments
Of truth and love and care,
And may we bring encouragement
As your good news we share. —Sper

Many are brought to faith by trouble.

Six Words from Solomon

READ: 1 Kings 10:23; 11:1–10

Fear God and keep His commandments,
for this is man's all. —ECCLESIASTES 12:13

SMITH Magazine, an online community that "celebrates the joy of storytelling," invited readers to submit six-word memoirs that describe their lives. Thousands responded with brief biographies ranging from the lighthearted "Sweet wife, good sons—I'm rich" to the painful "Sixty. Still haven't forgiven my parents."

Based on Scripture, I tried to imagine how King Solomon might have summed up his life in six words. As a young man, he could have written: God has given me great wisdom. But in his later years, he might have said: Should have practiced what I preached.

During a reign distinguished by peace and prosperity, Solomon developed spiritual heart problems. When he was old, "his wives turned his heart after other gods; and his heart was not loyal to the Lord his God, as was the heart of his father David" (1 Kings 11:4). The result was God's displeasure and a sad end to a previously exemplary life (v. 9).

The multiple times Solomon used the word *vanity* (or *meaningless*) in Ecclesiastes may indicate his disillusionment about life. This once-wise king, who had it all, lost it all, and pondered it all, ended the book with this final conclusion: "Fear God and keep His commandments" (12:13).

Those are six words worth heeding. —DM

The pleasures of this sinful world
Are meaningless and vain;
But if we love and follow God
True purpose we will gain. —Sper

Obedience to God is the key to a life of blessing.

Looking and Learning

READ: Deuteronomy 11:18–21

Train up a child in the way he should go. —PROVERBS 22:6

As an umpire stood behind the plate at a girls' softball game, he heard a player's mother start chanting: "We want a new ump! We want a new ump!" Soon, other parents took up the chant. The ump smiled, then turned toward the crowd and yelled, "I want new parents! I want new parents!" The heckling died away.

It's important for parents to set a good example, because their children are watching them. Christian parents can encourage good habits and behavior by doing things like:

- Praying for and with them—so they learn how to talk with God. "Continue earnestly in prayer, being vigilant in it" (Colossians 4:2).
- Reading and teaching them the Bible—so they learn God's truth. "Teach [God's commands] diligently to your children . . . talk of them when you sit in your house, when you walk by the way, when you lie down, and when you rise up" (Deuteronomy 6:7).
- Telling them about Jesus—and leading them to faith in Him. "Unless one is born again, he cannot see the kingdom of God" (John 3:3).

The best way to set a good example for our children is to live out our faith in front of them. While they're looking, they're learning about what matters most. —CHK

Take stock of yourself and consider your child—
Your time and your thoughts are his due;
How would you reply to the Lord should He ask,
"What kind of parent are you?" —Anonymous

Children may not inherit their parents' talent, but they will absorb their values.

Ignoring Grace

READ: Matthew 7:13–23

Narrow is the gate and difficult is the way which leads to life, and there are few who find it. —MATTHEW 7:14

In the hectic downtown of one of Asia's great cities, I marveled at the busy sidewalks filled with people. There seemed to be no room to move in the crush of humanity, yet it also seemed that everyone was moving at top speed.

My attention was drawn to the soft, almost mournful sound of a single trumpeter playing "Amazing Grace." The crowds appeared oblivious to both the musician and the music. Still, he played—sending a musical message of the love of God out to whoever knew the song and would think about the words as he played.

I thought of this experience as a parable. The music seemed to be an invitation to the masses to follow Christ. As with the gospel message, some believe in God's amazing grace and choose the narrow way. Others ignore His grace, which is the broad way that leads to everlasting destruction. Jesus said, "Enter by the narrow gate; for wide is the gate and broad is the way that leads to destruction, and there are many who go in by it. Because narrow is the gate and difficult is the way which leads to life, and there are few who find it" (Matthew 7:13–14).

Jesus died so that "whoever calls" on His name (Romans 10:13) can find forgiveness in His grace. —BC

Amazing grace—how sweet the sound—
That saved a wretch like me!
I once was lost but now am found,
Was blind but now I see. —Newton

Christ believed is salvation received.

Counterfeits of the Heart

READ: Jeremiah 17:5–11

The heart is deceitful above all things. —JEREMIAH 17:9

True stories about deceit and deception can sound stranger than fiction. According to an AP news item, a Georgia woman was arrested after trying to pay for more than $1,500 in purchases with a million-dollar counterfeit bill. When questioned, the woman claimed to have been misled, saying that the fake money had been given to her by her ex-husband, who was a coin collector.

The size of the bill makes us question whether anyone could really have been misled into thinking it was real. But maybe that makes it a good illustration of the almost unbelievable problem of self-deception that the prophet warns us about. When Jeremiah said, "The heart is deceitful above all things, and desperately sick; who can understand it?" (17:9 ESV), he expresses a sense of amazement that is beyond our ability to grasp. Here the prophet is not saying that some of us have a problem being honest with ourselves; he is claiming that everyone does.

Thankfully, God searches our hearts and understands what we cannot see (v. 10). He gives us every reason to say, "Lord, we need your help. Please show us whether we are being honest with ourselves and you. If we aren't, help us to change and rely on you rather than on ourselves." —MD

> *Search me, O God, and know my heart today;*
> *Try me, O Savior, know my thoughts I pray.*
> *See if there be some wicked way in me;*
> *Cleanse me from every sin and set me free.* —Orr

The only way to survive in a world of deception
is by trusting the One who will never deceive us.

Defragment

READ: Psalm 55:1–8

*Cast your burden on the Lord, and
He shall sustain you.* —PSALM 55:22

Every so often, my computer becomes sluggish. Frequent use of certain programs and documents causes pieces of information to become scattered, requiring my computer to search for the pieces before I can use them. To fix it, I need to run a program that retrieves the pieces and groups them together where they are easily accessible. This process is called "defragmentation."

Like my computer, my life gets fragmented. One situation tugs on my emotions while I'm trying to concentrate on something else. Demands from every direction bombard me. I want to accomplish everything that needs to be done, but my mind won't stop and my body won't start. Soon I begin to feel weary and useless.

Recently I attended a retreat where one of the handouts included a prayer with words that expressed how I felt: "Lord, I am scattered, restless, and only half here."

King David also went through such times (Psalm 55:2). In prayer, David presented his needs to God morning, noon, and evening, confident that he would be heard (v. 17).

Prayer can help to defragment our lives. When we cast our cares on the Lord, He will show us what we need to do and what only He can do.
—JAL

*O Lord, we bring our restless hearts
To you in fervent prayer;
Now help us wait expectantly
While resting in your care.* —Sper

We need prayer the most when we have the least time to pray.

Good Wishes

READ: Philippians 1:9–18

This I pray, that your love may abound still more and more in knowledge and all discernment. —PHILIPPIANS 1:9

In Singapore, the Chinese New Year season's social and business dinners often begin with a dish consisting of salads, dressings, pickles, and raw fish. The name of the dish, Yu Sheng, is a pun that sounds like "year of prosperity." It is traditional for those present to toss the salad together. As they do, certain phrases are repeated to bring about good fortune.

Our words may express our hopes for others for the year ahead, but they can't bring about good fortune. The important issue is—what does God want to see in us in the coming year?

In his letter to the Philippians, Paul expressed his desire and prayer that their love "may abound still more and more in knowledge and all discernment" (1:9). The church had been a great tower of support for him (v. 7), yet he urged them to continue to grow to love others. Paul wasn't talking about intellectual knowledge but knowledge of God. Love for others starts with a closer relationship with Him. With a fuller knowledge of God, we can then discern between right and wrong.

Giving our best wishes to others for the coming year is fine. But our heartfelt prayer should be that we abound in love, so that we may be "filled with the fruits of righteousness . . . to the glory and praise of God" (v. 11). —CPH

Teach me Thy patience! still with Thee
In closer, dearer company,
In work that keeps faith sweet and strong,
In trust that triumphs over wrong. —Gladden

People with a heart for God have a heart for people.

When Royalty Comes to Town

READ: 1 Corinthians 6:12–20

*Your body is the temple of the Holy Spirit who is in you . . .
and you are not your own.* —1 CORINTHIANS 6:19

My friend Tim Davis tells the story of being in Trinidad as a little boy when Queen Elizabeth came to visit their town. He recalls going with his missionary parents to join hundreds of others who gathered to greet the queen. Waving his little flag, he watched as the entourage came down the street—first the soldiers, then the mounted guard, and then the limousine from which she waved to the cheering crowd. He looked on as the queen drove out of town, leaving everyone to return to life as usual. In Tim's words, "Royalty came to town and nothing changed!"

For those of us who have accepted Jesus as Savior, there was a day when royalty arrived—in our heart. As Paul put it, our body is "the temple of the Holy Spirit" (1 Corinthians 6:19), a reality that has huge ramifications. His residence in our life is intended to transform us to live in a way that brings glory to Him. Our relationships, the way we serve our employer, how we use our money, how we treat our enemies, and everything else in our lives should reflect the wonderful reality that royalty lives within.

Has anything changed since King Jesus came into your heart? Does your world notice, or do they think He was just passing through? —JS

> *By this shall every person know
> That we serve God above:
> His Spirit dwells within our hearts
> And fills us with His love.* —D. DeHaan

If Jesus has taken up residence in us, the world should notice a lasting change.

Fault Line

READ: Matthew 7:24–27

Whoever hears these sayings of Mine, and does them, I will liken him to a wise man who built his house on the rock. —MATTHEW 7:24

In 1931, the city of Hayward, California, built its first permanent city hall building. Costing $100,000 at the time, the structure with its square Corinthian columns and Roman arch entry was considered a marvel. There was only one problem—it was built on the Hayward Fault and is gradually splitting in two. In 1989, an earthquake forced its closure, and it is now unsafe and unoccupied.

Building on an unstable foundation is not wise. This is also true of our spiritual lives. Jesus taught His disciples this truth with an illustration: "Everyone who hears these sayings of Mine, and does not do them, will be like a foolish man who built his house on the sand: and the rain descended, the floods came, and the winds blew and beat on that house; and it fell. And great was its fall" (Matthew 7:26–27).

The shifting morals of our present world can be confusing. We may be tempted to let culture or the opinions of society be the foundation for the decisions we make. But obeying the unwavering truth of God's Word brings stability unavailable anywhere else. "Therefore whoever hears these sayings of Mine, and does them, I will liken him to a wise man who built his house on the rock" (v. 24). —DF

The Bible stands though the hills may tumble,
It will firmly stand when the earth shall crumble;
I will plant my feet on its firm foundation,
For the Bible stands. —Lillenas

Build your life on the solid foundation—Jesus Christ.

Overcoming Bias

READ: Colossians 3:8–17

There is neither Greek nor Jew, circumcised nor uncircumcised . . .
slave nor free, but Christ is all and in all. —COLOSSIANS 3:11

A *Washington Post* article reported that recent studies of the nature of prejudice found that almost everyone harbors biases, and these attitudes affect even those who actively resist them. A University of Kentucky psychologist says that much of our self-esteem comes from feeling better about ourselves than about others because of the group we belong to. Prejudice is not easy to overcome, even within the family of God.

Paul's words to the believers at Colosse instruct us today, saying that our speech and behavior toward fellow Christians should reflect our oneness in Christ. "[You] have put on the new man," Paul said, "where there is neither Greek nor Jew, circumcised nor uncircumcised, barbarian, Scythian, slave nor free, but Christ is all and in all" (Colossians 3:10–11). Instead of superiority and favoritism, we should demonstrate compassion, kindness, humility, gentleness, and patience toward each other (v. 12). And above all, we are to "put on love, which is the bond of perfection" (v. 14).

In the body of Christ, no race, nationality, or class is better than another. Through the cross, Christ has made us one, and we are to treat each other with honesty, dignity, and love.   —DM

> *It matters not what race or gender,*
> *Rich or poor, or great or small,*
> *The God who made us is not partial—*
> *He sent Christ to die for all.* —D. DeHaan

Prejudice distorts what it sees, deceives when it talks, and destroys when it acts.

The Armies of God

READ: 2 Kings 6:8–17

*He shall give His angels charge over you, to
keep you in all your ways. —PSALM 91:11*

When our granddaughter Julia was very small, we took her on a driving trip over an Idaho mountain road. Afterward, she and her Nana were having a conversation about the "adventure." "I don't worry because I think Papa has a guardian angel," Nana said. "I think he must have a team of guardian angels!" Julia replied.

The mission of angels is to protect and serve the children of God (Hebrews 1:13–14). The psalmist said, "The chariots of God are . . . thousands of thousands; the Lord is among them" (Psalm 68:17). God is the "Lord of hosts," which means "armies." The angels are the Lord's army.

In 2 Kings we read about Elisha and his servant who were surrounded by the Syrian army. Elisha's servant cried out, "Alas, my master! What shall we do?" Elisha replied, "Do not fear, for those who are with us are more than those who are with them." Then the Lord opened the servant's eyes and he saw that "the mountain was full of horses and chariots of fire all around" (6:15–17). The Lord's army was at hand!

Even though we cannot see them with our natural eyes, we can rest in the confidence that the Lord of Hosts is constantly watching over us, and He has an invisible army at His bidding to send where He pleases.
—DR

*What ready help the Father gives
To struggling saints below!
He sends His heavenly ministers
To thwart our ancient foe. —D. DeHaan*

The angels of God protect the people of God as they do the work of God.

Space Scouts

READ: Ephesians 6:1–4

*You, fathers . . . bring [your children] up in the training
and admonition of the Lord.* —EPHESIANS 6:4

Many of the first astronauts were once Boy Scouts. The scouts were good at capturing the imagination of young boys and instilling discipline to reach their goals—even if it meant reaching for the stars.

On July 20, 1969, the Boy Scouts were busy celebrating at a conference. During the gathering, the scouts were delighted to hear from Eagle Scout Neil Armstrong, who sent them greetings from space. One of their own had grown up to realize a wonderful dream!

In some ways, the Christian home can be like a loving, spiritual scout camp. The Bible encourages parents to provide a positive growth environment for children in the home. Parents are exhorted to "bring [children] up in the training and admonition of the Lord" (Ephesians 6:4). "To bring up" refers to nourishing children by providing resources for their physical, mental, and spiritual needs. "Training" includes concern about all aspects of a child's development. And "admonition" speaks of providing direction by well-chosen words uniquely suited to each child.

Let's strive to make our home a place where loving discipline enables the children in our charge to reach their potential for God's glory. —DF

> *They are buds of hope and promise,*
> *Possessed by Him whose name is Love;*
> *Lent us here to train and nourish*
> *For a better life above.* —Crosby

**What you put into your children's hearts today
influences their character for tomorrow.**

Of Weeping and Rejoicing

READ: Romans 12:9–16

Rejoice with those who rejoice, and weep with those who weep. —ROMANS 12:15

Golda Meir knew both struggle and success during her life. As prime minister of Israel, she experienced many episodes of conflict and loss, as well as the periodic joy of successes and victory in the life of the fledgling State of Israel. She said of joy and sorrow, "Those who don't know how to weep with their whole heart don't know how to laugh either."

The apostle Paul called us to a life of both weeping and rejoicing—but with a twist. In Romans 12:15, the apostle challenged us to look outside our own experiences to the needs of others. He said, "Rejoice with those who rejoice, and weep with those who weep."

If we rejoice only in our own victories, we miss the wonder of celebrating the power of the Lord, who desires to accomplish His purposes in and through others as well. If we mourn only our own losses, we lose the opportunity to "be there" for those who are hurting by showing them compassion.

Life is filled with the extremes of joy and sorrow, victory and defeat. But we have been given the privilege of entering into those moments in people's lives to see the grace of God at work. Don't miss it!   —BC

Lord, give me sensitivity
To people in their grief and pain,
To weep with them and show your love
In ways mere words cannot attain. —Sper

Looking to the needs of others honors Christ.

Standing Ovation

READ: Acts 6:8–15; 7:54–60

*Look! I see . . . the Son of Man standing
at the right hand of God! —*ACTS 7:56

Susan Boyle spent most of her adult life living with her cat Pebbles, caring for her aging mother, and singing in church. She certainly didn't look like a musical superstar. That's probably why the audience laughed at this unassuming middle-aged woman before she performed in a talent show. Undeterred, Susan faced the unfriendly crowd, sang beautifully, and went on to receive a standing ovation.

Stephen was confronted by a hostile crowd in the days of the early church (Acts 6–7). A panel of religious authorities listened to lying witnesses accuse him of blasphemy (Acts 6:13). Stephen responded by speaking the truth of God's Word, which reinforced his faith in Christ. At the end of his speech, he said, "Look! I see the heavens opened and the Son of Man standing at the right hand of God!" (7:56). Then the crowd stoned him (v. 58). Jesus, who was watching from heaven, welcomed Stephen home.

Most Christians aren't confronted with this much hostility. Yet we all need to "stand fast in the Lord" when the pressure is on (Philippians 4:1). We can't let others silence our voice for Christ. Speaking up for Jesus does not always win the crowd's favor here on earth, but it does ensure His approval in heaven, where it matters the most.   —JBS

Stand up, stand up for Jesus, the strife will not be long;
This day the noise of battle—the next the victor's song.
To him that overcometh a crown of life shall be:
He with the King of glory shall reign eternally. —Duffield

If you meet opposition, maybe it shows
that you are doing something that counts.

Will I Have to Tell?

READ: 2 Corinthians 5:12–21

If anyone is in Christ, he is a new creation. —2 CORINTHIANS 5:17

Jim was sharing the gospel with Kerri. He told her she was separated from a holy God because of her sin, and that Jesus had died and risen for her salvation. She kept coming up with one reason not to believe: "But if I do receive Him, I won't have to tell other people about it, will I? I don't want to do that." She said that didn't fit her personality; she didn't want to have to tell others about Jesus.

Jim explained that promising to witness about Jesus wasn't a requirement before receiving Him. But he also said that once she came to know the Lord, Kerri would become His ambassador to the world (2 Corinthians 5:20).

After talking a little longer, Kerri acknowledged her need for salvation through Christ. She went home excited and at peace. Then a funny thing happened—within twenty-four hours she told three people about what God had done in her life.

Because we have been reconciled to God through Jesus, we now have "the ministry of reconciliation" (v. 18). We are His ambassadors, and therefore we implore people "on Christ's behalf, be reconciled to God" (v. 20).

When we're thankful, we want to share what God has done. —AC

> *I love to tell the story,*
> *For some have never heard*
> *The message of salvation*
> *From God's own holy Word.* —*Hankey*

There's no better news than the gospel—spread the word!

Volcanic Activity

READ: Ephesians 4:29–32

*An angry man stirs up strife, and a furious man
abounds in transgression.* —PROVERBS 29:22

It erupts. It melts everything in its path. Its blast is as powerful as a nuclear explosion!

Well, maybe not—but a temper can feel as intense as a volcano when it is aimed directly at another person. The moment may be quickly over, but it can leave emotional devastation and bitter feelings behind.

It's sad that the people we love the most are often the target of our hurtful words. But even when we feel we've been provoked, we have a choice. Will we respond in anger or in kindness?

The Bible tells us to rid ourselves of bitterness and anger, and to "be kind to one another, tenderhearted, forgiving one another, even as God in Christ forgave you" (Ephesians 4:32).

If you are struggling with chronic anger that is hurting your relationships, surrender this vulnerable part of your emotions to Christ's strength (Philippians 4:13). Ask God to forgive you for an uncontrolled temper, to show you how to moderate your emotions, and to teach you how to honor others above yourself (Romans 12:10). Seek out help from others to learn how to deal with your strong emotions in appropriate ways.

As we earnestly seek to love others and to please God, we can win the victory over a volcanic temper. —CHK

*Spirit of God, please change my heart,
And give me a new desire;
I want to be a man of peace,
Not controlled by anger's fire.* —K. DeHaan

Losing your temper is no way to get rid of it.

Exalt Him

READ: Psalm 46

I am God; I will be exalted. —PSALM 46:10

Be still, and know that I am God; I will be exalted among the nations" (Psalm 46:10). These words from a song sung long ago at the temple in Jerusalem remind us of one of our main tasks—worshiping our awesome God.

One way to do that is to meditate on His many attributes. Exalt God, for He is faithful, eternal, all-knowing, just, unchangeable, gracious, holy, merciful, longsuffering, impartial, and infinite. Our God is perfect.

Exalt God also by realizing that He is all-powerful, almighty, personal, righteous, unsearchable, wise, triune, accessible, self-existent, glorious, and compassionate.

Another way to worship God is to contemplate His names. Exalt God, for He is Creator. He is Love. He is Redeemer. He is Shepherd. He is Savior, Lord, and Father. He is Judge. He is Comforter. He is Teacher. He is I AM. Our God is the Mighty One.

Dwell on His identity. God is our shield. Our stronghold. Our light. Our strength. Our sustainer. Our rescuer. Our fortress.

Meditate on God's attributes. Contemplate His names. Dwell on His identity. Adore Him. Respect Him. Honor Him. Love Him. Exalt Him. Use the rest of your life getting ready to worship our awesome God forever.   —DB

O worship the King,
All glorious above,
And gratefully sing
His power and His love. —*Grant*

Let everything that has breath praise the Lord. —Psalm 150:6

Friending

READ: John 15:9–17

You are My friends if you do whatever
I command you. —JOHN 15:14

Facebook.com, the social networking Web site, was launched in 2004 as a way for college students to connect with each other online. It is now open to people of all ages, and currently there are an estimated 500 million users. Each user has an individual page with photos and personal details that can be viewed by "friends." To "friend" a person means opening the door to communication and information about who you are, where you go, and what you do. Facebook friendships may be casual or committed, but each one is "by invitation only."

Just before Jesus was crucified, He told His disciples: "You are My friends if you do whatever I command you. No longer do I call you servants, for a servant does not know what his master is doing; but I have called you friends, for all things that I heard from My Father I have made known to you" (John 15:14–15).

Unselfishness, oneness of purpose, and confident trust are the hallmarks of true friendship, especially in our relationship with the Lord. Christ has taken the initiative by giving His life for us and inviting us to know and follow Him.

Have we responded to the Lord Jesus' invitation of friendship by opening our hearts to Him with nothing held back?   —DM

> *Friendship with Jesus,*
> *Fellowship divine;*
> *O what blessed, sweet communion—*
> *Jesus is a Friend of mine.* —Ludgate

Jesus longs to be our Friend.

Heat and Holiness

READ: Isaiah 43:1–13

When you walk through the fire, you shall not be burned. —ISAIAH 43:2

Why is it taking my hair so long to get dry? I wondered. As usual, I was in a hurry, and I didn't want to go outside into the wintry weather with wet hair. Then I realized the problem. I had changed the setting on the hairdryer to "warm" instead of "hot" to accommodate my niece's preferences.

I often wish I could control the conditions of life as easily as I can change the setting on my hairdryer. I would choose a comfortable setting—not too hot, not too cold. I certainly wouldn't choose the heat of adversity or the fire of affliction. But in the spiritual realm, warm doesn't get the job done. We are called to holiness, and holiness often involves "heat." To be holy means to be set apart for God—separated from anything unclean or impure. To refine and purify us, God sometimes uses the furnace of affliction. The prophet Isaiah said, "*When* you walk through the fire, you shall not be burned"; he didn't say *if* (Isaiah 43:2). And the apostle Peter said that we should not be surprised by trials (1 Peter 4:12).

None of us knows when we'll be called to walk through the fire or how hot the furnace will be. But we do know this: God's purpose for the flames is to purify us, not to destroy us.   —JAL

When through fiery trials thy pathway shall lie,
My grace, all-sufficient, shall be thy supply.
The flames shall not hurt thee; I only design
Thy dross to consume and thy gold to refine. —Keen

The only way God hurries holiness is by turning up the heat.

Buried Treasure

READ: Leviticus 19:9–15

Open my eyes, that I may see wondrous things from Your law. —PSALM 119:18

Growing up in rural Missouri where American outlaw Jesse James (1847–1882) had lived, my friends and I were convinced he had buried treasure nearby. We wandered the woods in dreamy hopes of digging up a saddlebag or other treasure. Often we'd run into an elderly man chopping firewood with a giant axe. For years, we watched this mysterious "axe man" trudge the highways in search of soda cans, his own kind of treasure. Redeeming the cans for cash, he'd retire to his run-down, roofless, unpainted shack with a bottle in a brown paper bag. After his death, his family found bundles of money stored in his ramshackle home.

Like the axe man who ignored his treasure, we Christians sometimes ignore parts of Scripture. We forget that all of Scripture is ours to use; that each passage has a reason for its inclusion in the canon. Who knew Leviticus held so much buried treasure? In an efficient seven verses in chapter 19, God teaches us how to provide for the poor and disabled without stripping them of their dignity (vv. 9–10, 14), how to run our businesses ethically (vv. 11, 13, 15), and how to embed respect for Him into our daily life (v. 12).

If a few verses can contain so much treasure, think of all that can be ours if we dig into our Bibles every day. —RK

FOR FURTHER STUDY

Mine the treasure in Leviticus 19, and then search for more treasure in other parts of Leviticus to put into practice in your Christian walk.

Every word in the Bible was placed with a purpose;
any part you've not read is your buried treasure.

Change

READ: Matthew 3:1–12

Repent, for the kingdom of heaven is at hand! . . . Therefore bear fruits worthy of repentance. —MATTHEW 3:2, 8

Medical studies have shown that even though people who have had heart-bypass surgery are told that they must change their lifestyle or die, about 90 percent do not change. Typically, two years after surgery the patients haven't altered their lifestyle. It seems that most would rather die than change.

Just as doctors preach a message of physical change to prevent death, John the Baptist came preaching a message of spiritual change. "Repent, for the kingdom of heaven is at hand!" (Matthew 3:2). He was preparing the way for the ultimate manifestation of God's reign—the Messiah, Jesus.

Repentance means to change one's mind and attitude about God, which ultimately changes a person's actions and decisions. Those who repent and accept Christ's provision of forgiveness from their sins through His death on the cross will escape spiritual death (John 3:16). Repentance involves confessing sin with godly sorrow, and then forsaking sin. John the Baptist was calling people to turn from one way of living to ways that honor God.

Today, the Lord is still calling us to repent and then to respond with the "fruits worthy of repentance" (Matthew 3:8).　　　—MW

> *Repentance is to leave the sin*
> *That we had loved before,*
> *And showing we are grieved by it*
> *By doing it no more.* —Anonymous

Repentance means hating sin enough to turn from it.

Dreams or Choices?

READ: Philippians 1:1–11

*Approve the things that are excellent, that you may
be sincere and without offense.* —PHILIPPIANS 1:10

I've received a lot of good advice in my life. Near the top of the list is this wise observation from a friend: "Life is not made by the dreams that you dream but by the choices that you make."

He's right—your life today is the sum total of all the choices you've made up to this point. The apostle Paul gave similar advice in Philippians when he said to "approve the things that are excellent" (1:10). In any given situation we have a whole continuum of choices, ranging from really rotten choices, to the mediocrity of average choices, to choices that are good, and then to those that are excellent. God wants to move us across the continuum, past our natural impulses, all the way to excellent choices.

Often it's challenging to make the most excellent choice, especially if there aren't many others joining us. Sometimes it may feel as if our desires and freedoms have been suppressed. But if you follow Paul's advice, you'll notice some really positive outcomes—like being pure and blameless and fruitful (v. 11).

Make the choice to live a life filled with love, joy, peace, patience, kindness, goodness, faithfulness, gentleness, and self-control (Galatians 5:22–23). Then revel in the result!   —JS

> *The little choices we must make
> Will chart the course of life we take;
> We either choose the path of light,
> Or wander off in darkest night.* —D. DeHaan

Make an excellent choice and watch the ripple effect of blessing.

Emergency Room Fellowship

READ: Galatians 6:1–10

*Bear one another's burdens, and so fulfill
the law of Christ.* —GALATIANS 6:2

Not long ago, my wife, Janet, and I accepted an invitation to dine with a Christian woman who attends our Sunday school class. In her zeal to prepare a meal for us, she cut her index finger deeply. As we drove her to the emergency room, we prayed for her, and then we kept her company in the waiting room. Several hours later, our friend finally saw the doctor.

After we returned to her home, our hostess insisted we stay for the meal she had prepared. What followed was a great time of lively conversation and spiritual fellowship. While we ate, she shared with us some of the heartaches she had suffered, and how through the ups and downs she had found God's wonderful grace invading her life.

Later, my wife and I reflected on the unexpected trip to the hospital and the shared fellowship that had resulted. This verse came to mind: "Bear one another's burdens, and so fulfill the law of Christ" (Galatians 6:2). By providing support for our injured hostess, she was blessed. Then afterward, she became a blessing to us through her hospitality and a delicious meal.

In retrospect, painful experiences can be a marvelous gateway to rich fellowship as we "bear one another's burdens." —DF

*Beautiful lives are those that bear
For other lives their burden of care;
Beautiful souls are those that show
The Spirit of Christ wherever they go.* —Abbott

A helping hand can lighten another's burden.

Holy Fruit

READ: 2 Peter 1:1–8

If these things are yours and abound, you will be neither barren nor unfruitful in the knowledge of our Lord Jesus Christ. —2 PETER 1:8

Billy Graham told about the conversion of H. C. Morrison, the founder of Asbury Theological Seminary. He said that Morrison, a farm worker at the time, was plowing in a field one day when he saw an old Methodist preacher coming by on his horse. Morrison knew the elderly gentleman to be a gracious, godly man. As he watched the old saint go by, a great sense of conviction of sin came over Morrison and he dropped to his knees. There between the furrows in his field, alone, he gave his life to God.

When he concluded the story, Billy Graham earnestly prayed, "Oh, God, make me a holy man."

Augustine said, "Do you wish to be great? Then begin by *being.*" True and lasting greatness stems from what we are. Though we may seem to be doing nothing at all, we can be doing everything worthwhile if our lives are being styled by God's grace. Even if we are set aside through old age, sickness, or seclusion, we can still be productive. Are you bedridden or housebound? Your holy life can still bear fruit.

This can happen only as we stay in close relationship with Jesus (John 15:1–11). Only then will we have the fruit that "remains" (v. 16). —DR

> *I lived so that all whom I met could see*
> *His Holy Spirit shining through me;*
> *O friend, is this what our hearts can say*
> *As we sit and think at the close of day?* —*Nicholson*

The most powerful testimony is a holy life.

Resolution

READ: Acts 15:36–41; 1 Corinthians 9:1–6

The contention became so sharp that they parted from one another. —ACTS 15:39

In May 1884, two young parents disagreed about what middle name to give their newborn son. The mom preferred Solomon; the dad, Shippe—both family names. Because John and Martha couldn't agree, they compromised on "S." Thus Harry S. Truman would become the only US president with an initial for a middle name.

Over 120 years later, we still know about this conflict, but we also know that a reasonable resolution was reached.

In the New Testament, we read about another disagreement that has lived on in history. This one was between two missionaries: Paul and Barnabas (Acts 15). Barnabas wanted to take Mark with them on a trip to check on some churches they had helped previously (v. 37). But Paul did not trust Mark because of an earlier incident (v. 38). Paul and Barnabas disagreed so sharply that they parted ways (v. 39).

We still read about this argument 2,000 years later. What's important is not that it lived on in history, but that it didn't leave permanent relationship scars. Paul apparently reconciled with Barnabas, and in his final days asked for Mark to be with him because "he is useful to me for ministry" (2 Timothy 4:11).

Arguments happen. But let's make sure they are resolved. Grudges are a burden too heavy to carry.   —DB

> *Arguments can lead to grudges,*
> *Which, if left, will cause a rift;*
> *But if we bring resolution,*
> *Our relationships won't drift.* —Sper

A grudge is one thing that doesn't get better when it's nursed.

Greater Compassion

READ: Isaiah 49:13–18

Can a woman forget her nursing child, and not have compassion on the son of her womb? Surely they may forget, yet I will not forget you. —ISAIAH 49:15

I met my wife, Marlene, in college. I was majoring in pastoral studies, and she was working on a degree in elementary education. The first time I saw her working with children, I knew what a natural fit this was for her. She loved children. It became even more obvious when we got married and had children of our own. Seeing her with them was an education in unconditional love and acceptance. It was clear to me that there is nothing in all the world like the tender love and compassion of a mother for her newborn child.

That's what makes Isaiah 49:15 so remarkable. It's here that God told His people, who were feeling forsaken and forgotten (v. 14), that His compassion is even greater than a mother's: "Can a woman forget her nursing child, and not have compassion on the son of her womb? Surely they may forget, yet I will not forget you."

Sometimes we face struggles in life, and we are tempted to think that God has forgotten us. We may even believe that God no longer loves us. But God's love for us is as expansive as the open arms of Christ on the cross. And the tender compassion of our heavenly Father is more dependable and more enduring than the love of a nursing mother for her infant. Be comforted—His love never fails.   —BC

God will not forget His children
Nor will He forsake our care;
His compassion is enduring—
Even when we're unaware. —Sper

God's love for us is as expansive as the open arms of Christ on the cross.

The Variety of Creation

READ: Job 12:7–13

In [God's] hand is the life of every living thing. —JOB 12:10

Have you ever stopped to consider the amazing features God placed in the animals He created? Job did, and one of the most interesting he wrote about is the ostrich. Despite its apparent lack of good sense and its eccentric parenting skills, its offspring survive (Job 39:13–16). And despite its membership in the bird family, it can't fly—but it can outrun a horse (v. 18).

Another remarkable creature is the bombardier beetle. This African insect shoots two common materials, hydrogen peroxide and hydroquinone, from twin storage tanks in its back. Apart, these substances are harmless; together, they blind the beetle's predators. A special nozzle inside the beetle mixes the chemicals, enabling it to bombard its foe at amazing speeds! And the little guy can rotate his "cannon" to fire in any direction.

How can this be? How is it that a rather dull-witted ostrich survives despite a seeming inability to care for its young while the bombardier beetle needs a sophisticated chemical reaction to ensure its continued presence on earth? It's because God's creative abilities know no boundaries. "He commanded and they were created," the psalmist tells us (Psalm 148:5). From the ostrich to the beetle, God's creative work is clear for all to see. "Praise the name of the Lord" (148:13). —DE

> *All things bright and beautiful,*
> *All creatures great and small,*
> *All things wise and wonderful;*
> *The Lord God made them all.* —Alexander

The design of creation points to the Master Designer.

What Really Matters

READ: Matthew 16:21–28

For what profit is it to a man if he gains the whole world, and loses his own soul? —MATTHEW 16:26

Several years ago a friend of mine visited an exhibit of relics from the disastrous *Titanic* voyage. Exhibit visitors were given a replica ticket with the name of an actual passenger or crew member who, decades earlier, had embarked on the trip of a lifetime. After the tour group walked through the exhibit viewing pieces of silver dinnerware and other artifacts, the tour ended with an unforgettable twist.

A large board listed the names of all the passengers, including their status—first class, second class, crew. As my friend looked for the name of the person whose ticket he was holding, he noticed a line across the board dividing the names. Above the line were the names of those who were "saved" and below the line all those who were "lost."

The parallel to our life on earth is profound. It really doesn't make any difference how the world ranks your status. The only thing that ultimately matters is whether you are "saved" or "lost." As Jesus said, "What profit is it to a man if he gains the whole world, and loses his own soul?" (Matthew 16:26). Perhaps you've already trusted in Christ for your salvation. But what about your fellow passengers? Instead of sizing them up by the externals, talk to them about their ultimate destination.   —JS

It's not what I achieve that qualifies,
It matters not if I gain wealth or fame;
The only thing I must be certain of
Is "Have I put my trust in Jesus' name?" —Hess

In light of eternity, what one believes is far
more important than what one achieves.

Perfect Peace and Rest

READ: Psalm 71:19–24

*You, who have shown me great and severe
troubles, shall revive me again.* —PSALM 71:20

The psalmist had seen "great and severe troubles" (Psalm 71:20). Yet hovering in the back of his mind was the thought that God would "revive" him again. The literal meaning of this phrase is "bring him to life again." He elaborated: "[You shall] bring me up again from the depths of the earth [the grave]. You shall increase my greatness, and comfort me on every side" (vv. 20–21). If the troubles didn't end in this life, certainly in heaven they would.

This thought—that someday we shall be in God's presence and enjoy Him forever—crowns many of the psalms and is an assurance that helps life's present troubles fade away (see Psalms 16, 17, 49, 73).

Perhaps no one but God knows the trouble you've seen, but this is not all that shall be. Someday, your Father will "increase [your] greatness"— you will be clothed with unspeakable glory. There will be comfort "on every side." His presence and love will bring perfect peace and rest.

Richard Baxter writes, "O what a blessed day that will be when I shall . . . stand on the shore and look back on the raging seas I have safely passed; when I shall review my pains and sorrows, my fears and tears, and possess the glory which was the end of all!"   —DR

> *When all my labors and trials are o'er,*
> *And I am safe on that beautiful shore,*
> *Just to be near the dear Lord I adore*
> *Will through the ages be glory for me.* —Gabriel

When God wipes our tears, sorrow will give way to eternal song.

Not Without Hope

READ: Exodus 6:1–13

I will rescue you from their bondage, and I will redeem you with an outstretched arm and with great judgments. —Exodus 6:6

Sixteen Tons," written by Merle Travis and recorded by Tennessee Ernie Ford, became one of America's most popular songs in the mid-1950s. People seemed to identify with this coal miner's lament about feeling trapped and unable to change his situation no matter how hard he worked. Coal miners often lived in company-owned houses and were paid in "scrip"—coupons valid only at the company-owned store. Even if summoned to heaven, the miner said, he couldn't go because he owed his soul to the company store.

That sense of hopeless resignation may help us understand the feelings of the Hebrew people during their four hundred years of bondage in Egypt. When Moses told them of God's promise to release them from slavery, they didn't listen to him "because of anguish of spirit" (Exodus 6:9). They were so far down they couldn't look up.

But God did something for them that they could not do for themselves. And the Lord's miraculous deliverance of His people foreshadowed His powerful intervention on our behalf through His Son, Jesus Christ. It was when "we were powerless to help ourselves that Christ died for sinful men" (Romans 5:6 Phillips).

When life is at its lowest ebb, we are not without hope because of the wonderful grace of God. —DM

When trouble seeks to rob your very breath,
When tragedy hits hard and steals your days,
Recall that Christ endured the sting of death;
He gives us hope, and merits all our praise. —Gustafson

No one is hopeless whose hope is in God.

A Bouquet of Praise

READ: 1 Peter 4:7–11

That in all things God may be glorified
through Jesus Christ. —I PETER 4:11

Corrie ten Boom (1892–1983) was a World War II concentration camp survivor who became a popular Christian speaker around the world. Thousands attended her meetings as she talked about how she had learned to forgive her captors just as Christ had forgiven her sins.

After each meeting, people surrounded her and heaped accolades on her for her godly qualities and thanked her for encouraging them in their walk with the Lord. Corrie said she would then return to her hotel room, get down on her knees, and present those compliments in thanks to God. She called it giving God "a bouquet of praise."

The Lord has given each of us gifts to use to minister to one another (1 Peter 4:10) so that "in all things God may be glorified through Jesus Christ, to whom belong the glory and the dominion forever and ever" (v. 11). We have nothing to offer others that we have not first received from the Lord (1 Corinthians 4:7), so the glory does belong to Him.

To learn humility, perhaps we could follow Corrie's example. If we receive a compliment for something we've said or done, let's privately give a bouquet of praise to God for the glory He alone deserves.   —AC

Immortal, invisible, God only wise,
In light inaccessible hid from our eyes,
Most blessed, most glorious, the Ancient of Days,
Almighty, victorious—Thy great name we praise. —Smith

Praise is the fairest blossom which springs from the soul.

The Core of the Problem

READ: Romans 3:10–18

For I know that in me (that is, in my flesh) nothing good dwells; for to will is present with me, but how to perform what is good I do not find. —ROMANS 7:18

One of my favorite television cartoons as a boy was *Tom Terrific.* When Tom faced a challenge, he would put on his thinking cap and work through the matter with his faithful sidekick Mighty Manfred, the Wonder Dog. Usually, those problems found their source in Tom's arch-enemy, Crabby Appleton. To this day, I remember how this villain was described on the show. He was "Crabby Appleton—rotten to the core."

The fact is that all of us share Crabby Appleton's primary problem—apart from Christ, we're all rotten to the core. The apostle Paul described us this way: "There is none righteous, no, not one; there is none who understands; there is none who seeks after God" (Romans 3:10–11). None of us are capable of living up to God's perfect standard of holiness. Because of our condition of being separated from a holy God, He sent His Son Jesus to give himself to die on the cross for the punishment we deserve, and then rise again. Now we can be "justified freely by His grace" through faith in Him (v. 24).

Jesus Christ has come to people "rotten to the core" and makes us "a new creation" by faith in Him (2 Corinthians 5:17). In His goodness, He has fixed our problem completely—all the way down to our core. —BC

I know I'm a sinner and Christ is my need;
His death is my ransom, no merit I plead.
His work is sufficient, on Him I believe;
I have life eternal when Him I receive. —Anonymous

We need more than a new start—we need a new heart.

True Self-Denial

READ: Luke 9:18–25

If anyone desires to come after Me, let him deny himself,
and take up his cross daily, and follow Me. —LUKE 9:23

Lent is a period of forty days prior to Easter (excluding Sundays). For many people it commemorates Jesus' fasting in the wilderness. They "give up something" for Lent every year, like sweets or TV. This can yield spiritual benefits, but denying yourself *things* and denying *yourself* aren't the same. In Luke 9:23, Jesus taught the latter.

This verse can be broken down into three parts. In the statement "If anyone desires to come after Me," the word *desires* indicates that this is for sincere disciples only. In the phrase "let him deny himself," the words *let* and *deny himself* imply a willingness to renounce one's selfish will and ways. And in the statement "take up his cross daily," the word *daily* emphasizes a continual dying to self-will.

It's easier to give things than to give ourselves. Yet Jesus gave himself, and so must we. To those who deny themselves in obedient service, He has promised, "Whoever loses his life for My sake will save it" (v. 24). And to His question, "What profit is it to a man if he gains the whole world, and is himself destroyed?" we are called to answer, "There is no profit!" We show that we believe this when we deny ourselves and follow Christ. —JY

To follow Christ we must let go
Of all that we hold dear;
And as we do deny ourselves,
Our gains become more clear. —Sper

By living for ourselves we die; by dying to ourselves we live.

Win or Lose

READ: 2 Timothy 4:1–8

I have fought the good fight, I have finished the race, I have kept the faith. —2 TIMOTHY 4:7

During the 2009 college football season, University of Texas quarterback Colt McCoy began every postgame interview by thanking God for the opportunity to play. When he was injured early in the national championship game, he was forced to watch from the sidelines as his team lost.

After the game, he told a television reporter, "I'd have given everything I have to be out there with my team . . . I always give God the glory. I never question why things happen the way they do. God is in control of my life and I know that if nothing else, I'm standing on the Rock."

The apostle Paul experienced God's deliverance many times, but he didn't insist on things going his way. From prison in Rome he wrote to Timothy: "I am already being poured out as a drink offering, and the time of my departure is at hand" (2 Timothy 4:6). Some might say that Paul had failed to accomplish his goals and that his life was ending in defeat. But he saw it differently: "I have fought the good fight, I have finished the race, I have kept the faith" (v. 7). He looked forward to an eternal crown (v. 8).

As we walk with God, we can praise Him for His faithfulness—win or lose. —DM

> *I can always count on God, my heavenly Father,*
> *For He changes not; He always is the same.*
> *Yesterday, today, forever, He is faithful,*
> *And I know He loves me, praise His holy name!* —Felten

In every change He faithful will remain. —Katharina von Schlegel

Virtuoso

READ: 1 Corinthians 10:31–11:1

*Therefore . . . whatever you do, do all to
the glory of God.* —1 CORINTHIANS 10:31

A major US newspaper has called Christopher Parkening "the leading guitar virtuoso of our day, combining profound musical insight with complete technical mastery of his instrument." There was a time, however, when Parkening gave up playing the guitar professionally. At the height of his career as a classical guitarist, he retired at age thirty, bought a ranch in Montana, and spent his days fly-fishing. But early retirement did not bring him the satisfaction he had hoped for.

Then, during a visit to California, he was invited to a church where he heard a clear presentation of the gospel. Of this he wrote: "That night I lay awake, broken over my sins . . . I had lived very selfishly and it had not made me happy . . . It was then that I asked Jesus Christ to come into my life, to be my Lord and Savior. For the first time, I remember telling Him, 'Whatever You want me to do with my life, Lord, I'll do it.'"

One of Parkening's favorite verses is 1 Corinthians 10:31, "Therefore . . . whatever you do, do all to the glory of God." He has taken up the guitar again, but this time with the motivation to glorify God.

Each of us has been given gifts; and when we use them for God's glory, they bring satisfaction and joy. —DF

*The gifts we offer to the Lord
Are by His standards measured;
Our sacrifice and lives of praise—
Such gifts are highly treasured.* —Sper

We were created to give God the glory.

Who and How

READ: Mark 8:27–33

You are the Christ. —MARK 8:29

Whenever I read the Gospels, I identify with the disciples. Like me, they seemed slow to catch on. Jesus kept saying things like "Don't you understand it yet?" and "Are you still so dull?" (see Mark 7:18). Finally, however, Peter "got it," at least one part of it. When Jesus asked, "Who do you say that I am?" Peter answered, "You are the Christ" (8:29).

Peter was right about the "who"—Jesus—but he was still wrong about the "how." When Jesus predicted His death, Peter rebuked Him for it. Jesus, in turn, rebuked Peter: "Get behind Me, Satan! For you are not mindful of the things of God, but the things of men" (v. 33).

Peter was still thinking in human ways of establishing kingdoms. One ruler would overthrow another and set up a new government. He was expecting Jesus to do the same. But Christ's kingdom was going to come in a new way—through service and the sacrifice of His life.

The method God uses today hasn't changed. Whereas Satan's voice tempts us to gain power, the voice of Jesus tells us that the meek will inherit the earth (Matthew 5:5). To gain citizens for God's kingdom, we must follow the example of Jesus, who set aside selfish ambitions, served others, and called people to repent of their sin. —JAL

> *We say we love humanity,*
> *But can we really claim*
> *A readiness to sacrifice*
> *For them in Jesus' name?* —Sper

A Christian is an ambassador who speaks for the King of Kings.

Anticipation

READ: 1 Thessalonians 4:13–18

I will come again and receive you to Myself. —JOHN 14:3

At the beginning of March, my friend began a countdown. Marked on the calendar in her office were the twenty days left until the first day of spring. One morning when I saw her, she volunteered, "Only twelve more days!" A few days later, "Only six!" Her enthusiasm started to rub off on me, and I began to keep track as well. "Just two more days, Jerrie!" She beamed. "I know!"

As believers, we have something to look forward to that is even more exciting than the anticipation of budding flowers and lots of sunshine after a long winter. God has made many promises in His Word, and each one has been or will be fulfilled. But the certainty that Christ will return is one of the greatest promises of all. "For the Lord Himself will descend from heaven with a shout, with the voice of an archangel, and with the trumpet of God . . . Then we who are alive and remain shall be caught up together with them in the clouds to meet the Lord in the air," and we'll be with Him forever (1 Thessalonians 4:16–17).

Although no one can know the exact day, we have God's promise that Jesus will come back (Acts 1:7–11). As we celebrate the spring and coming Easter season, let's encourage each other in anticipation of that day!   —CHK

> *He is coming! Oh, the rapture*
> *To behold His lovely face,*
> *And to tell Him how I love Him,*
> *Who has saved me by His grace.* —Dimmock

Christ is coming—perhaps today!

Fearful Tears

READ: Revelation 5:1–12

*So I wept much, because no one was found worthy
to open and read the scroll.* —REVELATION 5:4

John, the great apostle and the one Jesus loved, was reduced to tears. In a vision he received while imprisoned (Revelation 5:1–12), he found himself in God's throne room as future events unfolded. In heaven, John saw God hold up a sealed scroll. He wept because as he observed the glories of God's presence, he saw no one who could open the scroll—no one with the power to reveal God's final revelation and to complete the concluding chapter of history's drama.

As an apostle, John had observed the power of sin in the world. He had witnessed Jesus' life and death on earth to conquer sin. He had seen Him ascend into heaven. But now he was fearful when he saw that no one was worthy to open the scroll and vanquish sin forever (v. 4).

Imagine the drama of what happened next. An elder approached John and said, "Do not weep," and pointed him toward Someone he knew: "Behold, the Lion of the tribe of Judah" (v. 5). John looked, and he saw Jesus—the only One with the power to take the scroll, open the seals, and complete the story. Soon John's tears were dry, and millions of angels were proclaiming, "Worthy is the Lamb!" (v. 12).

Are you crying? Behold, John's friend—Jesus. He is worthy. Turn things over to Him.   —DB

> *Our Lord is worthy all our days*
> *Of all our love and highest praise;*
> *He died to take our sin and shame—*
> *Oh, bless the Savior's holy name!* —Egner

The Lamb who died to save us is the Shepherd who lives to lead us.

God's Flannelgraph

READ: Psalm 19

The heavens declare the glory of God; and the firmament shows His handiwork. —PSALM 19:1

In this age of new video technology it might be hard to believe that some teachers still feel the best way to depict Bible stories is the low-tech flannelgraph board. I recall that my childhood Sunday school teachers used those flat boards covered with flannel, which enabled them to display cutouts of David, Daniel, Jonah, Jesus, and all the other Bible characters. The flannelgraphs helped my teachers capture the essence of the Bible story in an artistic way.

Those old-school flannelgraphs aren't the oldest graphic teaching devices, however. God has long had a kind of "flannelgraph" of His own, and it is called creation. God uses the marvel of creation to instruct us and to display His power.

In Psalm 19:1, David wrote, "The heavens declare the glory of God; and the firmament shows His handiwork." In creation, God has revealed himself so clearly that Paul declared, "His invisible attributes are clearly seen." Those who have the witness of creation are "without excuse" (Romans 1:20). Why? On the flannelgraph of God's creation, we see God's order and design. We see His power and glory. This should lead us to worship. "O Lord, our Lord, how excellent is Your name in all the earth!" (Psalm 8:1). —BC

With words of great power God formed the world—
By the strength of His voice heaven's hosts were unfurled;
Now in His honor we worship His name
And in heartfelt devotion His glory proclaim. —Branon

Creation is the canvas on which God has painted His character.

Forgetting Ourselves

READ: Philippians 2:1–4

Let every man be swift to hear, slow to speak. —JAMES 1:19

I was fishing a local trout stream last summer, my attention fixed on a fish that was feeding nearby. I looked up and there on the bank I spied an acquaintance—nationally known fly-fishing guide and outfitter Dave Tucker. Immediately I became aware of my own performance, bungled the next cast, and lost the fish. So it is when we turn our attention away from the activity at hand and think about ourselves.

W. H. Auden has an engaging little poem about those who forget themselves in an activity—a cook mixing a sauce, a surgeon making an incision, a clerk completing a bill of lading. He says that all "wear the same rapt expression, forgetting themselves in a function." That phrase "forgetting themselves in a function" brings Philippians 2:3–4 to mind: "Let nothing be done through selfish ambition or conceit, but in lowliness of mind let each esteem others better than himself. Let each of you look out . . . for the interests of others."

When I'm listening to a friend, I need to remind myself to focus on him, not to begin wondering how I look, what he thinks of me, what I should say next. Let's put others first by listening in rapt attention, concentrating on the one in front of us, forgetting ourselves.   —DR

> *When we hold our tongues and listen,*
> *We communicate our care;*
> *For an open ear speaks volumes*
> *To a heart that's in despair. —Sper*

Listening may be the most loving thing you do today.

Small Things

READ: John 6:4–14

There is a lad here who has five barley loaves and two
small fish, but what are they among so many? —JOHN 6:9

Skeptical about the usefulness of a small lunch, Andrew said to Jesus, "What are [these five loaves and two fish] among so many?" (John 6:9). Yet the little lunch in the hands of Jesus turned out to be a huge blessing. So, before you think that you don't have much to offer Jesus, consider this:

Edward Kimball, a Sunday school teacher in Boston, decided to visit a young man in his class to be sure he was a Christian. That day he led that man, Dwight L. Moody, to the Lord.

Moody, the Billy Graham of the nineteenth century, had a major impact on Wilbur Chapman. Chapman, a prominent evangelist, recruited Billy Sunday to join in his evangelistic campaigns. In turn, Sunday launched a national ministry that had great results in cities like Charlotte, North Carolina. An organization that started as a result of Sunday's revival invited evangelist Mordecai Ham to Charlotte. In one of those meetings, Billy Graham received Christ as his Savior and later became the most prominent evangelist of our time.

When you think you don't have much to offer, remember Sunday school teacher Edward Kimball, who spent a Saturday afternoon reaching out to someone in his class. God has a special way of using routine faithfulness in the "small things" to accomplish great things!   —JS

What may seem insignificant,
Mundane, routine, or small
Is often used by God to show
His power over all. —Sper

God uses small things to accomplish great things for His glory.

Are We There Yet?

READ: Deuteronomy 8

The Lord your God led you all the way these forty years in the wilderness, to humble you and test you, to know what was in your heart. —DEUTERONOMY 8:2

If there is any such thing as a universal question, it may be this: Are we there yet? Generations of children have asked it. They have then grown into adults who have to answer the same question when their children ask.

Whenever I read the books of Moses, I wonder how many times he heard that question from the Israelites. Before rescuing them from slavery and leading them out of Egypt, Moses told them that the Lord would lead them to "a land flowing with milk and honey" (Exodus 3:8). He did, but first they spent forty years wandering in the wilderness. This was no ordinary wandering, however. They were not lost; they were wandering for a purpose. After four hundred years of slavery, the children of Israel needed to have their hearts, souls, and minds reoriented toward God. This was accomplished in the wilderness (Deuteronomy 8:2, 15–18), but not before an entire generation died because of their disobedience (Numbers 32:13).

In life, it sometimes seems as if we are wandering in circles. We feel lost. We want to ask God, "Are we there yet? How much longer?" At such times, it helps to remember that the journey, not just the destination, is important to God. He uses it to humble us, test us, and show us what is in our hearts. —JAL

All God's testings have a purpose—
Someday you will see the light;
All He asks is that you trust Him,
Walk by faith and not by sight. —Zoller

It's the journey, not just the destination, that's important.

Five-Minute Rule

READ: Psalm 102:1–17

He shall regard the prayer of the destitute, and
shall not despise their prayer. —PSALM 102:17

I read about a five-minute rule that a mother had for her children. They had to be ready for school and gather together five minutes before it was time to leave each day. They would gather around Mom, and she would pray for each one by name, asking for the Lord's blessing on their day. Then she'd give them a kiss and off they'd run. Even neighborhood kids would be included in the prayer circle if they happened to stop by. Many years later, one of the children said that she learned from this experience how crucial prayer is to her day.

The writer of Psalm 102 knew the importance of prayer. This psalm is labeled, "A prayer of the afflicted, when he is overwhelmed and pours out his complaint before the Lord." He cried out, "Hear my prayer, O Lord . . . in the day that I call, answer me speedily" (vv. 1–2). God looks down "from the height of His sanctuary; from heaven [He views] the earth" (v. 19).

God cares for you and wants to hear from you. Whether you follow the five-minute rule asking for blessings on the day, or need to spend more time crying out to Him in deep distress, talk to the Lord each day. Your example may have a big impact on your family or someone close to you.   —AC

The issue isn't how much time
We spend with God in prayer,
But seeking Him throughout each day
And knowing that He's there. —Sper

Prayer is an acknowledgment of our need for God.

The Overflow

READY: Psalm 103:1–10

Forget not all His benefits. —PSALM 103:2

Joyful shouts filtered into our house from outside, and I wanted to know what was so wonderful out there. I peeked through the curtains and watched two young boys splashing in a thick stream of water that gushed from a fire hydrant.

The overflow of water reminded me of how God pours out blessings on His children and how important it is to recognize that "the Lord . . . daily loads us with benefits" (Psalm 68:19).

Although I know He has furnished countless good things for me, when the car blows a gasket, when the flu infects my family, and when relationships threaten to unravel, dissatisfaction threatens my view of God's blessings. They seem more like infrequent drips from a faucet than a flood of water from a hydrant!

Maybe that's why in Psalm 103 David reminds us to "forget not all His benefits" (v. 2). And then, to help us, he lists a torrent of blessings for believers. He reminds us that God forgives all our iniquities, heals all our diseases, redeems our lives from destruction, crowns us with lovingkindness, and satisfies our mouths with good things (vv. 3–5).

Today, let's take time to acknowledge God's abundance instead of overlooking the overflow of His blessings. —JBS

We're loaded with benefits daily,
Sent down from the Father above;
His mercies and blessings abounding
Are gifts of His marvelous love. —Anonymous

Adding up your blessings will multiply your joy.

A Clear View

READ: Matthew 5:1–12

Blessed are the pure in heart, for they shall see God. —MATTHEW 5:8

The Gran Telescopio Canarias, one of the world's most powerful telescopes, sits atop an extinct volcano on La Palma, Canary Islands. Inaugurated in July 2009 by King Carlos of Spain, it offers astronomers an unusually clear view of the heavens. Located at 7,870 feet, the telescope is above the cloud cover, where the prevailing winds are dry and turbulence-free. Here, near the equator, scientists can study all of the Northern Celestial Hemisphere and part of the Southern.

Jesus chose a mountainside to teach His followers about the characteristics of a life yielded to God. There He taught them that attitude, not altitude, was the key to having a clear view of the Father.

Tucked into the passage known as the Beatitudes, Jesus said: "Blessed are the pure in heart, for they shall see God" (Matthew 5:8). This is not just for the few who try to achieve it, but for all who will humbly receive it. To have a heart that is clean in God's eyes, we need to accept the Father's pardon through Christ His Son. "If we confess our sins, He is faithful and just to forgive us our sins and to cleanse [purify] us from all unrighteousness" (1 John 1:9).

A mountaintop is a great place to see the stars, but to clearly see God requires a change of heart.   —DM

> *Since by faith I have clear vision,*
> *Your blest Word is rich and new;*
> *Men with eyes by sin distorted*
> *Cannot all its treasures view.* —Bosch

To get a clear view of God, focus on Jesus Christ.

Chocolate-Fueled Car

READ: 1 Kings 19:1–8

*The testimony of the Lord is sure,
making wise the simple.* —PSALM 19:7

Many people like both the sweetness and the energy they get from chocolate. Yet British auto technicians have found a surprising use for this sweet food. Scientists at the University of Warwick have built a race car that runs on vegetable oils and chocolate. The fuel provides energy so that the car can reach top speeds of 135 mph.

The Bible also records a surprising source of energy from food. When Elijah had been used by God on Mt. Carmel to call fire down from heaven, this spiritual high was followed by persecution and melancholy. In response to Elijah's depression, God sent an angel to provide food, drink, and rest for the weary prophet. The sustaining power of that food from heaven was remarkable: "So he arose, and ate and drank; and he went in the strength of that food forty days and forty nights as far as Horeb, the mountain of God" (1 Kings 19:8).

Just as we need food to sustain our physical lives, we also need nourishing food for our spiritual lives. God's Word is "sweeter . . . than honey and the honeycomb" (Psalm 19:10) and feeds our souls. It makes "wise the simple" (v. 7) and provides both nourishment and energy for life's long journey. Take time to feed on it.   —DF

*God's Word provides the nourishment
That every Christian needs to grow,
Supplying strength from day to day
By teaching what we need to know.* —Sper

God feeds us through His Word.

A Dream of Answers Forgotten

READ: Job 42:1–6

I have heard of You by the hearing of the ear, but now my eye sees You. —JOB 42:5

A friend quit two jobs to become a full-time caregiver when his adult son was seriously hurt in a car accident. That same year his wife of over thirty years contracted a terminal illness and died. Since then, he says, he has no answers when his son asks "why" this happened to them. But he told me of a reassuring dream he had along the way.

He dreamed that he was in a place that was awash with sunlight. There were crowds of people around him, and a man was answering all of his "why" questions. Each answer made so much sense that he clearly understood why he was not to know the answers now. Then he was with his son in the dream. But when he tried to help him with his questions, he couldn't remember the answers. But even that seemed okay. And then he woke up.

My friend's experience reminds me of another friend of God who suffered with unanswered questions (Job 7:20–21). Only when God finally broke His silence and gave Job a vision of himself in the wonder of creation did Job find something that was better than answers (42:1–6). Only then did Job find peace in knowing that our God has good and even wonderful reasons to trust Him.   —MD

What God is doing you may not know now,
But someday you'll understand why;
Questions that taunt you and trouble your mind
Will one day have heaven's reply. —Hess

What's better than answers to our "why" questions?
Trusting a good God who has His reasons.

A Matter of Perspective

READ: Revelation 3:14–22

[You] do not know that you are wretched, miserable, poor, blind, and naked. —REVELATION 3:17

One of my favorite stories is about the Texas rancher who was doing agricultural consulting for a farmer in Germany. He asked the German farmer about the size of his property, to which he replied, "About a mile square." When the German asked the Texan about the size of his ranch, the rancher explained that if he got in his pick-up truck at dawn and drove until sunset he would still be on his ranch. Not to be outdone, the farmer replied, "I used to have an old truck like that!"

All joking aside, it's important to have the right perspective. Unfortunately, the Christians in Laodicea had the wrong perspective about wealth (Revelation 3:14–22). By all appearances, they were rich. They had plenty of earthly goods and thought they needed nothing—not even Jesus. But Jesus had a different perspective. In spite of their material prosperity, He saw that they were "wretched, miserable, poor, blind, and naked" (v. 17). So He invited them to become truly rich by seeking what only He could provide: purity, character, righteousness, and wisdom.

Let's not make the Laodicean mistake. Instead, let's keep our perspective right about what it means to be rich. True wealth is not measured by what you have but by who you are in Christ.   —JS

In Christ we're rich beyond belief
With wealth the world cannot see;
We have new strength and character,
New righteousness and purity. —Sper

The poorest person is he whose only wealth is money.

God's Answers

READ: Daniel 9:20–27

While I was speaking in prayer, the man Gabriel . . . reached me. —DANIEL 9:21

Daniel poured out his heart to God (Daniel 9:2). He had read Jeremiah and rediscovered God's promise that Israel's captivity in Babylon would last seventy years. So, in an effort to represent his people before God, Daniel fasted and prayed. He pleaded with God not to delay in rescuing His people (v. 19).

When we pray, there are things we can know and other things we cannot. For instance, we have the assurance that God will hear our prayer if we know Him as our heavenly Father through faith in Jesus, and we know that His answer will come according to His will. But we don't know when the answer will come or what it will be.

For Daniel, the answer to his prayer came in miraculous fashion, and it came immediately. While he was praying, the angel Gabriel arrived to provide the answer. But the nature of the answer was as surprising as the quick reply. While Daniel asked God about "seventy years," the answer was about a prophetic "seventy weeks of years." Daniel asked God for an answer about the here and now, but God's answer had to do with events thousands of years into the future.

Focused as we are with our immediate situation, we may be shocked by God's answer. Yet we can know that the answer will be for His glory. —DB

I know not by what methods rare,
But this I know—God answers prayer;
I leave my prayers with Him alone,
Whose will is wiser than my own. —Hickok

God's answers to our prayers may exceed our expectations.

Becoming a Go-To Person

READ: Luke 7:1–10

When he heard about Jesus, he sent elders of the Jews to Him, pleading with Him to come and heal his servant. —LUKE 7:3

Would you pray for my sister?" the burly worker asked awkwardly. I eyed him suspiciously.

Months earlier, muggy August heat intensified emotions in the pre-strike atmosphere of the assembly plant where I was working that summer. Managers drove production at a frenzied pace, and union members resisted. During breaks, we were coached by union officials on slowing down our output. My faith and idealism got me in the doghouse because I didn't think God would accept anything but my best effort. I naively tried to explain.

My coworkers' response was harassment, and this burly worker asking for prayer had been the ringleader. An undesirable task? I got the assignment. Off-color jokes had me as the star.

So now I greeted this prayer request with suspicion. "Why me?" His answer jarred me: "Because she's got cancer," he said gruffly, "and I need someone God will hear." The bitter rancor between us eased as I prayed for his sister.

Like the centurion in Luke 7, people in the storms of life don't waste time or mince words. They go directly to the people whose faith they've tagged as real. We need to be those people. Do our lives mark us as a go-to person in touch with God?　　　　　　　　　　　　　　—RK

> *We give to others what they need*
> *No greater help and care*
> *Than when we intercede for them*
> *And bear them up in prayer.* —D. DeHaan

Even the hardest of souls might ask for help when someone they love is at risk.

Forsaking Wrath

READ: Psalm 37:8–11

Cease from anger, and forsake wrath. —PSALM 37:8

I have a friend whose note cards are imprinted with a picture of Rodin's *The Thinker*, the famous sculpture depicting a man in sober reflection. Below the picture is this inscription: "Life is not fair."

Indeed, it is not. And any theory that insists that this life is fair is illusory and deceptive.

Despite the overwhelming unfairness of life, however, David in Psalm 37 prays that he will not retaliate but will instead rest in the Lord and wait patiently for Him to bring justice to the earth in due time (v. 7). "For evildoers shall be cut off; but those who wait on the Lord, they shall inherit the earth" (v. 9).

Our wrath tends to be vindictive and punitive. God's wrath is untainted by self-interest and tempered by mercy. His wrath can even be His relentless love that brings our antagonists to repentance and faith. We must not then avenge ourselves, "for it is written, 'Vengeance is Mine, I will repay,' says the Lord . . . Do not be overcome by evil, but overcome evil with good" (Romans 12:19, 21).

This must begin in the heart, the wellspring from which the issues of our lives flow. May we cease from anger, forsake wrath, and wait patiently for the Lord. —DR

> *Lord, help me not retaliate*
> *When someone wants to pick a fight;*
> *Instead, give me the strength and faith*
> *To show your love and do what's right.* —Sper

Revenge restrained is a victory gained.

Suit Up

READ: Ephesians 6:13–21

Take up the whole armor of God, that you may be able to withstand in the evil day, and having done all, to stand. —EPHESIANS 6:13

When I played American football as a kid, one thing that took some getting used to was all the equipment we had to wear. Running effectively in a helmet, shoulder pads, and a variety of other protective items can feel awkward and clumsy at first. But over time the protective gear becomes like a familiar friend that provides welcome protection against serious injury. When a football player suits up, he knows that his equipment is designed to protect him against an opponent who could do him physical harm.

As followers of Christ, we face a dangerous foe—a spiritual enemy who seeks our downfall and destruction. Fortunately, our Lord has provided us with protection, and He challenges us to suit up for spiritual battle.

In Ephesians 6:13, we read, "Take up the whole armor of God, that you may be able to withstand in the evil day, and having done all, to stand." Paul then describes our armor: helmet, breastplate, shield, sword, belt, and shoes. These pieces of spiritual equipment are effective only if we put them on and use them, even if they might feel uncomfortable at first. Faithfulness in the Word (v. 17), in prayer (v. 18), and in witness (vv. 19–20) are critical to making our armor feel like a part of us. So suit up! The battle is on!   —BC

> *Be not weary, Christian warrior,*
> *Buckle on thine armor tight;*
> *Be ye strong and face the battle*
> *In the power of His might.* —Iler

God's armor is tailor-made for you, but you must put it on.

The Stones

READ: Joshua 4

*When your children ask . . . "What are these stones?"
then you shall let [them] know, saying, "Israel crossed
over this Jordan on dry land."* —JOSHUA 4:21–22

Not long ago our friends had a gathering at their house and invited a group of people who were music lovers. Kevin and Ilse, who are both gifted musicians, requested that each person or couple bring a rock for a fire pit that was often the site for their evening musical jams. But they didn't want just plain ol' rocks. They asked that each one be marked with a name or date or event that indicated how or when we had become friends.

God felt that the Israelites needed a reminder of an amazing event in their lives. Although the Jordan River had been at flood stage, the Israelites had been able to cross over on dry ground because God had stopped the water from flowing (Joshua 3:13–17). Something similar had happened years before in an escape from Egypt (see Exodus 14:21–31). On this occasion, however, God instructed His people to build a memorial of stones so that in the future when children would ask about the stones, parents could remind them of the mighty hand of God (Joshua 4:23–24).

Just as God continually cared for the Israelites, so He continues to provide for us today. What "stones of remembrance" will you use to remind your children, grandchildren—and even yourself—of the evidence of God's might? —CHK

> *God's faithfulness we've known throughout the years,*
> *His oneness with us in our joys and tears;*
> *So many times the Lord has helped us through,*
> *Has answered prayer and given strength anew.* —F. Hess

Remembering God's goodness is a good cure for doubt.

Free Compliments

READ: Proverbs 16:20–30

*Pleasant words are like a honeycomb, sweetness to
the soul and health to the bones.* —PROVERBS 16:24

During a time of economic crisis and depressing news, two students
at Purdue University decided to lift the spirits of people on campus
with some encouraging words. For two hours every Wednesday afternoon, Cameron Brown and Brett Westcott stood along a busy walk-
way holding a large "Free Compliments" sign and saying nice things
to everyone who passed by. "I like your red coat." "Cool snow boots."
"Very nice smile." Some students said they deliberately walked past "the
compliment guys" every Wednesday just to hear a kind word.

I was struck by these two young men who looked at people with the
goal of commending them, rather than finding fault or being critical. Is
that how I, as a follower of Christ, view others each day?

Instead of being like the person who is focused on evil and whose
speech is "like a burning fire" (Proverbs 16:27), we can take a different
approach, knowing that what we say begins deep inside us. "The heart
of the wise teaches his mouth, and adds learning to his lips. Pleasant
words are like a honeycomb, sweetness to the soul and health to the
bones" (vv. 23–24).

Kind words may be free, but they give a priceless lift of spirit. Why
not encourage someone today?   —DM

> *The power in words can build up or tear down—*
> *Create a big smile or produce a sad frown;*
> *So in all your contacts with people each day,*
> *Be sure to encourage in all that you say.* —Fitzhugh

A gentle word of compliment falls lightly but it carries great weight.

How to Bloom

READ: 1 Peter 1:1–9

*Rejoice to the extent that you partake
of Christ's sufferings.* —1 PETER 4:13

My family and I live in an apartment, so our "flower garden" consists of what we can grow in indoor pots. For a long time our plants would not flower despite watering and fertilizing. Then we discovered that the soil had to be raked and turned over if the plants were to bloom. Now our potted plants are a pure joy to look at with their healthy leaves and blooming flowers.

Sometimes we need a little raking and turning in our own lives to make us bloom. Writing to the harassed believers in his day, Peter said, "Beloved, do not think it strange concerning the fiery trial which is to try you, as though some strange thing happened to you; but rejoice" (1 Peter 4:12–13).

Like the soil in our potted plants, these Christians were having their lives "turned over." God's purpose in doing that was to allow their faith to result in praise and glory to Him at the revelation of Jesus Christ (1:7).

God wants to loosen the things that can choke our lives and that prevent us from radiating joy. To do this, He sometimes has to allow pain and trouble—trials that help stir up the soil of our lives. If this is what you are experiencing today, rejoice. Surrender to His touch and acquire a joy and fruitfulness you never imagined possible.   —CPH

*Turning the soil and pulling the weeds
Helps garden flowers to grow,
And if we're to see growth in our lives
Trials and testings we'll know.* —Sper

Those who bless God in their trials will be blessed by God through their trials.

Gracias!

READ: 1 Chronicles 16:7–10, 23–36

Oh, give thanks to the Lord! —1 CHRONICLES 16:8

When I visited Mexico, I wished I knew how to speak Spanish. I could say gracias (thank you), muy bien (very good), and hola (hello). But that was about it. I grew tired of just saying gracias to everyone who talked with me or did something for me.

But we should never grow tired of giving words of thanks to God. David knew the importance of saying thanks. After he became king over Israel and had a tent constructed to house the ark of the covenant (where God's presence dwelt), he appointed some of the Levites "to commemorate, to thank, and to praise the Lord" (1 Chronicles 16:4). Many people remained there to offer sacrifices and give thanks to God daily (vv. 37–38).

David also committed to Asaph and his associates a song of thanks (1 Chronicles 16:8–36). His psalm gave thanks for what the Lord had done: "His deeds among the peoples" (v. 8); "His wondrous works" (v. 9); "His wonders, and the judgments of His mouth" (v. 12); and His "salvation" (v. 35). David's song also gave praise for who the Lord was: good, merciful, and holy (vv. 34–35).

Like David, we should never grow tired of saying gracias to God for who He is and for all He's done for us. Take time today to offer your sacrifice of praise to Him.   —AC

> *Praise, my soul, the King of heaven,*
> *To His feet thy tribute bring;*
> *Ransomed, healed, restored, forgiven,*
> *Evermore His praises sing.* —Lyte

The heart filled with praise brings pleasure to God.

Imperfect Leaders

READ: 2 Corinthians 3:1–5

Our sufficiency is from God. —2 CORINTHIANS 3:5

God's ways are not our ways. We tend to equate leadership with lordship; He equates leadership with servanthood. We want strength so we can help God with His work; He makes us weak so He can demonstrate His power. We advertise our credentials so others can be more certain of us; He lets us fail so they can see that apart from God we're not much at all.

We are inclined to focus on personalities, to be impressed by the intellect, education, and strength of a leader's will. Followers begin to believe that a particular leader can do no wrong. Such adulation, however, is nothing more than humanism—making a human being the measure of all things. What's worse, it's idolatry—centering our devotion on someone other than God.

So God lets leaders fall off their pedestal. Failure, indecision, and underachievement bring them to a humbling realization of their own inadequacy—and can cause followers to lose their illusions and overdependence on those leaders. This is a good reminder that all of us, leaders and followers alike, walk through life on "feet of clay." Ultimately, the only good thing about any one of us is the goodness of God. That's why we need to recognize that "our sufficiency is from God" (2 Corinthians 3:5).　　　　　　　　　　　　　—DR

If you rely upon God's strength
And live a life that's true,
Then what you do in Jesus' name
Will be His work through you. —D. DeHaan

Only as we see our weakness can we draw upon God's strength.

Failures Anonymous

READ: John 21:3–17

As soon as they had come to land, they saw a fire of coals there, and fish laid on it, and bread. —JOHN 21:9

It's my duty to grill the burgers, brats, steaks, or whatever else my wife has on the menu. And while I'm not the greatest chef when it comes to outdoor cooking, I love the aroma of grilling over a charcoal fire. So the mention of a "fire of coals" in John 21:9 catches my attention. And I find myself wondering why John would include this detail in the story about Jesus calling a failing Peter back to serve and follow Him.

In John 21:1–3, it's apparent that Peter had reopened his fishing business. Just a few days before, Peter was warming his hands over a charcoal fire when he denied Jesus to save his own skin (John 18:17–18). So why not go back to fishing?

While Peter and his cohorts were casting nets, Jesus built a fire on the beach. Coincidence? I doubt it! And as Peter approached Jesus, I wonder if the pungent aroma of the burning charcoal brought back memories of that other fire where he had failed Christ. Yet Jesus in His mercy took the initiative to call Peter back into His service.

Think of it: Jesus is willing to forgive our failures and call us into His service. After all, if only perfect people qualified to serve Him, He wouldn't have anyone to choose from!   —JS

> *Although we are imperfect,*
> *The Lord can use us still,*
> *If we confess our sins to Him*
> *And seek to do His will.* —Sper

Being imperfect doesn't disqualify us from serving God;
it just emphasizes our dependence on His mercy.

Columbus's Eclipse

READ: 2 Corinthians 2:14–17

We are not, as so many, peddling the Word of God. —2 CORINTHIANS 2:17

On one of Christopher Columbus's voyages, he found that his crew's food supply was almost depleted. Anchored off the island of Jamaica, he was grateful to be given food by the islanders. But as time went on, the gifts of food decreased so that the crew began to starve.

Columbus knew from an astronomy book that a lunar eclipse would soon occur. He called the native chiefs together and told them God was angry about their selfishness and would blot out the moon. At first the islanders scoffed. But when they watched the night's silver disc slowly become dark, they became terrified and quickly brought food. Columbus said that if he prayed, the moon would be restored. Though we may empathize with his circumstances, Columbus's "message from God" was dishonest and self-serving.

Aware of religious charlatans who "peddled" God's Word for their own desires, the apostle Paul wrote, "We are not, as so many, peddling the word of God; but as of sincerity, but as from God, we speak in the sight of God" (2 Corinthians 2:17).

At all times we must be on guard not to misrepresent God's message to acquire what we want from others. With a heart yielded to God, we must honestly share spiritual truths that will benefit those who hear. —DF

Don't compromise the Word of God
Or twist what He has said;
For blessing comes from faithfully
Proclaiming truth instead. —Sper

The purpose of sharing God's truth is to profit others, not to prosper ourselves.

Theology Is for Everyone

READ: Jeremiah 23:25–32

*I am the Lord, exercising lovingkindness, judgment,
and righteousness in the earth.* —JEREMIAH 9:24

Some say that theology is only for "professionals." But the situation in the days of the prophet Jeremiah illustrates why it's important for everyone to know what God says about himself.

The religious experts in Jeremiah's day were misrepresenting God by prophesying "the delusions of their own minds" (Jeremiah 23:26 NIV) and leading people astray with their lies (v. 32). Due to their dishonesty, the people did not know the true nature of God.

Today there are people who portray God as angry, vengeful, and eager to punish people for every minor offense. God, however, describes himself as "merciful and gracious, longsuffering, and abounding in goodness and truth" (Exodus 34:6). Others show the world a picture of a loving God who is too kind to punish wrongdoing. But God describes himself as one who exercises judgment and righteousness (Jeremiah 9:24). He is both a just judge and a loving father. If we emphasize one over the other, we paint a false picture of God.

The most important thing we can know about God and proclaim to the world is that God does not want to punish people; He wants them to repent so that He can forgive (2 Peter 3:9). But to be truly loving, He must also be absolutely just.   —JAL

*Though love for God should always move
My heart to do what's good and right,
It's wise to fear His judgments true
And stand in awe of His great might.* —D. DeHaan

Everyone must face God as Savior or as Judge.

Gold-Medal Effort

READ: Philippians 2:4–11

Let each of you look out not only for his own interests,
but also for the interests of others. —PHILIPPIANS 2:4

At the 2009 Kansas high school state track championship, an unusual thing happened. The team that won the girls 3,200-meter relay was disqualified. But what happened next was even more unusual. The team that was awarded the state championship by default turned right around and gave their medals to the team that had been disqualified.

The first school, St. Mary's Colgan, lost first place because judges ruled that a runner had stepped out of her lane as she handed off the baton. That meant the second team, Maranatha Academy, moved up to first. After receiving their medals, the girls from Maranatha saw the downtrodden looks on the faces of the St. Mary's girls, so they gave them their individual medals.

Why did they do this? As Maranatha's coach Bernie Zarda put it: "Our theme for the year was to run not for our glory, but for God's glory." As a result of the girls' action, their story was told throughout Kansas, and God's name was lifted up.

When we set aside our own interests and accomplishments to recognize that it's better to care for the interests of others (Philippians 2:4), we see God's name glorified. Acting with grace and kindness toward others is one of the best ways to point people to God.   —DB

Love is not blind but looks
Abroad through others' eyes,
And asks not, "Must I give?"
But, "May I sacrifice?" —Ziegler

When we love God, we will serve people.

Talk Low, Talk Slow

READ: Judges 7:24–8:3

A soft answer turns away wrath. —PROVERBS 15:1

John Wayne, famous American actor and film icon, once said, "Talk low, talk slow, and don't say too much." His advice is hard for me to follow since I'm a fast talker and I don't always speak quietly or limit my words. However, this idea of controlling our speech can be a useful tool when dealing with anger. The Bible says we are supposed to be "slow to speak" (James 1:19), and that "a soft answer turns away wrath" (Proverbs 15:1).

Gideon gave a soft answer during a verbal scuffle with some fellow Israelites (Judges 8). Just after his army defeated the Midianites, a group of his countrymen criticized him sharply (v. 1). They were miffed because they missed out on the main part of the battle. Gideon did not fling back a rough response. Instead, he reminded them that they had captured and killed the Midianite princes. He also honored the men by asking, "What was I able to do in comparison with you?" Finally, "their anger toward him subsided when he said that" (v. 3).

With the Lord's help, we can defuse heated situations by reining in our words. Responding gently and carefully to angry people can promote unity, for God's glory. —JBS

> Lord, set a guard upon my lips,
> My tongue control today;
> Help me evaluate each thought
> And watch each word I say. —Hess

Bite your tongue before your tongue bites others.

Serve Him Today

READ: 1 Samuel 12:19–25

You have done all this wickedness; yet do not turn aside from following the Lord, but serve the Lord with all your heart. —1 SAMUEL 12:20

Most of us, at some time, have wanted something so badly that even though we knew it was wrong, we plunged after it anyway. Later we have felt sorrow for our spiritual stubbornness and stupidity. In the aftermath of willfully disobeying God, we may become angry with ourselves, numbed by regret, or resigned to the consequences of our foolish mistake. But there is another choice.

When the people of Israel insisted on having a king despite the warnings of Samuel the prophet (1 Samuel 8:4–9), God allowed them to have their way. But when they realized the tragic results of their choice, they asked for Samuel's help and prayers (12:19). Samuel told the people, "Do not fear. You have done all this wickedness; yet do not turn aside from following the Lord, but serve the Lord with all your heart" (12:20).

We can't undo yesterday, but we can act today to influence tomorrow. Samuel promised to pray for them and teach them the right way. He urged them, "Only fear the Lord, and serve Him in truth with all your heart; for consider what great things He has done for you" (v. 24).

God invites us to serve Him today, humbly acknowledging His forgiveness and His faithfulness. —DM

Sins confessed you must forget;
Look not back to yesterday—
Full of failure and regret;
Look ahead and seek God's way. —D. DeHaan

Don't let yesterday's failures bankrupt tomorrow's efforts.

Valid Entry

READ: John 14:1–10

*Jesus said to him, "I am the way, the truth, and the life. No one comes to the Father except through Me." —*JOHN 14:6

On a teaching trip outside the US, my wife and I were denied entry into our country of destination because of visa problems. Although we were under the assumption that our visas had been correctly issued by the country we planned to visit, they were deemed invalid. Despite the efforts of several government officials, nothing could be done. We weren't allowed in. We were placed on the next flight back to the States. No amount of intervention could change the fact that we did not have the proper validation for entrance.

That experience with my visa was inconvenient, but it can't begin to compare with the ultimate entry rejection. I'm speaking of those who will stand before God without valid entry into heaven. What if they were to present the record of their religious efforts and good deeds? That would not be enough. What if they were to call character references? That wouldn't work. Only one thing can give anyone entry into heaven. Jesus said, "I am the way, the truth, and the life. No one comes to the Father except through Me" (John 14:6).

Christ alone, through His death and resurrection, paid the price for our sins. And only He can give us valid entry into the presence of the Father. Have you put your faith in Jesus? Make sure you have a valid entry into heaven.   —BC

There aren't many ways into heaven;
The Bible says there's only one;
Good works won't gain anyone entrance;
It's only through faith in God's Son. —Sper

Only through Christ can we enter the Father's presence.

Who Is This?

READ: Luke 19:28–40

Blessed is [He] who comes in the name of the Lord! —LUKE 19:38

I magine standing shoulder to shoulder with onlookers by a dirt road. The woman behind you is on her tiptoes, trying to see who is coming. In the distance, you glimpse a man riding a donkey. As He approaches, people toss their coats onto the road. Suddenly, you hear a tree crack behind you. A man is cutting down palm branches, and people are spreading them out ahead of the donkey.

Jesus' followers zealously honored Him as He entered Jerusalem a few days before His crucifixion. The multitude rejoiced and praised God for "all the mighty works they had seen" (Luke 19:37). Jesus' devotees surrounded Him, calling out, "Blessed is the King who comes in the name of the Lord!" (v. 38). Their enthusiasm affected the people of Jerusalem. When Jesus finally arrived, "all the city was moved, saying, 'Who is this?'" (Matthew 21:10).

Today, people are still curious about Jesus. Although we can't pave His way with palm branches or shout praises to Him in person, we can still honor Him. We can discuss His remarkable works, assist people in need (Galatians 6:2), patiently bear insults (1 Peter 4:14–16), and love each other deeply (v. 8). Then we must be ready to answer the onlookers who ask, "Who is Jesus?" —JBS

> *So let our lips and lives express*
> *The holy gospel we profess;*
> *So let our works and virtues shine,*
> *To prove the doctrine all divine.* —Watts

We honor God's name when we call Him our Father and live like His Son.

Too Good to Be True?

READ: Luke 24:1–12

Their words seemed to [the disciples] like idle tales,
and they did not believe them. —LUKE 24:11

In the 1980s, John Knoll and his brother Thomas began experimenting with a computer program to manipulate images. Software companies thought they were crazy, because photographers didn't use computers at that time. Initially the brothers called their program Display, then Imaginator, and finally they settled on Photoshop®. Today Photoshop® is used by amateurs at home and professionals in business around the world. A *San Jose Mercury News* article noted its place in popular language. When something looks too good to be true, people say, "It must have been Photoshopped."

On the first Easter morning, the women who took spices to anoint the body of Jesus found the tomb empty and heard angels say, "He is not here, but is risen!" (Luke 24:6). When the women told this to the disciples, "Their words seemed to them like idle tales, and they did not believe them" (v. 11). Nonsense! Mind-boggling! Too good to be true!

If someone manipulated the evidence, then millions of people around the world celebrate a myth. But if Jesus conquered death, then all He said about forgiveness, power to change, and eternal life is real.

Because Christ has risen and lives today, this news is too good not to be true! —DM

Up from the grave He arose,
With a mighty triumph o'er His foes;
He arose a Victor from the dark domain,
And He lives forever with His saints to reign. —Lowry

The resurrection is a fact of history that demands a response of faith.

Time for a Checkup

READ: 1 Corinthians 11:27–29

Let a man examine himself, and so let him eat of the bread and drink of the cup. —1 CORINTHIANS 11:28

Every year I have a physical, that periodic visit to the doctor's office where I'm poked and prodded, screened and studied. It is something that can be easy to dread and even to fear. We aren't sure what the tests will show or what the doctors will say. Still, we know that we need this evaluation to understand our physical well-being and what is needed as we move forward.

The same is true spiritually in the life of the Christ-follower. We need to pause from time to time and reflect on the condition of our hearts and lives.

One place for an important self-study is at the Lord's Table. Paul wrote this to the Corinthians, some of whom were eating in an unworthy manner: "Let a man examine himself, and so let him eat of the bread and drink of the cup" (1 Corinthians 11:28). In the remembrance of Christ's death for us, there can be a sobering clarity of thought and understanding, for as we consider the price Jesus paid for us, it is the best time to consider the condition of our heart and our relationships. Then, with honest understanding of our spiritual well-being, we can turn to Him for the grace we need to move forward in His name.

Is it time for your checkup?   —BC

Search me, O God, my heart discern;
Try me, my inmost thoughts to learn.
Help me to keep from sin, I pray,
Guarding my mind throughout this day. —*Anonymous*

Self-examination is one test from which no Christian is excused.

An Attached Fuel Hose

READ: 2 Timothy 2:1–7

*No one engaged in warfare entangles himself
with the affairs of this life.* —2 TIMOTHY 2:4

Felipe Massa of Brazil should have won the Formula One Grand Prix in Singapore in September 2008. But as he drove off from a refueling stop while in the lead, the fuel hose was still attached. By the time his team removed the hose, he had lost so much time that he finished thirteenth.

The apostle Paul warned Timothy of another kind of attachment that would cause him defeat—"the affairs of this life" (2 Timothy 2:4). He urged Timothy not to let anything slow him down or distract him from the cause of his Lord and Master.

There are many attractive things in our world that are so easy to get entangled with—hobbies, sports, TV, computer games. These may start off as "refueling" activities, but later they can take up so much of our time and thought that they interfere with the purpose for which God created us: to share the good news of Christ, serve Him with our gifts, and bring glory to Him.

Paul told Timothy why he should not be entangled with this world's affairs: So that he could "please Him" (v. 4). If your desire is to please the Lord Jesus, you will want to stay untangled from the world. As John reminds us, "The world is passing away, and the lust of it; but he who does the will of God abides forever" (1 John 2:17).   —CPH

Although we live in this world, we must declare our allegiance to heaven.

The Last Jelly Bean

READ: Psalm 34:1–10

Oh, taste and see that the Lord is good . . . Those who seek the Lord shall not lack any good thing. —PSALM 34:8, 10

One afternoon Angela gave her young daughter four jelly beans and let her know that was all the candy she was going to receive. After practically inhaling the first three candies, Eliana lingered over the final one. She sucked on it, took it out of her mouth, bit into it, sucked on it some more, then gnawed at the outer shell. Knowing that this was her last jelly bean, she took a full forty-five minutes to ingest the treat completely.

Angela observed her little girl with amusement. It occurred to her that she was watching Eliana learn the value of savoring—enjoying taste and texture and learning to draw out every possible bit of flavor from the pleasurable experience.

When we read, "Oh, taste and see that the Lord is good" (Psalm 34:8), we can be sure that God wants us to "savor" His presence. He allows us to gain intimate and satisfying knowledge of Him. And when we meditate on His Word, we will draw out a deeper understanding of who He is (Ezekiel 3:1–3). As we taste His goodness and love, He will reveal the distinctive flavor of His creativity, sovereignty, holiness, and faithfulness.

Our Father must look on with enjoyment as we learn how to enjoy and savor Him.   —CHK

> *Oh, taste the goodness of the Lord*
> *And savor all that He has done;*
> *Draw close and give your praise to Him—*
> *The holy, sovereign, faithful One.* —Sper

Our greatest privilege is to enjoy God's presence.

Spiritual Superstars

READ: 1 Corinthians 3:1–15

When one says, "I am of Paul," and another, "I am of Apollos," are you not carnal? —1 CORINTHIANS 3:4

Superstars abound in today's culture. Great soccer players can create such excitement that fans have been known to riot in the bleachers. Popular musicians have fans who stand with adoration throughout entire concerts. And Hollywood celebrities hire bodyguards to protect themselves from adoring stalkers.

The first-century Corinthian believers had become divided over their own "spiritual superstars." Paul viewed such favoritism as a reflection of the sinful nature in a believer's unyielded heart. "For when one says, 'I am of Paul,' and another, 'I am of Apollos,' are you not carnal?" he asked (1 Corinthians 3:4).

The apostle's teaching on how we view Christian leaders puts the topic in a biblical perspective that provides mutual appreciation for those who minister: "I planted, Apollos watered, but God gave the increase" (v. 6). Each person did his part. Paul had planted spiritual seed through evangelism, and Apollos had watered it with his eloquent Bible teaching. But it was God alone who made the seed of spiritual life grow. He alone is the "superstar."

We should be careful not to put any Christian leader on a pedestal. Instead, let's appreciate how God is using a variety of spiritual leaders for His honor and His glory. —DF

*Lord, give us wisdom. We know it's good to follow the
example of our godly leaders, but help us not to think so
highly of them that we worship them instead of you.*

**Each person has his or her place in God's
service, and only God deserves the glory.**

School of Hard Knocks

READ: Hebrews 12:3–11

No chastening seems to be joyful for the present . . . nevertheless, afterward it yields the peaceable fruit of righteousness. —HEBREWS 12:11

Of all my childhood memories, one stands out above the others. While I have no idea what my teacher said, I clearly remember telling her to "shut up." She sent me home, so I got up and left my kindergarten class to walk the half-block home. Walking down the sidewalk, I saw my mother weeding in the garden behind our house. I was now faced with a strategic decision—continue on my way and tell my mother why I was home early from school, or turn around and go back to face my teacher.

When I returned to the classroom, I was immediately escorted to the restroom, where my teacher washed my mouth out with soap. That kind of discipline probably wouldn't happen today, but take it from me, it was effective! To this day I am acutely sensitive about the impact of my words.

God is passionately interested in our positive growth as His children. At times He needs to confront us with unpleasant circumstances to catch our attention and reorient our lives to more consistently produce the "peaceable fruit of righteousness" (Hebrews 12:11).

Don't resist God's corrective hand. Respond to His reproofs with thankfulness that He loves you enough to care about what kind of a person you are becoming. —JS

> *Because our Father's heart is grieved*
> *Each time we go astray,*
> *He lifts His chastening hand in love*
> *To help us walk His way.* —D. DeHaan

God's correction is our hope for a better life.

Second-Chance Champions

READ: Hebrews 11:17–32

By faith Abraham . . . offered up Isaac, and he who had received the promises offered up his only begotten son. —HEBREWS 11:17

The Senior PGA Tour, often called the "Second-Chance Tour," has given many teaching pros a new golfing career after age fifty. Sportswriter Jack Cavanaugh says, "In no other sport does an athlete who never made it to the world-class level in his prime get a second chance in middle age to prove himself and amass riches that he could only dream about in his twenties, thirties, or forties."

Are you looking for a second chance? There's a widespread idea that if you once miss "God's best" you can never again render gold-medal service to Him. But in Hebrews 11, faith's "hall of fame," we read of several who failed yet came back strong for the Lord.

Abraham, often willful and impatient in waiting for the son God had promised, demonstrated amazing faith in offering up Isaac (vv. 17–19). Jacob, the schemer who stole his brother's birthright and blessing, became a man of faith who blessed his children and worshiped God (v. 21). Moses spent forty years in Midian before leading God's people out of Egypt (vv. 24–28).

Our previous mistakes do not necessarily exclude us from serving God. His best for us is that we turn away from our sin, learn from our failures, and begin anew to follow Christ. That's the way to be a second-chance champion. —DM

Our Savior does not cast us off
Because we fail or turn aside;
He will forgive when we repent,
Then in His love we will abide. —D. DeHaan

Champions of faith are people who have learned from their failures.

Bel Bows Down

READ: Isaiah 46:1–9

I will carry you! —ISAIAH 46:4

The prophet Isaiah draws a picture for us in Isaiah 46 of the siege of Babylon and the evacuation of its idols. The carts and carriages that carry them creak, and the weary animals groan under the load (v. 1).

In contrast, Isaiah says that God carries His children from birth (v. 3). "Even to your old age, I am He, and even to gray hairs I will carry you!" God declares (v. 4). The contrast is precise and vivid in the Hebrew text: The carts and carriages are "loaded" with the weight of the idols (v. 1), but we are loaded upon God (v. 3). Idols are a "burden," a thing carried (v. 1), but God has gladly "carried" us from the womb (v. 3).

The Lord has made us (v. 4). Nothing could be more comforting, for our Father loves and cares for His children. He promises, "I will carry you!" and that includes every care and worry that comes our way throughout our lifetime. So we may let Him carry us and our every burden.

This song by Annie Johnson Flint challenges us to experience God's care: "Fear not that thy need shall exceed His provision, / Our God ever yearns His resources to share; / Lean hard on the arm everlasting, availing; / Thy Father both thee and thy load will upbear."   —DR

Heavenly Father, I want to unload my burdens on you today. Help me to leave them with you. I trust you with my past, present, and future. Thank you for your goodness to me.

Our work is to cast care; God's work is to take care!

A Forever Service

READ: Revelation 22:1–7

Behold, I make all things new. —REVELATION 21:5

Two young brothers sat on the front row in church every Sunday, observing their dad as he led the worship service. One night after sending the boys to bed, the dad overheard one of his boys crying. He asked him what was wrong, but the boy was hesitant to answer. Finally, he confessed, "Daddy, the Bible says we're going to worship God in heaven forever. That's an awfully long time!" Because he pictured heaven as one long worship time with his dad up front leading, heaven sounded pretty boring to him!

While I sometimes wish we had more information about what heaven will be like, we know this for sure: boring can't possibly be the right word to describe it. We will see beauty like we've never seen before, including "a pure river of water of life, clear as crystal" (Revelation 22:1). We will experience "the glory of God," which will illuminate heaven (21:23; 22:5). And we will enjoy a life without pain or sorrow (21:4).

Yes, we will definitely worship in heaven. People "out of every tribe and tongue and people and nation" (5:9) will rejoice in praising Jesus, the worthy Lamb who died for us and rose again (5:12). We will bask in the glory of the Lord's presence—forever. But not for one second will we be bored! —AC

In heaven we'll see our Savior
And like Him we will be;
We'll praise Him and we'll serve Him
For all eternity! —Fitzhugh

The pleasures of earth cannot be compared to the joys of heaven.

The Penny Syndrome

READ: 1 Samuel 17:32–37

*The Lord, who delivered me from the paw of
the lion . . . He will deliver me from the
hand of this Philistine.* —1 SAMUEL 17:37

The penny has been called the most despised unit of US currency. Many people will not bother to pick up a one-cent coin if they see it lying on the ground. But some charities are finding that pennies add up to significant sums and that children are generous givers. As one participant said, "Small contributions can make a huge difference."

The Bible account of David and Goliath describes a seemingly insignificant person whose confidence in God was greater than any of the powerful people around him. When David volunteered to face the giant Goliath, King Saul said, "You are not able to go against this Philistine" (1 Samuel 17:33). But David had faith in the Lord who had delivered him in the past (v. 37).

David did not suffer from "the penny syndrome"—a sense of inferiority and helplessness in the face of an overwhelming problem. If he had listened to the pessimism of Saul or the threats of Goliath, he would have done nothing. Instead, he acted with courage because he trusted God.

It's easy to feel like a penny in a trillion-dollar deficit. But when we obey the Lord in every circumstance, it all adds up. Collectively, our acts of faith, large or small, make a big difference. And every penny counts. —DM

*It matters not how large or small
Your faith may seem to be;
What really counts is whom you trust
In life's uncertainty.* —Fitzhugh

Courage will follow when faith takes the lead.

Pay Attention to Signs

READ: Luke 11:29–45

*As Jonah became a sign to the Ninevites, so also the
Son of Man will be to this generation.* —LUKE 11:30

The road was smooth and we were making good progress as we headed for Jay's dad's house in South Carolina. As we drove through the mountains in Tennessee, I began seeing detour signs. But Jay kept going, so I assumed that they didn't apply to us. Shortly before we reached the North Carolina border, however, we came to a sign that said the highway ahead was closed due to a rock slide. We would have to turn around.

Jay was surprised. "Why wasn't there any warning?" he wanted to know.

"There were lots of warnings," I said. "Didn't you see the signs?"

"No," he said, "why didn't you mention them?"

"I assumed that you saw them," I answered. We now tell this story to entertain our friends.

Throughout history, God provided plenty of "signs" to show people the way to live, but they kept going their own way. When God finally sent His Son as a sign (Luke 11:30), the religious leaders paid little attention to His warnings. Life for them was good. They were recognized and respected (v. 43). They resented being told that they were wrong (v. 45).

We can be the same way. When life is going well, we tend to ignore warnings that we need to turn around and change our sinful ways. It's important to remember that we may be wrong even though life is good. —JAL

*God gives us warnings to prevent
Our falling into sin;
But if we do ignore—and fall—
Confession cleanses us within.* —Sper

God sends warnings to protect us, not to punish us.

Sourdough Bread

READ: Luke 12:1–7

Beware of the leaven of the Pharisees,
which is hypocrisy. —LUKE 12:1

Sourdough bread became popular during the California Gold Rush of the mid-1800s. In the 1890s, it was a favorite during the great Gold Rush in Alaska. Prospectors would carry with them a small portion of sourdough mix that contained a natural yeast. It could then be used as a starter to make more of their favorite sourdough bread.

In the Bible, though, yeast or leaven can have a negative connotation. For example, in the New Testament "leaven" is often referred to as a corrupting influence. This is why Jesus said: "Beware of the leaven of the Pharisees, which is hypocrisy" (Luke 12:1).

Hypocrites put on a show of righteousness while hiding sinful thoughts and behavior. Christ warned His disciples and us that secret sins will someday be exposed to full disclosure. He said, "There is nothing covered that will not be revealed, nor hidden that will not be known" (v. 2). Because of this, we are to reverentially fear God, to ask for His grace to forsake any sin, and to grow as authentic believers.

Yeast may be a blessing in the bakery, but it can also remind us to guard against the permeating influence of sin in our hearts.   —DF

The holiness of God demands
A heart that's pure within,
Yet grace unites with holiness
To purge the heart from sin. —D. DeHaan

Be sure your sin will find you out. —Numbers 32:23

Breath of Life

READ: Psalm 139:13–18

*The Spirit of God has made me, and the breath
of the Almighty gives me life.* —JOB 33:4

In his book *Life After Heart Surgery*, David Burke recalls his brush with death. Lying in his hospital bed after a second open-heart surgery, he found himself in incredible pain, unable to draw a full breath. Feeling that he was slipping toward eternity, he prayed one last time, trusting God and thanking Him for forgiveness of his sin.

David was thinking about seeing his dad, who had died several years earlier, when his nurse asked how he was feeling. He replied, "I'm okay now," explaining he was ready to go to heaven and meet God. "Not on my shift, buddy!" she said. Soon the doctors were opening his chest again and removing two liters of fluid. That done, David began to recover.

It's not unusual for any of us to ponder what it will be like when we face our final moments on earth. But those who "die in the Lord" have the certainty that they are "blessed" (Revelation 14:13) and that their death is "precious in the sight of the Lord" (Psalm 116:15).

God fashioned our days even before we existed (Psalm 139:16), and we exist now only because "the breath of the Almighty gives [us] life" (Job 33:4). Though we don't know how many breaths we have left, we can rest in the knowledge that He does. —CHK

> *God holds our future in His hands*
> *And gives us every breath;*
> *Just knowing that He's by our side*
> *Allays our fear of death.* —Sper

From our first breath to our last, we are in God's care.

Dealing with Delay

READ: Isaiah 26:1–9

You will keep him in perfect peace, whose
mind is stayed on You. —ISAIAH 26:3

In April 2010, clouds of ash spewed by a volcano in Iceland closed airports across the UK and Europe for five days. Nearly 100,000 flights were canceled, and millions of passengers around the world found themselves in an enormous holding pattern on the ground. People missed important events, businesses lost money, and no one knew when it would end.

When our plans fall apart and there is no remedy, how do we deal with frustration and delay? Isaiah 26:3–4 is an anchor for our souls in every storm of life: "You will keep him in perfect peace, whose mind is stayed on You, because he trusts in You. Trust in the Lord forever, for in [Jehovah], the Lord, is everlasting strength." Whether we're facing annoying inconvenience or heartbreaking loss, this rock-solid promise is worth memorizing and repeating every night when we close our eyes to sleep.

Today, when plans are shattered, do our minds dwell on the circumstances or on the Lord? During frustrating delay, can we still trust the loving heart of God? In the hymn "Like a River Glorious," Frances Havergal so beautifully expressed what we long for. —DM

Hidden in the hollow of His blessed hand,
Never foe can follow, never traitor stand;
Not a surge of worry, not a shade of care,
Not a blast of hurry touch the spirit there.
Stayed upon Jehovah, hearts are fully blest,
Finding as He promised, perfect peace and rest. —Havergal

When we put our problems in God's hands, He puts His peace in our hearts.

Of Pain and Gain

READ: Psalm 32

Many sorrows shall be to the wicked; but he who trusts in the Lord, mercy shall surround him. —PSALM 32:10

During summer training camp, the coaches on one football team wore T-shirts intended to urge their players to exert maximum effort. The shirts bore the motto, "Each day you must choose: The pain of discipline or the pain of regret."

Discipline is tough—and something we may try to avoid. But in sports and in life, short-term pain is often the only path to long-term gain. In the heat of battle it is too late to prepare. Either you are ready for the challenges of life or you will be haunted by the "what ifs," "if onlys," and "I should'ves" that accompany the failure to be prepared. That's the pain of regret.

One source defines regret as "an intelligent and emotional dislike for personal past acts and behaviors." It's painful to look back at our choices through the lens of regret and feel the weight of our failures. This was the case for the psalmist. After a personal episode of sin and failure, he wrote, "Many sorrows shall be to the wicked; but he who trusts in the Lord, mercy shall surround him" (Psalm 32:10). In the clarity of hindsight, he saw the wisdom of a life that strives to honor the Lord—a life that does not need to be marked by regret.

May our choices today not result in regret, but rather be wise and God-honoring.   —BC

In you, O Lord, we take delight,
Our every need you can supply;
We long to do what's true and right,
So, Lord, on you we will rely. —D. DeHaan

Present choices determine future rewards.

Feeding Ourselves

READ: Hebrews 5:12–6:2

By this time you ought to be teachers. —Hebrews 5:12

The eaglets were hungry, and Mom and Dad seemed to be ignoring them. The oldest of the three decided to solve his hunger problem by gnawing on a twig. Apparently it wasn't too tasty, because he soon abandoned it.

What intrigued me about this little drama, which was being broadcast by webcam from Norfolk Botanical Garden, was that a big fish lay just behind the eaglets. But they had not yet learned to feed themselves. They still relied on their parents to tear their food in tiny pieces and feed it to them. Within a few weeks, however, the parents will teach the eaglets how to feed themselves—one of their first survival lessons. If the eaglets don't learn this skill, they will never be able to survive on their own.

The author of Hebrews spoke of a similar problem in the spiritual realm. Certain people in the church were not growing in spiritual maturity. They had not learned to distinguish between good and bad (Hebrews 5:14). Like the eaglet, they hadn't learned the difference between a twig and a fish. They still needed to be fed by someone else when they should have been feeding not only themselves but others as well (v. 12).

While receiving spiritual food from preachers and teachers is good, spiritual growth and survival also depend on knowing how to feed ourselves. —JAL

You've given us your Spirit, Lord,
To help us grow, mature, and learn,
To teach us from your written Word,
So truth from error we'll discern. —Sper

Spiritual growth requires the solid food of God's Word.

The Purpose of God's Goodness

READ: Psalm 67

*God be merciful to us and bless us, and cause
His face to shine upon us.* —Psalm 67:1

When I was growing up, we often sang a song in Sunday school that went like this: "God is good to me! God is good to me! He holds my hand and helps me stand! God is good to me!"

I need to say right away that I believe God is good and He takes delight in doing good things for people. He does indeed hold our hand in times of trouble and helps us stand against the onslaught of life's difficulties. But I wonder if you've ever asked yourself: Why is He good? It certainly is not because we deserve it or because He feels the need to buy our love and allegiance with His benefits.

The psalmist prays for God to bless him so that "[the Lord's] way may be known on earth, Your salvation among all nations" (Psalm 67:2). God's daily blessings are proof positive that He is indeed a good God who cares for His own. But how will our world know this about God if we never praise Him for His goodness to us (v. 3)?

So, the next time God blesses you, be sure to look for ways to appropriately give Him the credit. Consuming His blessings without communicating His goodness shortchanges the very purpose of His gifts of grace in our lives.   —JS

*As endless as God's blessings are,
So should my praises be
For all His daily goodnesses
That flow unceasingly!* —Adams

**Make sure the people in your world know
what our good God has done in your life.**

The Dividing Wall

READ: Ephesians 2:11–22; 4:1–3

He Himself is our peace, who has made both one, and has broken down the middle wall of separation. —EPHESIANS 2:14

November 9, 2010, marked the 21st anniversary of the fall of the Berlin Wall. On that day in 1989 an announcement over East German TV informed people that they were free to travel to West Germany. A day later, East German bulldozers began to dismantle the wall that for twenty-eight years had divided East and West Germany.

Jesus Christ "has broken down the middle wall of separation" between Jew and Gentile (Ephesians 2:14). But there was an even more impenetrable barrier that separated man from God. Jesus' death and resurrection made the reconciliation between man and man and between man and God possible (v. 16).

All believers are now "members of the household of God" (v. 19). Together, we are to grow into "a holy temple in the Lord" (v. 21) with God's Holy Spirit living among and within us (v. 22).

But sadly, Christians often re-erect walls between one another. That is why Paul urges us to "walk worthy of the calling . . . bearing with one another in love, endeavoring to keep the unity of the Spirit in the bond of peace" (4:1–3). Rather than building walls, let's work to dismantle what separates us. Let the world see that we are indeed of the same household. —CPH

We're members of Christ's body,
A blessed family;
So let's not fight or quarrel,
But live in harmony. —Fitzhugh

Unity among believers comes from their union with Christ.

Knowing God's Will

READ: Ephesians 5:17–21

That you may prove what is that good and acceptable and perfect will of God. —ROMANS 12:2

A young man facing the future and unsure of what the next year would bring, concluded, "Nobody knows what God's will is." Is he right? Does a lack of certainty about the future translate into not knowing God's will?

The concept of knowing God's will is often limited to discerning what specific situation we will be in at some future time. Although seeking God's specific leading is part of it, another aspect that is just as vital is to follow the clearly defined elements of God's will each and every day.

For instance, it is God's will for us to be good citizens as a challenge to those opposed to Christ (1 Peter 2:15), to give God thanks no matter what (1 Thessalonians 5:18), to be sanctified sexually, avoiding immorality (4:3), to live under the Holy Spirit's control (Ephesians 5:18), to sing to Him (v. 19), and to submit to other believers (v. 21).

As we submit to God in these and other areas, we are more likely to live in what Romans 12:2 calls God's "good and acceptable and perfect will." Living with God's smile of approval leads to His guidance for the future.

As we seek to know God's will for the future, we must also act on what we already know now.   —DB

Knowing God's will for the future
Comes when we follow today
What He's revealed in the Scriptures
As His commands to obey. —Sper

Love and obey the Lord every day, and He will unfold your future.

Moving Past Sinful Failure

READ: 2 Samuel 12:1–23

I, even I, am He who blots out your transgressions for My own sake; and I will not remember your sins. —ISAIAH 43:25

How should we handle moments of faith failure, when we've damaged the kingdom of God in the eyes of our friends and family or dishonored God in our actions?

We can learn from King David after his humiliation in the Bathsheba scandal. Though the terrible consequences of that sin could not be avoided, he found his way back to a relationship with God that made it possible for him to continue to serve Him. We too can find our way back.

David's pattern in 2 Samuel 12 serves us well: We need to declare our error candidly (v. 13) and seek God's forgiveness. Then we can ask God that others be spared the consequences of our actions (v. 16). Finally, we need to recognize that sometimes the consequences simply cannot be avoided and must be endured. While we always mourn those consequences, we can't allow them to so consume us that we cease to be servants of God (vv. 20–23).

Satan not only delights in the moment of our failure but also in the spiritual inactivity that sometimes snares us in our remorse. When we've blown our witness, we are and should be humbled. But we should not multiply the damage by retreating into silence and obscurity as ambassadors of Christ. We can move past failure.   —RK

―――――――――――― ACTION SUGGESTION ――――――――――――
If after you've confessed your sin to God, you still suffer with guilty feelings, memorize Proverbs 24:16 and 1 John 1:9 and ask God to help you believe His Word.

God forgives our sins completely to restore us to His presence and service.

Sin Hurts

READ: Hebrews 2:10–18

He poured out His soul unto death, and He was numbered with the transgressors, and He bore the sin of many. —ISAIAH 53:12

Sooner or later we all feel the painful effects of sin. Sometimes it's the weight of our own sin and the shame and embarrassment of having failed miserably. At other times, it's the load of someone else's sin that weighs us down—someone who betrayed, deceived, abandoned, ridiculed, cheated, or made a fool of us.

Think about a time when the weight of that guilt or pain was so heavy that you couldn't pull yourself out of bed. Now try to imagine the heaviness of the combined grief that everyone's sin has caused your family, your church, your neighborhood. Add to that all the suffering sin has caused everyone in your city, state, nation, and the world. Now try to imagine the accumulated grief that sin has caused throughout the centuries since creation.

Is it any wonder that the weight of all this sin began squeezing the life out of Jesus on the night He was called to bear it? (Matthew 26:36–44). The next day, even His beloved Father would forsake Him. No other suffering can compare.

Sin put Jesus to the ultimate test. But His love endured it, His strength bore it, and His power overcame it. Thanks to Jesus' death and resurrection, we know beyond a doubt that sin will not and cannot win.

—JAL

Is God aloof from human pain
That ravages our mortal frame?
Oh, no, Christ felt our agony
When sin and death He overcame! —D. DeHaan

Christ's empty tomb guarantees our victory over sin and death.

A Family in Trouble

READ: Malachi 4:4–6; Matthew 1:1–2

He will turn many of the children of
Israel to the Lord their God. —LUKE 1:16

Many of America's thirty million white-tailed deer find themselves endangered not by guns, but by the cars of our expanding suburbs. I was reminded of their plight when a mature doe dashed through traffic just ahead of me. As I watched, I wondered what had driven her to take such a chance, and why she then stopped on the other side and looked back over her shoulder. As I drove by her, I turned to follow her gaze and saw two small fawns looking helplessly at their mother across the busy street. Instead of following, they turned and walked back into the woods.

This family is not alone. We too can find ourselves in circumstances of separation and danger we did not anticipate. Reading Malachi and Matthew reminds us that we are troubled children of troubled parents who desperately need the help of our Father in heaven. Sometimes we need His help to see and avoid repeating the sins of our fathers (Nehemiah 9:2–3). Sometimes we need His help to turn back to the example and care of loving parents (Luke 15:18).

Only from our heavenly Father can we find the perfect forgiveness, example, and inner grace we need. He knows we are all fallen children of fallen parents, and even now He offers us the help of His Spirit and the rescue of His Son. —MD

Each day we learn from yesterday
Of God's great love and care;
And every burden we must face
He'll surely help us bear. —D. DeHaan

It's never too soon to turn back to God.

Known for Compassion

READ: Acts 11:19–26

He was a good man, full of the Holy Spirit and of faith. And a great many people were added to the Lord. —ACTS 11:24

During Major General Mark Graham's two years as commander of Fort Carson, Colorado, he became known and loved for the way he treated others. One US Army colleague said: "I have never come across another general officer who was so compassionate and so concerned about the well-being of soldiers and their families." After losing one son to suicide and another who was killed in action, Mark and his wife, Carol, dedicated themselves to helping soldiers and their families cope with service-related stress, depression, and loss.

In the book of Acts, a follower of Christ was well known for his care and concern toward others. His name was Joseph, but in the early church, the apostles called him Barnabas—"son of encouragement." It was Barnabas who vouched for the newly converted Saul when others doubted the sincerity of his faith (Acts 9:26–27). Later, Barnabas brought Saul from Tarsus to teach the believers in Antioch (11:25–26). And it was Barnabas who wanted to give John Mark a second chance after his failure on a previous missionary journey (15:36–38).

Compassion is an inner feeling resulting in outward action. It should be our daily uniform of service (Colossians 3:12). By God's grace, may we be known for it. —DM

> *Lord, help us be compassionate*
> *To people in their grief;*
> *Then tell them of the love of Christ,*
> *To bring their souls relief.* —Sper

True compassion is love in action.

Resurrection and Life

READ: 1 Corinthians 15:1–11

I am the resurrection and the life. —JOHN 11:25

Jesus said, "I am the resurrection and the life"! It's one thing to make such a bold assertion; it's another to back it up—and back it up Jesus did by rising from the dead.

"If you believe that the Son of God died and rose again," writes George MacDonald, "your whole future is full of the dawn of eternal morning, coming up beyond the hills of life, and full of such hope as the highest imagination for the poet has not a glimmer yet."

The Son of God died and rose again, and His resurrection is the guarantee that God will bring us up and out of the ground: A thinking, feeling, remembering, recognizable person will live forever.

Living forever means living out the thought of eternity that God has placed in our hearts; meeting again one's believing loved ones lost through separating death; living in a world without sorrow; seeing our Lord who loves us and gave everything to unite us to Him forever.

But I see another meaning. Since we have this life and the next, we don't have to "have it all" now. We can live in broken and ruined bodies for a time; we can endure poverty and hardship for a while; we can face loneliness, heartache, and pain for a season. Why? Because there is a second birth—life in heaven forever. —DR

Yes, Christ the Lord is risen,
Has come forth from the grave;
He breaks the chains of death for you
And now has power to save. —Woodruff

The resurrection is the foundation of our faith.

Hard to Imagine

READ: Philippians 1:19–26

I am hard-pressed between the two, having a desire to depart and be with Christ, which is far better. —PHILIPPIANS 1:23

Whenever my wife, Martie, and I get ready to go on vacation, we like to read about our destination, study the maps, and anticipate the joy of finally arriving at the place we've dreamed about for so long.

For those of us who know Jesus Christ, we have an incredible destination ahead of us—heaven. But I find it interesting that a lot of us don't seem to be very excited about getting there. Why is that? Maybe it's because we don't understand heaven. We talk about streets of gold and gates of pearl, but what is it really like? What is there to look forward to?

I think the most profound description of heaven is found in Paul's words to the Philippians. He said that to "depart and be with Christ" is "far better" (1:23). It's what I told my eight-year-old grandson when he asked what heaven is like. I started by asking him, "What is the most exciting thing in your life?" He told me about his computer game and other fun things he likes to do, and then I told him that heaven is far better. He thought for a minute, and then said, "Papa, that's hard to imagine."

What is it that you look forward to in life? What really excites you? Whatever it is, although it's hard to imagine, heaven will be far better!

—JS

To be in His presence! A glorious thought
So awesome I cannot conceive;
I'll bow down and worship the Lord on His throne
And add to the praise He'll receive. —Sper

The more you look forward to heaven, the less you'll desire on earth.

Whispering Gallery

READ: Proverbs 10:11–23

In the multitude of words sin is not lacking, but
he who restrains his lips is wise. —PROVERBS 10:19

London's domed St. Paul's Cathedral has an interesting architectural phenomenon called the "whispering gallery." One Web site explains it this way: "The name comes from the fact that a person who whispers facing the wall on one side can be clearly heard on the other, since the sound is carried perfectly around the vast curve of the Dome." In other words, you and a friend could sit on opposite sides of architect Sir Christopher Wren's great cathedral and carry on a conversation without having to speak above a whisper.

While that may be a fascinating feature of St. Paul's Cathedral, it can also be a warning to us. What we say about others in secret can travel just as easily as whispers travel around that gallery. And not only can our gossip travel far and wide, but it often does great harm along the way.

Perhaps this is why the Bible frequently challenges us about the ways we use words. The wise King Solomon wrote, "In the multitude of words sin is not lacking, but he who restrains his lips is wise" (Proverbs 10:19).

Instead of using whispers and gossip that can cause hurt and pain while serving no good purpose, we would do better to restrain ourselves and practice silence. —BC

> *Lord, help us bridle what we say*
> *And tend our conversations,*
> *Avoiding careless gossiping*
> *That murders reputations.* —Sper

Gossip ends at a wise person's ears.

Haters of God

READ: 2 Timothy 2:23–26

God gave them over to a debased mind. —ROMANS 1:28

Recently I listened to an audiobook by a militant advocate for atheism. As the author read his own work with spiteful sarcasm and contempt, it made me wonder why he was so angry.

The Bible tells us that a rejection of God can actually lead to a more hateful attitude toward Him: "Even as they did not like to retain God in their knowledge, God gave them over to a debased mind . . . [to become] haters of God" (Romans 1:28–30).

Turning one's back on God does not lead to secular neutrality. Indeed, recent militant atheists have shown their desire to remove any reference to a Creator from culture.

When we hear about atheists trying to remove crosses or the Ten Commandments from society, it's easy to respond to their hatred of God with our own hatred. But we're exhorted to defend the truth with an attitude of love, "in humility correcting those who are in opposition, if God perhaps will grant them repentance, so that they may know the truth" (2 Timothy 2:25).

The next time you see the works or hear the words of a hater of God, do an attitude check. Then ask God for a spirit of humility and pray that the offender might come to the knowledge of the truth.   —DF

> *Lord, help us not respond in kind*
> *To those who hate and turn from you;*
> *Instead, help us to love and pray*
> *That someday they'll accept what's true.* —Sper

Defend the truth with love.

Star Power

READ: Job 38:1–11, 31–33

Do you know the ordinances of the heavens? Can
*you set their dominion over the earth? —*Job 38:33

For all of us who, like Job, have suffered through tragedy and then
dared to aim our questions at God, chapter 38 of Job's book should
give us plenty to think about. Imagine what it must have felt like for the
great man of the East when "out of the whirlwind" he heard God say,
"Who is this who darkens counsel by words without knowledge? Now
prepare yourself like a man; I will question you, and you shall answer
Me" (vv. 1–3). Gulp!

Job must have felt as puny as an ant. As God unveiled His questions,
found in the verses that follow, what He said was as unexpected as it was
powerful. He didn't really answer Job's "why" questions. Instead, God
seemed to be telling him to notice the power and might with which He
created this world and to observe His ability to control every element of
it. Isn't that reason enough to trust Him?

As one example of His awesome power, God pointed to the sky
and told Job to observe two of His awe-inspiring creations: Pleiades
and Orion (v. 31). Highlighting His grandeur and man's relative insig-
nificance, God mentioned two constellations that demonstrate power
beyond our understanding.

This is Someone we can trust. If He has the stars in His hands,
surely He can take care of us as well. —DB

Creator of the universe
Who reigns in awesome majesty:
How can it be you love and care
For such a one as me? —Sper

He who holds the stars in space holds His people in His hands.

God at Work

READ: John 14:15–23

*If anyone loves Me, he will keep My word; and
My Father will love him, and We will come to him
and make Our home with him. —JOHN 14:23*

As I stood on the Golan Heights, with the Sea of Galilee sparkling in the distance, I listened to our Jewish guide tell about his participation in the 1967 Six-Day War. His vivid accounts of Israel's victories over bigger, more powerful enemies reminded me of Bible stories I learned as a child.

Even though I believe that God has been moving individuals and nations down through history to accomplish His purposes, sometimes I get the idea that God stopped working in people's lives when He finished writing the Bible. Now that He's less visible, I conclude that He's also less involved. But that's not true. Even though God has finished His book, He hasn't finished telling the story; He's simply using a different form of media to tell it.

In Bible times, God often communicated in tangible, visible, and audible ways—tablets of stone, a pillar of fire, a still small voice, to name a few. But when Jesus came, that changed. He told His followers that God's Spirit would live not only *among* them but also *within* them (John 14:17).

When I long for God to communicate in ways I can see and hear and feel, I need to remember that He is doing something even better. He is living in me, so that through my life the world will be able to see and hear and feel Him. —JAL

*By this shall every person know
That we serve God above:
His Spirit dwells within our hearts
And fills us with His love. —D. DeHaan*

God's Spirit lives in us in order to work through us.

If I Could Stop the Clock

READ: 1 Kings 10:23–11:4

The glory of the Lord filled the house of the Lord. —1 KINGS 8:11

Every year when May rolls around in Michigan, I want to stop the clock. I rejoice when death is defeated by fragile sprouts that refuse to be confined by hardened clay and brittle branches. Over a few weeks, the naked landscape transforms into fully clothed trees adorned by bright, fragrant flowers. I can't get enough of the sights, sounds, and scents of springtime. I want time to stop moving.

Also in May, I come to 1 Kings in my Bible reading schedule. When I get to chapter 10, I have the same feeling: I want the story to stop. The nation of Israel has bloomed. Solomon has become king and has built a magnificent dwelling place for God, who moved in with a blaze of glory (8:11). Finally united under a righteous king, they are at peace. I love happy endings!

But the story doesn't end there. It continues: "But King Solomon loved many foreign women," and "his wives turned his heart after other gods" (11:1, 4).

Just as the seasons of the year continue, so do the cycles of life—birth and death, success and failure, sin and confession. Although we have no power to stop the clock while we're enjoying good times, we can rest in God's promise that eventually all bad times will end (Revelation 21:4).   —JAL

Father, our days are filled with pleasures and struggles.
We would like for life just to have the joys, but we
know that's not realistic in this sinful world. Help
us to wait patiently for you to bring us Home.

In good times and bad, God never changes.

Two Rules to Live By

READ: Matthew 22:34–40

*On these two commandments hang all the
Law and the Prophets.* —MATTHEW 22:40

Have you ever felt overwhelmed by rules and expectations? Think of how the Jewish people must have felt as they tried to keep up with more than six hundred rules from the Old Testament and many more that had been imposed on them by the religious leaders of their day. And imagine their surprise when Jesus simplified the pursuit of righteousness by narrowing the list down to just two: "love the Lord your God," and "love your neighbor as yourself" (Matthew 22:37, 39).

In essence, Jesus is telling us that the way God knows we love Him is by how we treat people—all of them. Let's face it; loving our neighbor can be a challenge. But when we do it to express our love to God, we unleash a powerful motivation that loves whether the person deserves it or not. And as we love God and our neighbor, everything else falls into place. If I love my neighbor, I won't bear false witness against him, covet his wealth or his wife, or steal from him. Loving others for God's sake even provides the grace and strength to forgive those who have heaped injustices upon us.

Who needs to see God's love today through you? The more unlovable the person, the greater the statement about how much you love God!

—JS

*To love your God with all your heart,
Your soul, your strength, your mind,
Enables you to love someone
Who's hurtful and unkind.* —Sper

Loving God is the key to loving others.

Never Alone

READ: Hebrews 13:1–8

*Let your conduct be without covetousness; be content
with such things as you have. For He Himself has said,
"I will never leave you nor forsake you." —*HEBREWS 13:5

Having played intercollegiate soccer, I've never lost my love for "The
Beautiful Game." I especially enjoy watching the English Premier
League. One reason is the skill and speed with which the game is played
there. Also, I love the way the fans sing in support of their beloved
"sides." For instance, Liverpool has for years had "You'll Never Walk
Alone" as its theme. How moving to hear 50,000 fans rise as one to sing
the lyrics of that old standard! It's an encouragement to players and fans
alike that together they will see each other through to the end. Walk
alone? Never.

This sentiment has meaning for everyone. Because each of us is
made for community, isolation and loneliness are among the most painful of human experiences. During painful times, our faith is vital.

The child of God never needs to fear abandonment. Even if people
turn on us, friends forsake us, or circumstances separate us from loved
ones, we are never alone. God has said, "I will never leave you nor forsake
you" (Hebrews 13:5). This is not just a nice tune or clever lyrics offering
an empty sentiment. It is the promise of God himself to those who are the
objects of His love. He is there—and He isn't going away.

With Christ, you will never walk alone.   —BC

*God's unseen presence comforts me,
I know He's always near;
And when life's storms besiege my soul,
He says, "My child, don't fear." —D. DeHaan*

God's presence with us is one of His greatest presents to us.

Two Words

READ: James 4:7–10

Submit to God. —JAMES 4:7

In the annals of US advertising history, one of the most efficient slogans ever is the California milk producers' two-word question, "Got milk?" With that phrase, the group captured almost everyone's attention. In surveys, the slogan was recognized by more than 90 percent of the people polled.

If "Got milk?" is so good at reminding people to drink "cow juice," perhaps we can create some two-word slogans to remind ourselves to live more godly lives. Let's turn to James 4 and try it. This passage gives four specific guidelines.

1. Give in! Verse 7 tells us to submit to God. Our sovereign God loves us, so why not let Him run the show? Submission helps us resist the Devil. 2. Get close! Verse 8 reminds us of the value of drawing near to God. It's up to us to close the gap between us and God. 3. Clean up! Verse 8 also reminds us to make sure our hearts are clean. That happens through confessing our sins to God. 4. Get down! James says we need to be humble before God (v. 10). That includes viewing our sin as something to weep over.

Give in! Get close! Clean up! Get down! These pairs of words may not look as good on a T-shirt as "Got milk?" But they sure will look good on us. —DB

Lord, help me live a godly life
Of faith and love and purity
So those who watch my life will see
Reflections of your work in me. —Sper

The most powerful testimony is a godly life.

Time to Pray?

READ: Psalm 70

Make haste to help me, O Lord! —PSALM 70:1

One morning when I was a young child, I was sitting in the kitchen watching my mother prepare breakfast. Unexpectedly, the grease in the skillet in which she was frying bacon caught fire. Flames shot into the air, and my mother ran to the pantry for some baking soda to throw on the blaze.

"Help!" I shouted. And then I added, "Oh, I wish it was time to pray!"

"It's time to pray" must have been a frequent household expression, and I took it quite literally to mean we could pray only at certain times.

The time to pray, of course, is any time—especially when we're in crisis. Fear, worry, anxiety, and care are the most common occasions for prayer. It is when we are desolate, forsaken, and stripped of every human resource that we naturally resort to prayer. We cry out with the words of David, "Help me, O Lord!" (Psalm 70:1).

John Cassian, a fifth-century Christian, wrote of this verse: "This is the terrified cry of someone who sees the snares of the enemy, the cry of someone besieged day and night and exclaiming that he cannot escape unless his Protector comes to the rescue."

May this be our simple prayer in every crisis and all day long: "Help, Lord!"
—DR

Any hour when helping others,
Or when bearing heavy care,
Is the time to call our Father,
It's the proper time for prayer. —Zimmerman

There is no place or time we cannot pray.

The Wise Ant

READ: Proverbs 6:6–11

*[The ant] provides her supplies in the summer, and
gathers her food in the harvest.* —PROVERBS 6:8

Every year I do something special to celebrate the arrival of spring —I buy ant traps. Those little invaders continually march into our kitchen in search of any crumb left on the floor. They aren't picky; a shard of potato chip, a grain of rice, or even a speck of cheese will do.

Although ants may be a nuisance, Solomon praised them for their steadfast work ethic (Proverbs 6:6–11). He pointed out that ants are self-directed. They have "no captain, overseer, or ruler" (v. 7), yet they are very productive. The ants also keep busy even when it's not immediately necessary, providing supplies in the summer and gathering food in the harvest (v. 8). By the time winter arrives, they're not worried about what they will eat. Little by little, these hard workers have saved up enough to sustain themselves.

We can learn from the ant. When God gives us times of plenty, we can prepare for times when resources may be low. God is the provider of all that we have, including our ability to work. We are to work diligently, be wise stewards of what He has provided, and then rest in the promise of His care (Matthew 6:25–34).

Let's remember Solomon's advice: "Go to the ant . . . Consider her ways and be wise" (Proverbs 6:6).   —JBS

> *The humble ant's keen industry*
> *Can teach us all a lesson,*
> *If in creation we will see*
> *God's classroom is in session.* —*Gustafson*

Trust God for today—and prepare for tomorrow.

Peace and Reconciliation

READ: Matthew 18:21–35

Should you not also have had compassion on your fellow servant, just as I had pity on you? —MATTHEW 18:33

When the US Civil War ended in 1865, more than half a million soldiers lay dead, the economy was shattered, and people remained deeply divided politically. The observance of Mother's Day in the United States began with two women's efforts for peace and reconciliation during this time of anguish. In 1870, Julia Ward Howe called for an International Mother's Day on which women would unite in opposing war in all its forms. A few years later, Anna Reeves Jarvis began her annual Mother's Friendship Day in an effort to reunite families and neighbors alienated by the war.

There is always great suffering when friends and families are fractured and unwilling to forgive. The gospel of Jesus Christ brings the promise of peace and reconciliation with God and with each other. When Peter asked Jesus how often he should forgive a brother who sinned against him, the Lord surprised everyone with His answer of "seventy times seven" (Matthew 18:21–22). Then He told an unforgettable story about a servant who had received forgiveness and failed to pass it on (vv. 23–35). As God freely forgives us, so He requires that we extend what we have received to others.

With God's love and power, forgiveness is always possible.   —DM

Oh, what joy and peace we forfeit,
When forgiveness we withhold;
Fellowship with God is broken,
And the heart grows hard and cold. —D. DeHaan

Forgiveness is Christianity in action.

Learning to Trust

READ: Isaiah 66:7–13

*Trust in the Lord, and do good; dwell in the land,
and feed on His faithfulness.* —PSALM 37:3

When I stuck my camera into the bush to take a picture of the baby robins, they opened their mouths without opening their eyes. They were so used to having mama robin feed them whenever the branches moved that they didn't even look to see who (or what) was causing the disturbance.

That is the kind of trust that loving mothers instill in their children. That is the kind of mom I am blessed to have. Growing up, I could eat whatever food she put on the table without fear that it would harm me. Although she made me eat things I didn't like, I knew she did so because they were good for me. If she cared only about what was easy for her, she would have let me eat junk food. No matter what Mom told me to do, or not to do, I knew she had my best interest in mind. She wasn't trying to keep me from having fun; she was trying to protect me from being hurt.

That is the kind of relationship we have with God, who compared himself to a mother: "As one whom his mother comforts, so I will comfort you" (Isaiah 66:13). As His children, we have no reason to fear what happens to us or to envy what happens to others: "Do not . . . be envious of the workers of iniquity" (Psalm 37:1). When we trust His goodness, we are fed by His faithfulness.   —JAL

*Lord, we're thankful for this example of motherhood. But even
more, we're grateful for your faithful "mothering" of us displayed
in your compassion day by day. Help us to find rest in you.*

God's care surrounds us.

Helpful Love

READ: John 1:9–14

The Word became flesh and dwelt among us. —JOHN 1:14

At the end of my mother's earthly journey, she and Dad were still very much in love and shared a strong faith in Christ. My mother had developed dementia and began to lose memories of even her family. Yet Dad would regularly visit her at the assisted-living home and find ways to accommodate her diminished capacities.

For instance, he would take her some saltwater taffy, unwrap a piece, and place it in her mouth—something she could not do for herself. Then as she slowly chewed the candy, Dad would quietly sit with her and hold her hand. When their time together was over, Dad, beaming with a wide smile, would say, "I feel such peace and joy spending time with her."

Though touched by Dad's great joy in helping Mom, I was more affected by the reality that he was depicting God's grace. Jesus was willing to humble himself to connect with us in our weaknesses. In reflecting on Christ's incarnation, John wrote, "The Word became flesh and dwelt among us" (1:14). Taking on human limitations, He did countless acts of compassion to accommodate us in our weakness.

Do you know anyone who might benefit from Jesus' helpful, accommodating love that could flow through you to them today?　　—DF

> *Love is giving for the world's needs,*
> *Love is sharing as the Spirit leads,*
> *Love is caring when the world cries,*
> *Love is compassion with Christlike eyes.* —Brandt

To be a channel of blessing, let Christ's love flow through you.

Come and See

READ: John 1:35–46

Come and see. —JOHN 1:39

In many large stores, employees are instructed to take customers to find what they are looking for rather than simply giving them verbal directions.

"Can you tell me where I can find the lightbulbs?"

"Sure. Come with me, and I'll take you to them."

This common act of courtesy and walking alongside an inquiring person may help us expand our concept of what it means to lead others to Christ.

In John 1, the phrase "come and see" occurs twice. When two curious disciples of John the Baptist asked Jesus where He was staying, the Lord said, "Come and see" (v. 39). After spending the day with Him, Andrew found his brother, Simon Peter, and brought him to Jesus (vv. 40–41). Later, Philip told Nathanael he had found the Messiah. To Nathanael's skeptical reply, Philip said, "Come and see" (v. 46).

Witnessing for Christ can be a one-time event when we speak the good news about Him to others. But it may also involve walking alongside people who are seeking help and wholeness. Our genuine interest in their spiritual welfare, our prayers, and our involvement with them say without words, "Come and see. Let's walk together, and I'll take you to Him." —DM

The gospel has to be proclaimed,
Its truth we need to share;
But sometimes seekers also need
To see how much we care. —Sper

Kindness and compassion have led more
people to Christ than proclamation alone.

The Benefit of the Doubt

READ: 1 Corinthians 13

[Love] bears all things, believes all things, hopes all things, endures all things. —1 CORINTHIANS 13:7

In 1860, Thomas Inman recommended that his fellow doctors not prescribe a medicine for a cure if they weren't sure it would work. They were to give the patient "the benefit of our doubts." This phrase is also a legal term meaning that if a jury has conflicting evidence that makes the jurors doubtful, they are to give the verdict of "not guilty."

Perhaps, as Christians, we can learn from and apply this medical and legal phrase to our relationships. Better yet, we can learn from the Bible about giving the benefit of the doubt to others. First Corinthians 13:7 says that love "bears all things, believes all things, hopes all things, endures all things." Leon Morris, in the *Tyndale New Testament Commentaries*, says this about the phrase "believes all things": "To see the best in others . . . This does not mean that love is gullible, but that it does not think the worst (as is the way of the world). It retains its faith. Love is not deceived . . . but it is always ready to give the benefit of the doubt."

When we hear something negative about others or are suspicious about the motive for their actions, let's stop before we judge their intentions as wrong or bad. Let's give them the benefit of the doubt. —AC

Love gives others the benefit of the doubt.

Come Home

READ: Psalm 51:1–13

*Restore to me the joy of Your salvation, and uphold
me by Your generous Spirit.* —PSALM 51:12

As nineteen-year-old Amelia waited in her doctor's office, she recognized the familiar hymn "Softly and Tenderly Jesus Is Calling" playing over the speaker. It made her smile when she remembered the words. Perhaps a song with the lyrics "shadows are gathering, deathbeds are coming" was not the most appropriate background music for a doctor's office!

Some find this old hymn too sentimental for their taste. But the message of the chorus can be encouraging for the wayward sinner:

Come home, come home,
Ye who are weary, come home;
Earnestly, tenderly, Jesus is calling,
Calling, "O sinner, come home!"

When a believer replaces God's will with his own, he will find himself in a backslidden condition, out of fellowship with God, in an unenviable state. Although we sometimes yield to our self-centered nature, God is always ready to welcome us back. Because of His "lovingkindness" and "tender mercies," it gives Him joy when we forsake our rebellious ways, return to Him, and ask for forgiveness (Psalm 51:1–2; Luke 15).

Has your heart and mind slipped away from your Savior? Jesus is calling and waiting for you to come back home. —CHK

*O for the wonderful love He has promised,
Promised for you and for me;
Though we have sinned He has mercy and pardon,
Pardon for you and for me. —Thompson*

A child of God is always welcomed home.

The Mighty Toe

READ: 1 Corinthians 12:14–26

If the foot should say, "Because I am not a hand, I am not of the body," is it therefore not of the body? —1 CORINTHIANS 12:15

Recently I heard of a sport that challenges my imagination—I can't comprehend why anyone would play it. It's called "Toe Wrestling." Every year, people from across the globe gather in England for the world championships. Competitors sit on the ground facing each other and then lock the big toe of the other's bare foot. The object is to pin the opponent's foot in a manner similar to the way an arm wrestler pins a competitor's wrist. It sounds strange to me.

In a way, however, this unusual competition gives honor to a part of the body that's largely ignored—until we drop something on it. Our toes and feet are vital parts of our anatomy, yet we pay little attention to them unless they hurt.

Perhaps that's why Paul used the foot to remind us that there are no unimportant parts in the body of Christ. In 1 Corinthians 12:15 he said, "If the foot should say, 'Because I am not a hand, I am not of the body,' is it therefore not of the body?" The only correct answer: "Of course it's part of the body."

Paul wants us to realize that each person in the body of Christ is important. Even if you think of yourself as the most overlooked and ignored member of the body of Christ, you have value. And you can honor God like a true champion by using your unique skills for God's glory. —BC

God builds His church with different stones,
He makes each one belong;
All shapes and sizes fit in place
To make the structure strong. —Sper

The Lord uses small tools to perform large tasks.

Gone but Not Forgotten

READ: John 10:31–42

John performed no sign, but all the things that John spoke about this Man were true. —JOHN 10:41

John the Baptist had been dead for at least two years, and the memory of his ministry had begun to fade. But as the crowds gathered around Jesus near the place where John had taught, they remembered what he had said about Jesus and remarked, "All the things that John spoke about this Man were true" (John 10:41).

Most of us live fairly unremarkable lives. We're not miracle workers. We're not noted for anything in particular. We're ordinary and commonplace. But we can tell people about Jesus wherever we go. We can point to Him and say, "Behold! The Lamb of God who takes away the sin of the world!" (1:29).

Our duty is to tell people what we have come to know about Jesus and then leave the results with God. If we do so, we will have served one of life's essential purposes. After we're dead and gone, our words may come to someone's mind and bring that person to the Lamb of God. Like seed buried in the ground, God's Word may seem to lie dormant for years and then spring up to eternal life.

So let us be faithful in pointing others to Jesus. Then, after we are gone, the epitaph on our gravestone could read, "He did no miracles, but everything he said about Jesus was true." —DR

> *Lord, help me make my witness clear,*
> *And labor faithfully,*
> *So friends and neighbors turn to Christ*
> *Through what they hear from me. —Anonymous*

We sow the seed, and God produces the harvest.

Strong Words

READ: 1 John 3:10–18

Whoever does not practice righteousness is not of God. —1 JOHN 3:10

The book titled *UnChristian* lists reasons why some non-Christians don't like people who profess faith in Jesus Christ. Their major complaints have to do with the way some Christians act toward unbelievers. The unbelievers in the study tended to view Christians as being hypocritical, judgmental, harsh, and unloving toward people not like themselves. I'm sure you dislike hearing their view of Christians, just as I do. Sometimes there's more truth in their perceptions than we wish there was.

In 1 John 3, which begins with the words, "Behold what manner of love the Father has bestowed on us, that we should be called children of God!" (v. 1), John introduces a sharp contrast: Believers love righteousness, keep themselves from sin, and love one another; nonbelievers practice sin, hate others, and abide in death. These are strong words! We are either followers of Jesus Christ or of the Devil. We are like Cain or Abel (v. 12; Genesis 4:8–15).

John says that love for others is what proves we are genuine children of God (3:10, 18–19; 4:7–8). We can't continue to practice sin and claim to be followers of Christ. Let's always make sure our words and deeds back up our beliefs.   —DE

> O help us, Lord, to live our lives
> So unsaved people clearly see
> Reflections of your loving heart,
> Your kindness, and your purity. —Sper

Following Christ has two requirements: Believing, and acting like you do.

When Life Seems Unfair

READ: Psalm 73

*I was envious of the boastful, when I saw
the prosperity of the wicked.* —PSALM 73:3

Have you ever felt that life is unfair? For those of us who are committed to following the will and ways of Jesus, it's easy to get frustrated
when people who don't care about Him seem to do well in life. A businessman cheats yet wins a large contract, and the guy who parties all the
time is robust and healthy—while you or your loved ones struggle with
finances or medical issues. It makes us feel cheated, like maybe we've
been good for nothing.

If you've ever felt that way, you're in good company. The writer of
Psalm 73 goes through a whole list of how the wicked prosper, and then
he says, "Surely I have cleansed my heart in vain" (v. 13). But the tide of
his thoughts turns when he recalls his time in God's presence: "Then I
understood their end" (v. 17).

When we spend time with God and see things from His point of
view, it changes our perspective completely. We may be jealous of the
nonbelievers now, but we won't be at judgment time. As the saying goes,
what difference does it make if you win the battle but lose the war?

Like the psalmist, let's praise God for His presence in this life and
His promise of the life to come (vv. 25–28). He is all you need, even
when life seems unfair. —JS

*All wrongs will one day be set right
By God who sees both bad and good;
All motives and all deeds will then
Be fairly judged and understood.* —D. DeHaan

Spending time with God puts everything else in perspective.

Alternatives to Revenge

READ: Deuteronomy 19:16–21;
Matthew 5:38–45

*You shall not take vengeance . . . but you shall
love your neighbor as yourself.* —LEVITICUS 19:18

One Sunday while preaching, a pastor was accosted and punched by a man. He continued preaching, and the man was arrested. The pastor prayed for him and even visited him in jail a few days later. What an example of the way to respond to insult and injury!

While there is a place for self-defense, personal revenge was forbidden in the Old Testament: "You shall not take vengeance, nor bear any grudge against the children of your people, but you shall love your neighbor as yourself" (Leviticus 19:18; see also Deuteronomy 32:35). It was also forbidden by Jesus and the apostles (Matthew 5:38–45; Romans 12:17; 1 Peter 3:9).

The Old Testament law exacted like for like (Exodus 21:23–25; Deuteronomy 19:21), which ensured that judicial punishment was not unjust or malicious. But there was a larger principle looming when it came to personal revenge: Justice must be done, but it must be left in the hands of God or the authorities ordained by God.

Instead of returning injury and insult, may we live by Christ-honoring and Spirit-empowered alternatives. Live at peace with everyone (Romans 12:18), submit to a spiritual mediator (1 Corinthians 6:1–6), and leave it in the hands of authorities and, most of all, in God's hands.   —MW

*Lord, when I'm troubled by the insult of another,
help me to let go of my desire for revenge. May I seek
justice but also realize that it will happen in your time.
I want to learn to overcome evil with good.*

Leave final justice in the hands of a just God.

We Shall Be Changed

READ: 2 Corinthians 4:16–5:8

We shall be like Him, for we shall see Him as He is. —1 JOHN 3:2

Being afflicted with early-onset Alzheimer's disease, Thomas DeBaggio chronicled his gradual memory loss in the book *Losing My Mind*. This book records the disturbing process by which—little by little—tasks, places, and people are all forgotten.

Alzheimer's disease involves the failure of nerve cells in the brain, leading to gradual memory loss, confusion, and disorientation. It can be tragic to watch a person slowly forget how to dress or fail to recognize the faces of loved ones. It's like losing the person before he or she dies.

Memory loss can occur by other means as well, such as injury or life trauma. And for those of us who live into old age, the breakdown of our bodies is inevitable.

But for the Christian, there is hope. When believers receive their glorified bodies at the resurrection, they will be perfect (2 Corinthians 5:1–5). But even more important, in heaven we will recognize the One who died to redeem us. We will remember what He did and know Him by the nail prints in His hands (John 20:25; 1 Corinthians 13:12).

Forgetfulness may beset our earthly bodies, but when we see the Lord, "We shall be like Him, for we shall see Him as He is" (1 John 3:2). —DF

> *Our Savior's life for us was given*
> *That we might one day bloom in heaven,*
> *Our mortal bodies changed to be*
> *Like His through all eternity!* —Spicer

In the twinkling of an eye . . . we shall all be changed. —Paul the Apostle

Broken Relationships

READ: Philippians 4:2–7

*Let nothing be done through selfish
ambition or conceit.* —PHILIPPIANS 2:3

I watched from my balcony as a twenty-story apartment building was demolished. The demolition took barely a week to complete. In its place a new building is being constructed. It's been months now, and despite construction activities going on nights and weekends, it is still incomplete. How much easier it is to tear down than to build up!

What is true for demolition and construction of buildings is also true for personal relationships. In Philippians 4:2, Paul wrote to two women in the church, saying, "I implore Euodia and I implore Syntyche to be of the same mind in the Lord." The quarrel between these two women threatened to tear down the witness of the Philippian church if left unresolved. So Paul urged a "true companion" (v. 3) to help rebuild that relationship.

Sadly, Christians do quarrel, but we should seek to "live peaceably" with all (Romans 12:18). Unless our conflicts are resolved, the Christian witness so painstakingly built up can be destroyed. It takes much effort and time to reconcile broken relationships. But it is worth it. Like a new building rising from the ruins, reconciled believers can emerge stronger.

May we seek to build each other up through our words and actions today! —CPH

*We have a common enemy
Who wants to scar the life
Of Jesus' precious bride, the church,
Through worldliness and strife.* —Sper

Two Christians are better than one—when they're one.

Humbly Receive

READ: James 1:13–22

Lay aside all filthiness and overflow of wickedness,
and receive with meekness the implanted Word,
which is able to save your souls. —JAMES 1:21

While reading the first chapter of James, I was struck by the phrase "humbly accept the Word planted in you, which can save you" (v. 21 NIV). A decision with which I'd been struggling came to mind, and I thought: I don't need to read another book, attend another seminar, or ask another friend about this. I need to obey what the Bible tells me to do. My efforts to be better informed had become a means of resisting God's instruction rather than receiving it.

James was writing to followers of Christ when he said: "Lay aside all filthiness and overflow of wickedness, and receive with meekness the implanted Word, which is able to save your souls. But be doers of the Word, and not hearers only, deceiving yourselves" (James 1:21–22).

Bible scholar W. E. Vine said that the Greek word used here for *receive* means "deliberate and ready reception of what is offered." Meekness is an attitude toward God "in which we accept His dealings with us as good, and therefore without disputing or resisting." A humble heart doesn't fight against God or contend with Him.

God's powerful Word, implanted in our hearts, is a trustworthy source of spiritual wisdom and strength. It's available to all who will humbly receive it. —DM

God who formed worlds by the power of His Word
Speaks through the Scriptures His truth to be heard;
And if we read with the will to obey,
He by His Spirit will show us His way. —D. DeHaan

Open your Bible prayerfully, read it carefully, and obey it joyfully.

Fresh Fruit

READ: Psalm 92

The righteous . . . shall still bear fruit in old age. —PSALM 92:12, 14

I love the old photographs that are often printed on the obituary page of our local newspaper. A grinning young man in a military uniform and words such as: "92 years old, fought for his country in WWII." Or the young woman with sparkling eyes: "89 years young, grew up on a farm in Kansas during the Depression." The unspoken message is: "I wasn't always old, you know."

Too often, those who have had a long life feel sidelined when they reach their later years. Psalm 92, however, reminds us that no matter how old we are, we can have a fresh and fruitful life. Men and women who have been "planted" in the rich soil of God's vineyard will continue to "bear fruit" and be "fresh and flourishing" (v. 14). Jesus promised that "he who abides in Me, and I in him," will continue to bear "much fruit" (John 15:5).

Yes, muscles may ache and joints may hurt, and life may slow down a bit. But inwardly we can be "renewed day by day" (2 Corinthians 4:16).

I recently saw a T-shirt on a beautiful white-haired woman that said: "I'm not 80. I'm 18 with 62 years experience." No matter how old we get, we can still be young at heart—but with the benefit of a well-lived lifetime of knowledge and wisdom. —CHK

> *We can be young in heart and mind,*
> *To others we can yet be kind,*
> *Sing songs of praise to God through tears,*
> *And grow in grace through all our years.* —Zimmerman

Faithfulness is God's requirement; fruitfulness is His reward.

Sign Language

READ: John 1:14–18

May the Lord make you increase and abound in love to one another and to all. —1 THESSALONIANS 3:12

A friend of mine pastors a church in a small mountain community not far from Boise, Idaho. The community is nestled in a wooded valley through which a pleasant little stream meanders. Behind the church and alongside the stream is a grove of willows, a length of grass, and a sandy beach. It's an idyllic spot that has long been a place where members of the community gather to picnic.

One day, a man in the congregation expressed concern over the legal implications of "outsiders" using the property. "If someone is injured," he said, "the church might be sued." Though the elders were reluctant to take any action, the man convinced them that they should post a sign on the site informing visitors that this was private property. So the pastor posted a sign. It read: "Warning! Anyone using this beach may, at any moment, be surrounded by people who love you." I read his sign the week after he put it up and was charmed. "Exactly," I thought. "Once again grace has triumphed over law!"

This love for one's neighbor springs from God's kindness, forbearance, and patience with us. It's not the law, but the goodness of God that draws men and women to repentance (Romans 2:4) and to saving faith in His Son, Jesus Christ.   —DR

As you have loved me, let me love
Lost souls in darkness dwelling;
To draw the needy ones to you,
Lord, give a zeal compelling! —Bosch

Love is the magnet that draws believers
together and attracts unbelievers to Christ.

Our Dependency

READ: 1 John 2:24–3:3

In Him we live and move and have our being. —Acts 17:28

While enjoying the arrival of a new great-niece, I was reminded of how much work it is to take care of a newborn baby. They are needy little creations who want feeding, changing, holding, feeding, changing, holding, feeding, changing, holding. Totally unable to care for themselves, they depend on those older and wiser people surrounding them.

We're dependent children too—reliant on our Father in heaven. What do we need from Him that we can't provide for ourselves? "In Him we live and move and have our being" (Acts 17:28). He supplies our very breath. He also meets our needs "according to His riches in glory by Christ Jesus" (Philippians 4:19).

We need our Father for peace in our troubles (John 16:33), love (1 John 3:1), and help in time of need (Psalm 46:1; Hebrews 4:16). He gives victory in temptation (1 Corinthians 10:13), forgiveness (1 John 1:9), purpose (Jeremiah 29:11), and eternal life (John 10:28). Without Him, we "can do nothing" (John 15:5). And from Him "we have all received one blessing after another" (John 1:16 NIV).

Let's not think of ourselves as totally independent—because we're not. The Lord sustains us day by day. In many ways, we're as needy as a newborn baby. —AC

We are dependent on the Lord
Who showers us with blessing;
He gives us everything we need—
Without Him we are nothing. —Sper

Depending on God isn't weakness; it's acknowledging His strength.

Simplify

READ: Matthew 6:25–34

Do not worry about tomorrow, for tomorrow will worry about its own things. Sufficient for the day is its own trouble. —MATTHEW 6:34

In a radio interview, a basketball superstar was asked about his knack for making the game-winning shot in crucial situations. The reporter asked how he was able to be so calm in such pressure-packed moments. His answer was that he tried to simplify the situation. "You only have to make one shot," the player replied.

One shot. That is the essence of simplifying a difficult situation. Focus only on what is in front of you right now. Don't worry about the expectations of your coach or teammates. Simplify.

Recognizing that the challenges of life can be both overwhelming and suffocating, Jesus urged us to take matters in hand by simplifying. He said, "Do not worry about tomorrow, for tomorrow will worry about its own things. Sufficient for the day is its own trouble" (Matthew 6:34). This was His wise conclusion to His teaching on the debilitating power of worry.

Worry doesn't accomplish anything positive; it just adds to the sense that we are drowning in the troubles we are facing. We must take things as they come—one day at a time—and trust Him for the wisdom to respond properly.

If you feel overwhelmed by life, do what you can today and then entrust the rest to Him. As Jesus said, "Each day has enough trouble of its own" (NIV). —BC

Don't worry for your future needs,
It will only bring you sorrow;
But give them to the Lord instead—
He'll take care of your tomorrow. —Sper

We lose the joy of living in the present when we worry about the future.

The Real Prize

READ: Ephesians 5:22–33

Husbands, love your wives, just as Christ also loved the church and gave Himself for her. —EPHESIANS 5:25

I've been amazed at the impact that my wife, Martie, has had on the lives of our kids. Very few roles demand the kind of unconditional, self-sacrificing perseverance and commitment as that of motherhood. I know for certain that my character and faith have been shaped and molded by my mom, Corabelle. Let's face it, where would we be without our wives and mothers?

This reminds me of one of my favorite memories in sports history. Phil Mickelson walked up the 18th fairway at the Masters Golf Tournament in 2010 after his final putt to clinch one of golf's most coveted prizes for the third time. But it wasn't his victory leap on the green that had an impact on me. It was when he made a beeline through the crowd to his wife, who was battling life-threatening cancer. They embraced, and the camera caught a tear running down Phil's cheek as he held his wife close for a long time.

Our wives need to experience the kind of sacrificial, selfless love that has been shown to us by the Lover of our souls. As Paul put it, "Husbands, love your wives, just as Christ also loved the church and gave Himself for her" (Ephesians 5:25). Prizes come and go, but it's the people you love—and who love you—that matter most.   —JS

Life is not about the prizes we win, but the people we love.

Trust and Sadness

READ: 2 Corinthians 1:3–11

Even in laughter the heart may sorrow. —PROVERBS 14:13

In early 1994, when our family found out that the US soccer team would be playing in Michigan in the World Cup, we knew we had to go. And what a great time we had as we went to the Pontiac Silverdome to see the US take on Switzerland!

There was just one problem. One of our four children, nine-year-old Melissa, couldn't join us. While we enjoyed the event, it was not the same without her. Even in our joy at being there, we felt sadness because of her absence.

As I think back on that day, I'm reminded that our sadness then is a little like our sadness now that Melissa is gone from this life, having died in a car accident eight years after that game. While we cherish the help of the "God of all comfort" (2 Corinthians 1:3), even that great comfort doesn't change the reality of her empty chair at family gatherings. Scripture doesn't tell us that God wipes away our sadness in this life, but it does tell us that God is faithful and will comfort us.

If you have lost a loved one, lean heavily on God's comfort. Keep trusting Him. But know that it's okay to feel sadness for this absence. Consider it one more reason to place your burdens on your loving heavenly Father. —DB

> *I have been through the valley of weeping,*
> *The valley of sorrow and pain;*
> *But the God of all comfort was with me,*
> *At hand to uphold and sustain. —Garlock*

Earth has no sorrow that heaven does not feel.

The Pilot's Rutter

READ: Psalm 119:129–136

Direct my steps by Your Word. —PSALM 119:133

During the era of great sea exploration in the fifteenth and sixteenth centuries, sailing ships traversed vast, hazardous oceans and navigated dangerous coastlines. Pilots used various navigation techniques, including a book called a "rutter" (not the "rudder," the ship's steering device). This was a log of events kept by earlier voyagers who chronicled their encounters with previously unknown and difficult waters. By reading the sailing details in a rutter, captains could avoid hazards and make it through difficult waters.

In many ways, the Christian life is like a voyage, and the believer needs help in navigating life's perilous seas. We have that help because God has given us His Word as a "spiritual rutter." Often when we reflect on a meaningful passage, we can recall God's faithfulness through trying circumstances. As the psalmist suggests, perils are found not only in life situations but also in our inner tendency toward sin. Because of these dual concerns, he wrote, "Direct my steps by Your Word, and let no iniquity have dominion over me" (119:133).

As you reflect on the teaching in the Bible, you'll be reminded of God's past care, assured of the Lord's guidance in trying circumstances, and warned against sinfulness. That's the advantage of having a "spiritual rutter." —DF

> *My Bible is a guidebook true*
> *That points for me the way,*
> *That gives me courage, hope, and cheer*
> *And guidance for each day.* —Anonymous

With God's Word as your map and His Spirit as your compass, you're sure to stay on course.

Are You Listening?

READ: Numbers 20:1–13

Speak to the rock before their eyes, and it will yield its water. —NUMBERS 20:8

He was frustrated. He was angry. He was tired of being blamed for everything that went wrong. Year after year, he had gotten them through one disaster after another. He was continually interceding on their behalf to keep them out of trouble. But all he got for his efforts was more grief. Finally, in exasperation, he said, "Hear now, you rebels! Must we bring water for you out of this rock?" (Numbers 20:10).

That suggestion might sound preposterous, but it wasn't. Forty years earlier, the previous generation had the same complaint: no water. God told Moses to strike a rock with his staff (Exodus 17:6). When he obeyed, water gushed out—plenty of water. When the grumbling started again so many years later, Moses did the thing that worked before. But this time it was the wrong thing to do. What Moses told the Israelites to do—to listen—he himself had not done. God had told him to speak to the rock this time, not strike it.

Sometimes, in exhaustion or exasperation, we don't pay close attention to God. We assume He will always work the same way. But He doesn't. Sometimes He tells us to act; sometimes He tells us to speak; sometimes He tells us to wait. That is why we must always be careful to listen before we take action. —JAL

Lord, help us to obey your Word,
To heed your still small voice;
And may we not be swayed by men,
But make your will our choice. —D. DeHaan

Listen—then obey.

Keeping the Wonder

READ: 2 Peter 1:2–11

If these things are yours and abound, you will be neither barren nor unfruitful in the knowledge of our Lord Jesus Christ. —2 PETER 1:8

On a recent trip, my wife was seated near a mother with a young boy on his first flight. As the plane took off, he exclaimed, "Mom, look how high we are! And everything's getting smaller!" A few minutes later he shouted, "Are those clouds down there? What are they doing under us?" As time passed, other passengers read, dozed, and lowered their window shades to watch the in-flight video. This boy, however, remained glued to the window, absorbed in the wonder of all he was seeing.

For "experienced travelers" in the Christian life, there can be great danger in losing the wonder. The Scriptures that once thrilled us may become more familiar and academic. We may fall into the lethargy of praying with our minds but not our hearts.

Peter urged the early followers of Christ to continue growing in their faith, virtue, knowledge, self-control, perseverance, godliness, brotherly kindness, and love (2 Peter 1:5–7). He said, "If these things are yours and abound [or are increasing], you will be neither barren nor unfruitful in the knowledge of our Lord Jesus Christ" (v. 8). Without them we become blind and forget the marvel of being cleansed from our sins (v. 9).

May God grant us all grace to keep growing in the wonder of knowing Him.   —DM

> *On such love, my soul, still ponder*
> *Love so great, so rich, so free;*
> *Say, while lost in holy wonder,*
> *"Why, O Lord, such love to me?"* —Kent

Continual growing in Christ comes from a deepening knowledge of Him.

Let Honor Meet Honor

READ: Matthew 6:1–6

Take heed that you do not do your charitable deeds
before men, to be seen by them. Otherwise you have no
reward from your Father in heaven. —MATTHEW 6:1

I've always been impressed by the solemn, magnificent simplicity of the Changing of the Guard at the Tomb of the Unknowns at Arlington National Cemetery. The carefully choreographed event is a moving tribute to soldiers whose names and sacrifice are "known but to God." Equally moving are the private moments of steady pacing when the crowds are gone: back and forth, hour after hour, day by day, in even the worst weather.

In September 2003, Hurricane Isabel was bearing down on Washington, DC, and the guards were told they could seek shelter during the worst of the storm. Surprising almost no one, the guards refused! They unselfishly stood their post to honor their fallen comrades even in the face of a hurricane.

Underlying Jesus' teaching in Matthew 6:1–6, I believe, is His desire for us to live with an unrelenting, selfless devotion to Him. The Bible calls us to good deeds and holy living, but these are to be acts of worship and obedience (vv. 4–6), not orchestrated acts for self-glorification (v. 2). The apostle Paul endorses this whole-life faithfulness when he pleads with us to make our bodies "a living sacrifice" (Romans 12:1).

May our private and public moments speak of our devotion and wholehearted commitment to you, Lord.   —RK

Grant me the strength this day, O Lord, to persevere,
to return honor to your name where I am serving. My desire
is to give myself in selfless devotion because of your love for me.

The more we serve Christ, the less we will serve self.

Bad Choice

READ: Revelation 20:11–15

Many of those who sleep in the dust of the earth shall awake, some to everlasting life, some to shame and everlasting contempt. —DANIEL 12:2

An elderly TV star was asked by talk-show host Larry King about heaven. King prefaced his question by referring to Billy Graham, who had told King he "knew what would be ahead. It would be paradise. He was going to heaven." King then asked his guest, "What do you believe?"

The man replied, "I'd like a lot of activity. Heaven sounds too placid for me. There's a lot to do in hell."

Sadly, this man is not alone in thinking that an existence in Satan's realm is a preferred destination. I've heard people say that they'd rather be in hell because all their friends will be there. One person wrote, "If hell was real, I don't think it would be bad. There would be a lot of interesting people."

How can we convince folks who are deceived in this way that hell and its horrors are to be avoided? Perhaps by telling them of the realities of hell that are presented in the Scripture. In Daniel 12:2 hell is described as a place of "shame and everlasting contempt." Luke 16:23 talks about "torments." Matthew 8:12 describes "weeping and gnashing of teeth." And Revelation 14:11 says there will be "no rest."

Biblical truth doesn't allow anyone to think that hell might be a good place to be. Clearly, rejecting Jesus and facing an eternity in Satan's kingdom is a bad choice. —DB

Don't choose to spend eternity
Where pain will never dim;
Instead decide to trust in Christ
And choose to follow Him. —Sper

The same Christ who talks about the glories
of heaven also describes the horrors of hell.

Hidden Sin

READ: 1 John 1:5–10

*O God, You know my foolishness; and my sins
are not hidden from You.* —PSALM 69:5

Chuck had slowed to a stop when his car was hit from behind and was pushed into the vehicle ahead of him. A sickening, crunching sound indicated that additional vehicles had collided behind them.

As Chuck sat quietly for a moment, he observed that the vehicle directly behind him was pulling out into traffic. Obviously hoping to avoid an encounter with police, the escaping driver neglected to notice he had left something behind. When the police arrived, an officer picked up the hit-and-run driver's license plate from the ground and said to Chuck, "Someone will be waiting for him when he arrives home. He won't get away with this."

Scripture tells us: "Be sure your sin will find you out," as this man who fled the accident discovered (Numbers 32:23). We may sometimes be able to hide our sin from the people around us, but nothing is ever "hidden from [God's] sight" (Hebrews 4:13). He sees each of our failures, thoughts, and motivations (1 Samuel 16:7; Luke 12:2–3).

Believers are given a wonderful promise: "If we confess our sins, [God] is faithful and just to forgive us our sins and to cleanse us from all unrighteousness" (1 John 1:9). So don't let unconfessed, so-called "hidden" sins come between you and God (vv. 6–7).   —CHK

*We cannot hide from God
No matter how we try;
For He knows all we think and do—
We can't escape His eye.* —Hess

Sin may be hidden from others, but never from God.

Sonrise!

READ: Malachi 4:1–6

The Sun of Righteousness shall arise with healing in His wings. —MALACHI 4:2

My state's name, "Idaho," according to one legend, comes from a Shoshone Indian word, "ee-dah-how." When translated into English, it means something like, "Behold! The sun rising over the mountain." I often think of that when the sun breaks over the eastern peaks and spills light and life into our valley.

Also, I think of Malachi's promise: "The Sun of Righteousness shall arise with healing in His wings" (Malachi 4:2). This is God's irrevocable promise that our Lord Jesus will come again and all creation "will be delivered from the bondage of corruption into the glorious liberty of the children of God" (Romans 8:21).

Each new sunrise is a reminder of that eternal morning when "bright heaven's Sun" will arise with healing in His wings. Then everything that has been made will be made over and made irrevocably right. There will be no throbbing backs or knees, no financial struggles, no losses, no aging. One Bible version says that when Jesus returns we will "go out and leap like calves released from the stall" (Malachi 4:2 NIV). This is my highest imagination and my hope.

Jesus said, "Surely I am coming quickly" (Revelation 22:20). Even so, come, Lord Jesus!   —DR

High King of heaven, my victory won,
May I reach heaven's joys, O bright heaven's Sun!
Heart of my own heart, whatever befall,
Still be my Vision, O Ruler of all. —Irish hymn

You have reason for optimism if you're looking for Christ's return.

Two Tales of One City

READ: Nahum 1

The Lord is good, a stronghold in the day of trouble;
and He knows those who trust in Him. —NAHUM 1:7

The book of Jonah has the makings of a great movie plot. It contains a runaway prophet, a terrible storm at sea, the prophet swallowed by a great fish, God sparing the prophet's life, and the repentance of a pagan city.

But the sequel—the book of Nahum—might not be so popular. Nahum ministered in Nineveh just as Jonah had, but about a hundred years later. This time, the Ninevites had no interest in repentance. Because of this, Nahum condemns Nineveh and proclaims judgment on the people.

To unrepentant Nineveh, the prophet preached: "The Lord is slow to anger and great in power, and will not at all acquit the wicked" (Nahum 1:3). But Nahum also had a message of mercy. To comfort the people of Judah, he proclaimed: "The Lord is good, a stronghold in the day of trouble; and He knows those who trust in Him" (v. 7).

We see in the stories of Jonah and Nahum that with every new generation comes the necessity of an individual response to God. No one's spiritual life can be handed off to another; we must each choose to serve the Lord from our own heart. God's message is as fresh today as it was hundreds of years ago: judgment for the unrepentant but mercy for the repentant. How will you respond? —DF

Your mercy, Lord, how great it is
To overrule our sin!
So help us know your righteousness
And choose to walk therein. —D. DeHaan

God's judgment is certain, but so is His mercy.

Impact for Christ

READ: 1 Timothy 4:10–16

Be an example to the believers in word, in conduct, in love . . . in faith, in purity. —1 TIMOTHY 4:12

Over the past several years, I've been privileged to travel with teenagers on eight mission trips. One thing I've learned in those excursions is that teens are not too young to make an impact for Jesus—either on me or on others whose lives they touch.

I've also noticed that the teens who make the biggest impact for Christ match the characteristics Paul told Timothy about in 1 Timothy 4:12. Trying to convince Timothy that his relative youth did not have to be a deterrent to his ministry, Paul told him to "be an example to the believers" in several areas.

In word: Young people who make a difference for Christ control what they say, avoid negative talk, and speak words that honor God. In conduct: Teens who practice discretion in their behavior shine for all the world to see. In love: By taking heed of Jesus' words to love God and their neighbor, teens please Jesus and touch hearts (Matthew 22:37–39). In faith: Those who put their faith into action change lives. In purity: It's tough to be morally pure and doctrinally sound, but kids who are can set the bar for the rest of us.

Paul's words aren't just for the young generation. All of us should be an example in word, conduct, love, faith, and purity. That's how we make an impact for Christ. —DB

O Christians, remember, you bear His dear name,
Your lives are for others to view;
You're living examples—men praise you or blame,
And measure your Savior by you. —Anonymous

The most valuable commentary on the Bible is a godly life.

Inside Out

READ: John 15:1–8

You are already clean because of the word
which I have spoken to you. —JOHN 15:3

During an international publishing conference, a young Frenchman described his experience at a book-signing event. A woman picked up one of his books, browsed through it, and exclaimed, "At last, a story that's clean!" He replied gently, "I write clean because I think clean. It's not an effort." What he expressed in print came from within, where Christ had altered the very core of his life.

John 15 records Jesus' lesson to His disciples about abiding in Him as the only means to a fruitful life. In the midst of His imagery of the vine and the branches, Jesus said: "You are already clean because of the word which I have spoken to you" (v. 3). Bible scholar W. E. Vine says that the Greek word for *clean* means "free from impure admixture, without blemish, spotless."

A pure heart is the work of Christ, and only in His power can we remain clean. We often fail, but "if we confess our sins, He is faithful and just to . . . cleanse us from all unrighteousness" (1 John 1:9). Renewal is an inside job.

Jesus has made us clean through His sacrifice and His Word. Our speech and actions that strike others as being fresh and pure flow from inside out as we abide in Christ. —DM

Admitting that we're guilty,
Acknowledging our sin,
Then trusting in Christ's sacrifice
Will make us clean within. —Sper

Confession to God brings cleansing from God.

Bull Sharks

READ: 1 Peter 4:12–19

Beloved, do not think it strange concerning the
fiery trial which is to try you. —1 PETER 4:12

Following a recent lunch discussion, I decided to research the comment that a bull shark attack had once occurred in Lake Michigan. It seemed like such an impossible thought that we all scoffed at the idea of sharks in a freshwater lake so far inland. I found one online site that claimed a bull shark attack did occur in Lake Michigan in 1955, but it was never verified. A shark attack in Lake Michigan? If the story were true, it would definitely be a rare occurrence.

Wouldn't it be great if hard times were like Lake Michigan bull shark attacks—rare or even untrue? But they aren't. Hardships and difficulties are common. It's just that when they happen to us, we think they shouldn't.

Perhaps that is why the apostle Peter, writing to first-century followers of Christ going through tough times, said, "Beloved, do not think it strange concerning the fiery trial which is to try you, as though some strange thing happened to you" (1 Peter 4:12). These trials are not abnormal, and once we get past our surprise, we can turn to the Father who ministers deeply to our hearts and in our lives. He has a love that never fails. And in our world filled with trials, that kind of love is desperately needed.   —BC

> *Underneath the restless surface*
> *Of each trial that comes in life*
> *Flows the Savior's love and power—*
> *They can calm our inner strife.* —D. DeHaan

By the sunshine of His love, God paints
on our clouds the rainbow of His grace.

God Is God

READ: Daniel 3:8–30

Women received their dead raised to life again. Others were tortured, not accepting deliverance, that they might obtain a better resurrection. —HEBREWS 11:35

When Polycarp (AD 69–155), who was bishop of the church at Smyrna, was asked by Roman authorities to curse Christ if he wanted to be released, he said, "Eighty-six years I have served Him, and He never did me any wrong. How can I blaspheme my King who saved me?" The Roman officer threatened, "If you do not change your mind, I will have you consumed with fire." Polycarp remained undaunted. Because he would not curse Christ, he was burned at the stake.

Centuries earlier, when three young men named Shadrach, Meshach, and Abed-Nego faced a similar threat, they answered, "O Nebuchadnezzar . . . our God whom we serve is able to deliver us from the burning fiery furnace, and He will deliver us from your hand, O king. But if not, let it be known to you, O king, that we do not serve your gods" (Daniel 3:16–18). A similar experience but two different outcomes. Polycarp was burned alive, but Shadrach, Meshach, and Abed-Nego left the furnace unsinged.

Two different results but the same display of faith. These men showed us that faith in God is not simply faith in what God can do. But it's the belief that God is God whether He delivers us or not. He has the final say. And it's our decision to choose to follow Him through it all.   —AL

Lord, help us trust you all the time
Regardless of what comes our way,
Accepting from your goodness that
You always have the final say. —Sper

Life is hard, but God is good—all the time.

Good for Nothing

READ: Revelation 2:1–7

Nevertheless I have this against you, that you have left your first love. —REVELATION 2:4

My wife, Martie, is a great cook. Sitting down after a busy day to enjoy her culinary delights is a real treat. Sometimes after dinner she runs errands, leaving me alone with the choice of grabbing the remote or cleaning up the kitchen. When I'm on my good behavior, I roll up my sleeves, load the dishwasher, and scrub the pots and pans— all for the joy of hearing Martie's grateful response, which is usually something like, "Wow, Joe! You didn't have to clean up the kitchen!" Which gives me a chance to say, "I wanted to show you how much I love you!"

When Jesus reproved the church at Ephesus for abandoning their "first love" (Revelation 2:4), it was because they were doing a lot of good things, but not out of love for Him. Although they were praised for their perseverance and patience, from Christ's point of view they were being "good" for nothing.

Good behavior should always be an act of worship. Resisting temptation, forgiving, serving, and loving each other are all opportunities to tangibly express our love for Jesus—not to get a star next to our name or a pat on the back.

When was the last time you did something "good" out of love for Jesus?　　　　　　　　　　　　　　　　　　　　　　　　　　—JS

> *For many, love is just a word,*
> *A passing phase, a brief emotion;*
> *But love that honors Christ our Lord*
> *Responds to Him with deep devotion.* —Hess

Love in deed is love indeed!

Stolen Thoughts

READ: Psalm 13; Colossians 3:1–4

How long, O Lord? Will You forget me forever? —PSALM 13:1

When my wife and I were traveling in another state, someone broke into our car after we stopped for lunch. With one look at the shattered glass, we realized that we had forgotten to put our GPS (global positioning system) out of sight. After a quick check of the backseat, I concluded that the thief also got my laptop, passport, and checkbook.

Then came the surprise. Later that evening, after phone calls and hours of growing worries, the unexpected happened. When I opened my suitcase, tucked between my clothes was what I thought I had lost. I couldn't believe my eyes! Only then did I recall that I had not put the items in the backseat after all. I had stuck them in the suitcase, which had been safely stored in the trunk of our car.

Sometimes, in the emotion of the moment, our minds play tricks on us. We think our loss is worse than it is. We may feel like the songwriter David who, in the confusion of the moment, thought God had forgotten him.

When David later recalled what he knew rather than what he feared, his sense of loss turned into a song of praise (Psalm 13:5–6). His renewed joy foreshadowed what is now ours to recall: Nothing can rob us of what is most important if our life is "hidden with Christ in God" (Colossians 3:3). —MD

> *When sorrows assail us or terrors draw nigh,*
> *His love will not fail us, He'll guide with His eye;*
> *And when we are fainting and ready to fail,*
> *He'll give what is lacking and make us prevail. —Anonymous*

Rest your assurance on God's love in your heart—not on the fear in your mind.

Business Card

READ: 1 Timothy 1:1, 12–17

Paul, an apostle of Jesus Christ, by the commandment of God our Savior and the Lord Jesus Christ. —1 TIMOTHY 1:1

In some cultures, the title below your name on your business card is very important. It identifies your rank. The way you are treated depends on your title as compared with others around you.

If Paul had a business card, it would have identified him as an "apostle" (1 Timothy 1:1), meaning "sent one." He used this title not out of pride but out of wonder. He didn't earn that position; it was "by the commandment of God our Savior and the Lord Jesus Christ." In other words, his was not a human but a divine appointment.

Paul had formerly been a "blasphemer, a persecutor, and an insolent man" (v. 13). He said that he considered himself to be the "chief" of sinners (v. 15). But because of God's mercy, he was now an apostle, one to whom "the King eternal" (v. 17) had committed the glorious gospel and whom He had sent out to share that gospel.

What is more amazing is that like the apostle Paul we are all sent out by the King of Kings to the world (Matthew 28:18–20; Acts 1:8). Let's recognize with humility that we don't deserve such a commission either. It is our privilege to represent Him and His eternal truth in word and in deed each day to all around us. —CPH

Let us go forth, as called of God,
Redeemed by Jesus' precious blood;
His love to show, His life to live,
His message speak, His mercy give. —Whittle

God gave you a message to share. Don't keep it to yourself!

A Royal Wedding

READ: Revelation 19:1–10

Let us be glad and rejoice and give Him glory, for the marriage of the Lamb has come, and His wife has made herself ready. —REVELATION 19:7

Weddings have long been an occasion for extravagance. Modern weddings have become a chance for young women to live out the fantasy of being "a princess for a day." An elegant gown, an elaborate hairstyle, attendants in color-coordinated dresses, bouquets of flowers, an abundance of food, and lots of celebrating with friends and family contribute to the fairy-tale atmosphere. Many parents start saving early so they can afford the high cost of making their daughter's dream come true. And royal weddings take extravagance to a level that we "commoners" seldom see. In 1981, however, many of us got a peek at one when the wedding of Prince Charles and Princess Diana was broadcast worldwide.

Another royal wedding is in the planning stages, and it will be more elaborate than any other. But in this wedding, the most important person will be the groom, Christ himself; and we, the church, will be His bride. John's revelation says that the bride will make herself ready (19:7) and that our wedding gown will be our righteous acts (v. 8).

Every bride works hard to make her wedding perfect. How much more, as the bride of Christ, should we be doing to prepare ourselves for a marriage that will last for eternity. —JAL

The church, the bride of Christ, will be
Arrayed in linen, clean and bright,
Through righteous acts that we have done—
Much to our Groom's delight. —Sper

Good deeds don't make a Christian, but a Christian does good deeds.

The Great Comeback

READ: Acts 2:14–21, 37–41

*But Peter, standing up with the eleven, raised his voice and said to them, "Men of Judea . . . heed my words." —*ACTS 2:14

We like to read about comebacks—about people or companies who face near disaster and turn things around. The Ford Motor Company is an example of that. In the 1940s, reluctance by leadership to modernize almost destroyed Ford. In fact, the government nearly took over the company lest its demise threaten the US war effort. But when Henry Ford II was released from his military duties to run the company, things turned around. Ford became one of the biggest corporations in the world.

Occasionally, we need a comeback. We need to correct wrong directions or compensate for wrong decisions. In those times, we have an example in Peter. He had failure written all over him. First, he nearly drowned when his faith faltered (Matthew 14:30). Then he said things that were so wrong Jesus called him "Satan" (16:22–23). And when Jesus needed Peter the most, he denied that he even knew Him (26:74).

But that's not the end of the story. In the power of the Spirit, Peter made a comeback. On the Day of Pentecost, he preached and 3,000 people came to faith in Christ (Acts 2:14, 41). Peter returned to effectiveness because his faith was renewed, he guarded what he said, and he stood up for Jesus.

Struggling? If Peter can come back, so can you. —DB

Today Christ calls, "Come follow Me!"
Do not look back to yesterday;
Fresh grace He'll give to do His will,
His joy you'll find as you obey. —D. DeHaan

To become whole, yield to the Holy Spirit.

Your Spiritual Pipeline

READ: Psalm 57

My soul trusts in You; and in the shadow of Your wings I will make my refuge. —PSALM 57:1

The Trans-Alaska Pipeline stretches eight hundred miles through Alaska. Because it was built through an earthquake zone, engineers had to be sure the pipe could withstand earth trauma. They decided on a network of Teflon sliders designed to ease the shock when the ground moved below the pipes. Engineers were delighted when the first big test came. In 2002, an earthquake occurred causing the ground to move eighteen feet to one side. The Teflon sliders moved gently to accommodate the movement without any damage to the pipe. The key was flexibility.

The believer's spiritual pipeline to heaven is built upon firm trust in God. But if we are inflexible in our expectations of how God should work, we can run into trouble. In a crisis, we can make the mistake of shifting our focus from God to our painful circumstances. Our prayer should be, "God, I don't understand why you have allowed this painful situation. But I am trusting in your ultimate deliverance despite all that's going on around me." The psalmist expressed this so well when he wrote: "My soul trusts in You . . . until these calamities have passed by" (Psalm 57:1).

When the earth seems to move under us, let's be flexible in our expectations but firmly confident in God's steadfast love and care.   —DF

> *Press forward and fear not! Though trials be near;*
> *The Lord is our refuge; whom then shall we fear?*
> *His staff is our comfort, our safeguard His rod;*
> *Then let us be steadfast and trust in our God.* —*Anonymous*

God may delay or deny our request, but He will never disappoint our trust.

Knowing the Creator

READ: Psalm 8:1–9

O Lord, our Lord, how excellent is Your name in all the earth,
who have set Your glory above the heavens! —PSALM 8:1

A tour bus along with several cars had stopped in front of the artist's house. People wandered around pointing at the towering steel sculptures glinting in the sun, while their cameras zoomed in on silver turbines spinning in the morning breeze. One person paused long enough to read the plaque on the wrought iron fence surrounding the sculpture garden.

This scene is repeated almost every day not far from where I live. Every time I drive past and see all the tourists and cameras, I think, *They'd appreciate it so much more if they knew the artist the way I did.* The artist had been a friend of mine for many years before he died. I often watched him at work transforming rusty oil-field pipe and truck axles into graceful works of art. When I see all that he made, I can't help but think of him.

As Christians, we are privileged to know the Creator of the universe. So when we study a tiny wildflower or marvel at the vastness of the Milky Way, we are reminded of the One who made all of it. In a deeply personal expression of praise, the psalmist wrote, "O Lord, our Lord, how excellent is Your name in all the earth" (Psalm 8:1).

How much more wonderful the marvels of this world appear when we know the One who made them all!   —DM

> *The wonder of creation speaks*
> *To everyone in different ways,*
> *But only those who know the Lord*
> *Can for His handiwork give praise. —Sper*

All creation points to the almighty Creator.

Do I Have to Read Leviticus?

READ: Isaiah 55:6–13

My Word . . . shall not return to Me void, but it shall accomplish what I please. —ISAIAH 55:11

Do I really have to read Leviticus?" A young executive asked me this in earnest as we talked about the value of spending time in reading the Bible. "The Old Testament seems so boring and difficult," he said.

Many Christians feel this way. The answer, of course, is that the Old Testament, including Leviticus, offers background and even contrasts essential to grasping the New Testament. While Isaiah challenges us to seek God (55:6), he also promises us that God's Word accomplishes what the Lord wants it to accomplish (v. 11). Scripture is alive and powerful (Hebrews 4:12), and it is useful to teach, correct, and instruct us (2 Timothy 3:16). God's Word never returns void (Isaiah 55:8–11), but sometimes it is not until later that God's words come to mind as we need them.

The Holy Spirit uses the truths we've stored from reading or memorization, and He helps us to apply them at just the right time. For example, Leviticus 19:10-11 speaks of business competition and even caring for the poor. The Spirit can remind us of these concepts, and we can use them, if we've spent time reading and contemplating that passage.

Reading the Bible turns our minds into storehouses through which the Spirit can work. That's a great reason to read Leviticus and the other sixty-five books as well. —RK

Lord, I want to learn to love your Word more and more. Teach me and help me to hide it in my heart so that I can live it, be encouraged by it, and help others to know it too.

To understand the Word of God, rely on the Spirit of God.

Rescued

READ: Colossians 1:3–18

He has delivered us from the power of darkness and conveyed us into the kingdom of the Son of His love. —COLOSSIANS 1:13

In the aftermath of Haiti's devastating earthquake in January 2010, the scenes of destruction and death were often punctuated by someone being pulled alive from the rubble, even after all hope seemed gone. Relief and tears of joy were followed by deep gratitude toward those who worked around the clock, often risking their own lives to give someone else another chance to live.

How would you feel if that happened to you? Have you ever been rescued?

In Colossians 1, Paul wrote to people who had come to know Jesus Christ and whose lives showed evidence of their faith. After assuring them of his prayers for them to know God's will and to please Him, Paul used a powerful word picture to describe what God had done for them all: "He has delivered us from the power of darkness and conveyed us into the kingdom of the Son of His love, in whom we have redemption through His blood, the forgiveness of sins" (vv. 13–14).

In Christ, we have been rescued! He has taken us from danger to safety, from one power and destiny to another, from death to life.

It's worth pondering all that being rescued means to us, as we thank God for His grace and power.   —DM

Amazing grace! How sweet the sound
That saved a wretch like me!
I once was lost but now am found;
Was blind, but now I see. —Newton

Those who've been rescued from sin are best able to help in the rescue of others.

True Wealth

READ: 1 Timothy 6:6–19

*Command those who are rich in this present age
not to be haughty, nor to trust in uncertain
riches but in the living God.* —1 TIMOTHY 6:17

Money is a powerful force. We work for it, save it, spend it, use it to satisfy our earthside longings, and then wish we had more. Aware of its distracting danger, Jesus taught more about money than any other topic. And, as far as we know, He never took an offering for himself. Clearly, He didn't teach about giving to fill His own pockets. Instead, Jesus warned us that trusting in wealth and using it to gain power clogs our spiritual arteries more readily than most other impediments to spiritual development. In telling the story of the "rich fool," He shamed His listeners for not being rich toward God (Luke 12:13–21), indicating that God has a far different definition of wealth than most of us.

So, what does it mean to be rich toward God? Paul tells us that those who are rich should not be conceited about their wealth, "nor to trust in uncertain riches" (1 Timothy 6:17). Rather, we are to "be rich in good works, ready to give, willing to share" (v. 18).

Interesting! God measures wealth by the quality of our lives and our generous disbursement of wealth to bless others. Not exactly Wall Street insider talk, but great advice for those of us who think that our security and reputation are tied up in the size of our bank account.   —JS

> *If we've been blessed with riches,*
> *We must be rich in deeds;*
> *God wants us to be generous*
> *In meeting others' needs.* —Sper

Riches are a blessing only to those who make them a blessing to others.

Getting Focused

READ: Philippians 3:8–16

Forgetting those things which are behind . . . I press toward the goal for the prize of the upward call of God in Christ Jesus. —PHILIPPIANS 3:13–14

I enjoy playing golf, so I occasionally watch instructional videos. One such video, however, left me disappointed. The teacher presented a golf swing that had at least eight steps and a dozen subpoints under each step. That was just too much information!

While I'm not a great golfer, years of playing have taught me this: The more thoughts you have in your head as you swing, the less likely you are to be successful. You must simplify your thought process and focus on what matters most—making solid contact with the ball. In this video the instructor's many points got in the way.

In golf and in life, we must focus on what matters most.

In Philippians 3, Paul describes how that relates to the Christian. Rather than being distracted by lesser things, he wanted to focus on what mattered most. He said, "One thing I do, forgetting those things which are behind and reaching forward to those things which are ahead, I press toward the goal for the prize of the upward call of God in Christ Jesus" (vv. 13–14).

"One thing I do." In a world of distractions, it's vital for the child of God to stay focused, and there is no better point of focus in the universe than Jesus Christ himself. Is He what matters most to you?   —BC

Lord, my focus is too easily distracted from you on to lesser things. Please draw me back to your ways and teach me what's most important. May I learn to always put you first.

We live most effectively for Christ when we keep our eyes on Him.

Dad's Hat

READ: Ephesians 6:1–4

Honor your father. —EPHESIANS 6:2

Amid the celebration, there was tragedy. It was the opening ceremonies of the 1992 Summer Olympic Games in Barcelona. One by one the teams entered the stadium and paraded around the track to the cheers of 65,000 people. But in one section of Olympic Stadium, shock and sadness fell as Peter Karnaugh, father of United States swimmer Ron Karnaugh, was stricken with a fatal heart attack.

Five days later, Ron showed up for his race wearing his dad's hat, which he carefully set aside before his competition began. Why the hat? It was the swimmer's tribute to his dad, whom he described as "my best friend." The hat was one his dad had worn when they went fishing and did other things together. Wearing the hat was Ron's way of honoring his dad for standing beside him, encouraging him, and guiding him. When Ron dove into the water, he did so without his dad's presence but inspired by his memory.

There are many ways to honor our fathers, as Scripture commands us to do (Ephesians 6:2). One way, even if they're no longer with us, is to show respect for the good values they taught us.

What can you do for your dad today to show him the kind of honor the Bible talks about? —DB

We're thankful for our fathers, Lord,
They're special gifts from you;
Help us to show we honor them
By what we say and do. —Sper

The best fathers not only give us life, they teach us how to live.

In Brief

READ: Psalm 117

His merciful kindness is great toward us. —PSALM 117:2

I counted once and discovered that Abraham Lincoln's Gettysburg Address contains fewer than three hundred words. This means, among other things, that words don't have to be many to be memorable.

That's one reason I like Psalm 117. Brevity is its hallmark. The psalmist said all he had to say in thirty words (actually just seventeen words in the Hebrew text).

> Praise the Lord, all you Gentiles!
> Laud Him, all you peoples!
> For His merciful kindness [love] is great toward us,
> And the truth of the Lord [faithfulness] endures forever.
> Praise the Lord!

Ah, that's the good news! Contained in this hallelujah psalm is a message to all nations of the world that God's "merciful kindness"— His covenant love—is "great toward us" (v. 2).

Think about what God's love means. God loved us before we were born; He will love us after we die. Not one thing can separate us from the love of God that is in Jesus our Lord (Romans 8:39). His heart is an inexhaustible and irrepressible fountain of love!

As I read this brief psalm of praise to God, I can think of no greater encouragement for our journey than its reminder of God's merciful kindness. Praise the Lord!　　　　　　　　　　　　　—DR

What we know about God should lead us to give joyful praise to Him.

Unexpected Blessing

READ: Ruth 2:11–23

Your daughter-in-law, who loves you . . . is better to you than seven sons. —RUTH 4:15

Naomi and Ruth came together in less-than-ideal circumstances. To escape a famine in Israel, Naomi's family moved to Moab. While living there, her two sons married Moabite women, Orpah and Ruth. Then Naomi's husband and sons died. In that culture, women were dependent on men, which left the three widows in a predicament.

Word came to Naomi that the famine in Israel had ended, so she decided to make the long trek home. Orpah and Ruth started to go with her, but Naomi urged them to return home, saying, "The hand of the Lord has gone out against me!" (Ruth 1:13). Orpah went home, but Ruth continued on with Naomi, affirming her belief in Naomi's God despite Naomi's own fragile faith (1:15–18).

The story started in desperately unpleasant circumstances: famine, death, and despair (1:1–5). It changed direction due to undeserved kindnesses: Ruth to Naomi (1:16–17; 2:11–12) and Boaz to Ruth (2:13–14).

It involved unlikely people: two widows (an aging Jew and a young Gentile) and Boaz, the son of a prostitute (Joshua 2:1; Matthew 1:5). It depended on unexplainable intervention: Ruth just "happened" to glean in the field of Boaz (2:3). And it ended in unimaginable blessing: a baby who would be in the lineage of the Messiah (4:16–17).

God makes miracles out of what seems insignificant: fragile faith, a little kindness, and ordinary people.   —JAL

In all the setbacks of your life as a believer,
God is plotting for your joy. —John Piper

Facing Our Fears

READ: Judges 6:11–23

The Angel of the Lord appeared to him, and said to him, "The Lord is with you, you mighty man of valor!" —JUDGES 6:12

A mother asked her five-year-old son to go to the pantry to get her a can of tomato soup. But he refused and protested, "It's dark in there." Mom assured Johnny, "It's okay. Don't be afraid. Jesus is in there." So Johnny opened the door slowly and seeing that it was dark, shouted, "Jesus, can you hand me a can of tomato soup?"

This humorous story of Johnny's fear reminds me of Gideon. The Lord appeared to Gideon, calling him a "mighty man of valor" (Judges 6:12) and then telling him to deliver Israel out of Midian's hand (v. 14). But Gideon's fearful reply was, "My clan is the weakest in Manasseh, and I am the least in my father's house" (v. 15). Even after the Lord told Gideon that with His help he would defeat the Midianites (v. 16), he was still afraid. Then Gideon asked the Lord for signs to confirm God's will and empowerment (vv. 17, 36–40). So, why did the Lord address fearful Gideon as a "mighty man of valor"? Because of who Gideon would one day become with the Lord's help.

We too may doubt our own abilities and potential. But let us never doubt what God can do with us when we trust and obey Him. Gideon's God is the same God who will help us accomplish all that He asks us to do. —AL

The Lord provides the strength we need
To follow and obey His will;
So we don't need to be afraid
That what He asks we can't fulfill. —Sper

We can face any fear when we know the Lord is with us.

Radical and Upside-Down

READ: Luke 14:7–14

There are last who will be first, and there are first who will be last. —LUKE 13:30

The values of the kingdom that Jesus came to establish were radically different than those of His day. The Pharisees and teachers of the law clamored for the spotlight and sought the adulation of the crowds. Many of us still do this today.

In Luke 14, Jesus told a parable that taught His followers not to be like that. The parable talks about people who chose the most honored seat for themselves at a wedding feast (vv. 7–8). He said they would be embarrassed when the host asked them publicly to take their rightful place (v. 9). Jesus went on in His story to talk about whom to invite to such dinners. He said they shouldn't invite friends and family, but "when you give a feast, invite the poor, the maimed, the lame, the blind. And you will be blessed, because they cannot repay you" (vv. 13–14).

Are you disappointed because you have not broken into the more elite group in your church or neighborhood? Or because you are stuck down on rung two when you'd rather be on rung eight or at least climbing the social ladder? Listen to what Jesus said: "Whoever exalts himself will be humbled, and he who humbles himself will be exalted" (v. 11). That's the radical and upside-down way of God's kingdom!   —DE

Blessed Savior, make me humble,
Take away my sinful pride;
In myself I'm sure to stumble,
Help me stay close by your side. —D. DeHaan

In Christ's kingdom, humility trumps pride every time.

Because

READ: Job 2

*Shall we indeed accept good from God, and
shall we not accept adversity?* —JOB 2:10

One day, my toddler exclaimed, "I love you, Mom!" I was curious about what makes a three-year-old tick, so I asked him why he loved me. He answered, "Because you play cars with me." When I asked if there was any other reason, he said, "Nope. That's it." My toddler's response made me smile. But it also made me think about the way I relate to God. Do I love and trust Him just because of what He does for me? What about when the blessings disappear?

Job had to answer these questions when catastrophes claimed his children and demolished his entire estate. His wife advised him: "Curse God and die!" (Job 2:9). Instead, Job asked, "Shall we indeed accept good from God, and shall we not accept adversity?" (v. 10). Yes, Job struggled after his tragedy; he became angry with his friends and questioned the Almighty. Still, he vowed, "Though He slay me, yet will I trust Him" (13:15).

Job's affection for his heavenly Father didn't depend on a tidy solution to his problems. Rather, he loved and trusted God because of all that He is. Job said, "God is wise in heart and mighty in strength" (9:4).

Our love for God must not be based solely on His blessings but because of who He is.   —JBS

*Shall we accept the good from God
But fuss when trials are in sight?
Not if our love is focused on
The One who always does what's right.* —Sper

Focusing on the character of God helps
us to take our eyes off our circumstances.

Recalculating

READ: 2 Timothy 3:10–17

All Scripture is given by inspiration of God, and is profitable for doctrine, for reproof, for correction, for instruction in righteousness. —2 TIMOTHY 3:16

On a road trip with a friend, we used his GPS navigation device to guide us as we drove each day. After entering our destination on the screen, we heard a voice telling us which road to follow, as well as when and where to make each turn. When we left the route, whether accidentally or deliberately, the voice would say, "Recalculating." Then it would tell us how to get back on the right road.

Second Timothy 3:16 describes the Bible as a spiritual navigation system for our journey through life. "All Scripture is given by inspiration of God, and is profitable for doctrine, for reproof, for correction, for instruction in righteousness." Doctrine tells us which road to travel; reproof tells us when we are off the road; correction tells us how to get back on; instruction in righteousness tells us how to stay on God's road.

The mistakes and choices that detour us from the Lord are not to be taken lightly. But failure is seldom fatal, and few decisions are final. The moment we veer off on our own, the Holy Spirit is "recalculating" and urging us to return to the Father's way.

If we've drifted off course, there's no better time than right now to heed God's voice and return to His road.   —DM

> *We need God's guidance from above,*
> *His daily leading and His love;*
> *As we trust Him for direction,*
> *To our course He'll give correction.* —Fitzhugh

To stay on course, trust the compass of God's Word.

Rest into It

READ: Romans 8:31–39

Come to Me, all you who labor and are heavy laden, and I will give you rest. —MATTHEW 11:28

The most enjoyable part of the stretch-and-flex exercise class I attend is the last five minutes. That's when we lie flat on our backs on our mats with the lights down low for relaxation. During one of those times, our instructor said softly, "Find a place where you can rest into." I thought of the best place to "rest into" mentioned in the words of a hymn by Cleland B. McAfee, "Near to the Heart of God."

> There is a place of quiet rest,
> Near to the heart of God,
> A place where sin cannot molest,
> Near to the heart of God.
> O Jesus, blest Redeemer,
> Sent from the heart of God,
> Hold us who wait before Thee
> Near to the heart of God.

This hymn was written in 1901 after the death of McAfee's two nieces from diphtheria. His church choir sang it outside the quarantined home of his brother, offering words of hope about God's heart of care.

The apostle Paul tells us that God has a heart of love for us (Romans 8:31–39). Nothing—tribulation, distress, persecution, famine, nakedness, peril, sword, death, life, angels, principalities, powers, height, nor depth—is able to separate us from the enduring love of our Lord. "If God is for us, who can be against us?" (v. 31).

Whatever our stresses or concerns, the heart of God is the place to "rest into." Leave it all with Him, "for He cares for you" (1 Peter 5:7).

—AC

When you're weary in life's struggles, find your rest in the Lord.

What Are You Known For?

READ: Philippians 2:25–30

Epaphroditus, my brother, fellow worker, and fellow soldier. —PHILIPPIANS 2:25

In the Roman Empire, pagans would often call on the name of a god or goddess as they placed bets in a game of chance. A favorite deity of the gambler was Aphrodite, the Greek name for Venus, the goddess of love. During the roll of the dice, they would say "epaphroditus!" literally, "by Aphrodite!"

In the book of Philippians we read of a Greek convert to the Christian faith by the name of Epaphroditus. He was a close companion of Paul who served him well in his missionary enterprise. Of his friend, Paul wrote: "Epaphroditus, my brother, fellow worker, and fellow soldier" (Philippians 2:25).

Epaphroditus was a spiritual brother in Christ, a faithful worker who shared ministry efforts, a brave soldier of the faith, and the carrier of the inspired letter to the church at Philippi. He modeled brotherhood, a work ethic, spiritual endurance, and service. Certainly, Epaphroditus had a well-deserved reputation that showed he did not live by a pagan deity but by faith in Jesus Christ.

Even more important than our name are the Christian qualities that are seen in our life: dependability, care, encouragement, and wisdom. What words would you like others to use to describe you?   —DF

O Lord, you see what's in my heart—
There's nothing hid from you;
So help me live the kind of life
That's loving, kind, and true. —D. DeHaan

If we take care of our character, our reputation will take care of itself!

Looking Ahead

READ: Hebrews 11:23–31

Moses . . . refused to be called the son of Pharaoh's daughter, choosing rather to suffer affliction. —HEBREWS 11:24–25

During the Cold War (1947–1991), a time of tension between the world's superpowers, Albert Einstein said, "I know not with what weapons World War III will be fought, but World War IV will be fought with sticks and stones." It was a moment of clarity that focused on the consequences of the choice to fight a nuclear war. Regardless of the motives for making such a choice, the results would be devastating.

Unfortunately, we don't always see ahead with such clarity. Sometimes the implications of our choices are hard to anticipate. And sometimes we are thinking only in the moment.

According to Hebrews 11:24–26, Moses looked ahead and made a choice based on possible consequences. "By faith Moses, when he became of age . . . [chose] rather to suffer affliction with the people of God than to enjoy the passing pleasures of sin, esteeming the reproach of Christ greater riches than the treasures in Egypt; for he looked to the reward."

Moses' choice wasn't easy, but its rightness was clear because he knew that the troubles he faced for godly living would be made bearable by his coming reward. As we look ahead, are we willing to bear "the reproach of Christ"—the tough times that come with being associated with Jesus—in exchange for the promised reward of pleasing God? —BC

Press on in your service for Jesus,
Spurred on by your love for the Lord;
He promised that if you are faithful,
One day you'll receive your reward. —Fasick

If we depend on Christ for everything, we can endure anything.

No Hope but God

READ: Romans 5:1–5

*But if we hope for what we do not see, we eagerly
wait for it with perseverance.* —ROMANS 8:25

In his book *Through the Valley of the Kwai*, Scottish officer Ernest Gordon wrote of his years as a prisoner of war during World War II. The 6' 2" man suffered from malaria, diphtheria, typhoid, beriberi, dysentery, and jungle ulcers, and the hard labor and scarcity of food quickly plunged his weight to less than 100 pounds.

The squalor of the prison hospital prompted a desperate Ernest to request to be moved to a cleaner place—the morgue. Lying in the dirt of the death house, he waited to die. But every day a fellow prisoner came to wash his wounds and to encourage him to eat part of his own rations. As the quiet and unassuming Dusty Miller nursed Ernest back to health, he talked with the agnostic Scotsman of his own strong faith in God and showed him that, even in the midst of suffering, there is hope.

The hope we read about in Scripture is not a vague, wishy-washy optimism. Instead, biblical hope is a strong and confident expectation that what God has promised in His Word He will accomplish. Tribulation is often the catalyst that produces perseverance, character, and, finally, hope (Romans 5:3–4).

Seventy years ago, in a brutal POW camp, Ernest Gordon learned this truth himself and said, "Faith thrives when there is no hope but God" (see Romans 8:24–25). —CHK

*Faith looks beyond this transient life
With hope for all eternity—
Not with some vague and wistful hope,
But with firm trust and certainty.* —D. DeHaan

Christ, the Rock, is our sure hope.

Lost and Found

READ: Luke 15:1–10

Rejoice with me, for I have found my sheep which was lost! —LUKE 15:6

Until the day I was found, I didn't know I was lost. I was going about business as usual, moving from task to task, distraction to distraction. But then I received an e-mail with the heading: "I think you're my cousin." As I read my cousin's message, I learned that she and another cousin had been searching for my branch of the family for nearly ten years. The other cousin promised her father, shortly before he died, that she would find his family.

I hadn't done anything to get lost, and I didn't have to do anything to be found except acknowledge that I was the person they had been looking for. Learning that they had spent so much time and energy searching for our family made me feel special.

This led me to think about the "lost and found" parables of Luke 15—the lost sheep, the lost coin, and the lost son. Whenever we wander away from God, whether intentionally like the prodigal son or unintentionally like the sheep, God looks for us. Even though we may not "feel" lost, if we have no relationship with God, we are. To be found, we need to realize that God is looking for us (Luke 19:10) and admit that we are separated from Him. By giving up our waywardness, we can be reunited with Him and restored to His family.   —JAL

The Lord has come to seek and save
A world that is lost in sin;
And everyone who comes to Him
Will be restored and changed within. —Sper

To be found, you must admit you are lost.

A Matter of Opinion?

READ: Matthew 16:13–20

[Jesus] said to them, "But who do you
say that I am?" —MATTHEW 16:15

We live in an age dominated by all kinds of public opinion polls. Decisions are being driven by the crowd, and some of that is good. Surveys can inform us about people's experiences with products, helping us make wiser purchases. Opinion polls can give government officials a sense of how their policy initiatives will be received. While information gleaned is a matter of personal opinion, it can be helpful in shaping decision-making on a variety of levels.

But when it comes to the most important question for all eternity, a public opinion poll cannot give us the answer. We must answer for ourselves. In Matthew 16, Jesus took His disciples to Caesarea Philippi and asked a question about public opinion: "Who do men say that I, the Son of Man, am?" (v. 13). The answers were varied and all were complimentary—but none was adequate. That's why Jesus then asked His disciples, "But who do you say that I am?" (v. 15). Peter got the answer right: "You are the Christ, the Son of the living God" (v. 16).

Public opinion can help answer certain questions, but not the one question that will determine your eternity: Who do you say that Jesus is? If you agree with Scripture, and place your trust in Christ, you will have eternal life.   —BC

> *It doesn't matter what the crowd*
> *Believes about the Lord.*
> *What matters is: Do you believe*
> *What God says in His Word?* —Sper

Opinion is no substitute for the truth of God's Word.

"Whatcha Doin'?"

READ: Colossians 3:12–17

Walk circumspectly, not as fools but as wise. —EPHESIANS 5:15

While staying at our house for a while, my granddaughter Addie began asking, "Whatcha doin', Grandpa?" over and over. Whether I was working at my computer, putting on my shoes to go outside, sitting down to read, or helping in the kitchen, she sidled up to me and asked what I was doing.

After answering her a few dozen times with, "Paying bills," "Going to the store," "Reading the paper," "Helping Grandma," I came to the conclusion that she was asking a key question.

Answering to a curious little girl about everything we do is one thing, but answering to God about our actions is infinitely more important. Wouldn't it be helpful to think of God coming alongside us at any time to ask, "What are you doing?" Imagine how often our answers would seem meaningless or empty.

"I'm spending the entire evening watching TV." "I'm eating more food than I should." "I'm going another day without talking to you." "I'm arguing with my spouse." The list could go on—to our embarrassment.

We are told to use our time carefully, with God's glory in sight (1 Corinthians 10:31; Colossians 3:23). Paul said, "Be very careful, then, how you live" (Ephesians 5:15 NIV). So, it's a good question. God wants to know: "Whatcha doin'?"   —DB

> *We're all accountable to God*
> *For how we use our time each day;*
> *Are moments chosen carefully,*
> *Or wasted mindlessly away?* —Sper

Beware of spending too much time on matters of too little importance.

Open Wide!

READ: 1 Peter 2:1–5

As newborn babes, desire the pure milk of the Word, that you may grow thereby. —1 PETER 2:2

Early in the spring, my wife and I watched a fascinating bird show outside our kitchen window. A couple of blackbirds with straw in their beaks entered a small vent in the house next door. A couple of weeks later, to our delight, we saw four baby birds stick their heads out of the vent. Mom and Dad took turns feeding their hungry babies.

Seeing the babies' wide-open mouths reminded me of how important it is for followers of Christ to eagerly desire spiritual food. In 1 Peter 2:2, the apostle Peter uses the analogy of babies longing to be fed: "As newborn babes, desire the pure milk of the Word, that you may grow thereby." The Greek word translated "desire" speaks of an intense yearning. It is a compound word meaning to "earnestly desire" or to "long after."

It might seem strange to be commanded to earnestly long for something. But unlike hungry birds and babies, we need to be reminded of our need for spiritual nourishment. Even though we may have fed on the Word in the past (v. 3), we need to realize that our need is ongoing and that without more nourishment we will grow spiritually weak. God is eager to feed His dear children. So, open wide!　　　　—DF

> *My hunger for the truth He satisfies;*
> *Upon the Word, the Living Bread, I feed:*
> *No parching thirst I know, because His grace,*
> *A pool of endless depth, supplies my need.* —Sanders

Neglecting the Word will famish your soul;
meditating on the Word will feed it.

Controversy of the Cross

READ: 1 Corinthians 1:17–25

The message of the cross is . . . the power of God. —1 CORINTHIANS 1:18

A case before the US Supreme Court focused on whether a religious symbol, specifically a cross, should be allowed on public land. Mark Sherman, writing for the Associated Press, said that although the cross in question was erected in 1934 as a memorial to soldiers who died in World War I, one veteran's group that opposed it called the cross "a powerful Christian symbol" and "not a symbol of any other religion."

The cross has always been controversial. In the first century, the apostle Paul said that Christ had sent him "to preach the gospel, not with wisdom of words, lest the cross of Christ should be made of no effect. For the message of the cross is foolishness to those who are perishing, but to us who are being saved it is the power of God" (1 Corinthians 1:17–18). As followers of Christ, we see the cross as more than a powerful Christian symbol. It is the evidence of God's power to free us from the tyranny of our sin.

In a diverse and pluralistic society, the controversy over religious symbols will continue. Whether a cross can be displayed on public property will likely be determined by the courts. But displaying the power of the cross through our lives will be decided in our hearts.   —DM

Christ takes each sin, each pain, each loss,
And by the power of His cross
Transforms our brokenness and shame
So that our lives exalt His name. —D. DeHaan

Nothing speaks more clearly of God's love than the cross.

He Calls Me Friend

READ: John 15:9–17

All things that I heard from My Father I have made known to you . . . that you should go and bear fruit. —JOHN 15:15–16

Someone has defined friendship as "knowing the heart of another and sharing one's heart with another." We share our hearts with those we trust, and we trust those who care about us. We confide in our friends because we have confidence that they will use the information to help us, not harm us. They in turn confide in us for the same reason.

We often refer to Jesus as our friend because we know that He wants what is best for us. We confide in Him because we trust Him. But have you ever considered that Jesus confides in His people?

Jesus began calling His disciples friends rather than servants because He had entrusted them with everything He had heard from His Father (John 15:15). Jesus trusted the disciples to use the information for the good of His Father's kingdom.

Although we know that Jesus is our friend, can we say that we are His friends? Do we listen to Him? Or do we only want Him to listen to us? Do we want to know what's on His heart? Or do we only want to tell Him what's on ours? To be a friend of Jesus, we need to listen to what He wants us to know and then use the information to bring others into friendship with Him. —JAL

Sweet thought! We have a Friend above,
Our weary, faltering steps to guide,
Who follows with His eye of love
The precious child for whom He died. —Anonymous

Christ's friendship calls for our faithfulness.

Touch a Life

READ: Galatians 6:6–10

Let us not grow weary while doing good. —GALATIANS 6:9

My friend Dan, who was soon to graduate from high school, was required to make a senior presentation. He had fifteen minutes to share how he had made it to the point of graduation and to thank those who had helped him along the way.

I gazed around the room before he started to talk. All kinds of people—young families, teachers, friends, church leaders, and coaches—were in attendance. He began to talk about the ways each person had touched his life. One woman had "been like an aunt and had always been there" for him. A thirty-something man "shared Scriptures often and gave counsel." Another man had "taught him discipline and hard work." A church friend had "taken him to football practice every day" because his mom couldn't. A couple had "treated him like he was their own son." One commonality—they were all just ordinary Christians who had reached out to make a difference in his life.

Paul called it doing "good to all, especially to those who are of the household of faith" (Galatians 6:10). We can help shape another person's life by showing an interest and taking action. And, as happened with Dan, we can reap a harvest (v. 9).

Look around. Is there someone whose life needs your touch? —AC

Lord, grant me a heart of compassion
So burdened for others' needs
That I will show your kindness
In attitudes, words, and deeds. —Fitzhugh

Do all the good you can, in all the ways you
can, for all the people you can, while you can.

Fusion Man

READ: Psalm 55:1–8

So I said, "Oh, that I had wings like a dove! I would fly away and be at rest." —PSALM 55:6

Yves Rossy accomplished something people have dreamed of since the ancient myth of Icarus. He has flown. Known as "Fusion Man," Rossy built a set of wings with an engine pack that uses his body as the fuselage of the aircraft, with the wings fused to the back of his heat-resistant suit. His first flight took place near Geneva, Switzerland, in 2004, and he has since had numerous successful flights.

The psalmist David longed to have wings so he could fly away. In a time when he was being pursued by enemies who were seeking to take his life, Israel's king cried, "Oh, that I had wings like a dove! I would fly away and be at rest" (Psalm 55:6).

Like David, when we're facing pressure, mistreatment, hardship, or grief, we might wish we could sprout wings and fly away. But Jesus offers a better way. Rather than fleeing our struggles, He invites us to flee to Him. He said, "Come to Me, all you who labor and are heavy laden, and I will give you rest. Take My yoke upon you and learn from Me . . . and you will find rest for your souls" (Matthew 11:28–29). Rather than wishing we could fly away and escape life's problems, we can bring them to Him.

Escape cannot give us rest, but Jesus can.   —BC

> *O give me a spirit of peace, dear Lord,*
> *Midst the storms and tempests that roll,*
> *That I may find rest and quiet within,*
> *A calm buried deep in my soul. —Dawe*

God gives us strength to face our problems, not to flee from them.

The Power of a Promise

READ: Genesis 2:18–25

*For this reason a man shall . . . be
joined to his wife.* —MATTHEW 19:5

I wear only two pieces of jewelry: a wedding band on my finger and a small Celtic cross on a chain around my neck. The ring represents my vow to be faithful to Carolyn, my wife, as long as I shall live. The cross reminds me that it is not for her sake alone, but for Jesus' sake that I do so. He has asked me to be faithful to her until death shall separate us.

A marriage vow is more than a contract that we can break by paying damages. It is a unique vow that is explicitly intended to be binding until death separates us (Matthew 19:6). The words "for better, for worse; for richer, for poorer; in sickness and in health" take into consideration the probability that it will not be easy to keep our vows. Circumstances may change and so may our spouses.

Marriage is hard at best; disagreements and difficult adjustments abound. While no one must live in an abusive and dangerous relationship, accepting the difficulties of poverty, hardship, and disappointment can lead to happiness. A marriage vow is a binding obligation to love, honor, and cherish one another for as long as we shall live because Jesus has asked us to do so. As a friend of mine once put it, "This is the vow that keeps us faithful even when we don't feel like keeping our vows." —DR

> *"For better or for worse," we pledge,*
> *Through sickness and through strife;*
> *And by the help and grace of God*
> *We'll keep these vows for life.* —D. DeHaan

Love is more than a feeling; it's a commitment.

A Family Reunion

READ: 1 Thessalonians 2:4–12

We were gentle among you, just as a nursing mother cherishes her own children. —1 THESSALONIANS 2:7

For the past twenty-nine years, the annual Celebration of Life reunion in our city has brought together members of a unique family. The festive gathering reunites doctors, nurses, and staff from Colorado Springs' Memorial Hospital for Children with former patients from its neonatal intensive care unit. Some are infants in strollers while others are young teens. Their parents come with them to say thank you to those who saved their children's lives and gave them a second chance. Edward Paik's article in *The Gazette* quoted Dr. Bob Kiley's heartfelt response: "Both professionally and personally, for all the staff, this solidifies why we're in this job."

I wonder if in heaven there will be many such times when spiritual caregivers and those they helped as "babes in Christ" will reunite to share stories and give praise to God. The New Testament describes how Paul, Silvanus, and Timothy worked among the young believers in Thessalonica with gentleness, "just as a nursing mother cherishes her own children," and with comfort and encouragement, "as a father does his own children" (1 Thessalonians 2:7, 11).

Helping new believers at a critical stage in their faith is a labor of love that will be cause for great rejoicing at the "family" reunion in heaven.   —DM

Friends will be there I have loved long ago,
Joy like a river around me will flow;
Yet, just a smile from my Savior, I know,
Will through the ages be glory for me. —Gabriel

One of heaven's pleasures will be to share our earthly stories.

Trouble Ahead

READ: Numbers 13:25–14:9

Only do not rebel against the Lord, nor fear the people of the land . . . the Lord is with us. Do not fear them. —NUMBERS 14:9

Inevitably, trouble will invade our lives: A bad report from a medical test, the betrayal of a trusted friend, a child who rejects us, or a spouse who leaves us. The list of possibilities is long, but there are only two options: forge ahead on our own, or turn to God.

Flying solo into the face of trouble is not a good idea. It can lead to bad behavior patterns, blaming God, and retreating into defeat. Like the Israelites, we may spin out of control and into despair (Numbers 14:1–4).

When the majority of the spies brought a report of intimidating giants and dangers ahead, they used the pronoun "we" seven times with no reference to the Lord (13:31–33). The Israelites were on the cusp of the ultimate blessing that God promised to them. They were eye-witnesses to the miracles in Egypt, and their feet had walked the dry bottom of the Red Sea in jaw-dropping victory. God's faithfulness had been amazingly evident. What short memories! What disappointing faithlessness! Sadly, they turned their backs on God and left the blessing behind.

Caleb and Joshua, on the other hand, opted to turn to the Lord with this confidence: "The Lord is with us" (14:9). When your giants show up, what will you do? —JS

In this world of sin and trouble
Where so many ills are known,
If I shun the ways of evil,
I am kept by Him alone. —Smith

God's presence is a life preserver that keeps
the soul from sinking in a sea of trouble.

Occupational Hazard

READ: Philippians 1:12–18

The things which happened to me have actually turned out for the furtherance of the gospel. —PHILIPPIANS 1:12

M y occupation is words. Whether I am writing or editing, I am using words to convey ideas so that readers can understand. I can usually see what's wrong with someone else's writing (though sometimes not with my own) and figure out how to fix it.

As an editor, I am paid for being critical. My job is to see what's wrong with the way words are used. This ability becomes a disability, however, when I carry it over into my personal life and always look for what is wrong. Focusing on what's wrong can cause me to miss everything that's good.

The apostle Paul had reason to focus on those who were causing him harm. Certain people were preaching the gospel out of selfish ambition to add to Paul's suffering (Philippians 1:16). But instead of concentrating on the negative, he chose to look at the positive and rejoice in it: Jesus Christ was being preached (v. 18).

God wants us to be discerning—we need to know good from bad— but He doesn't want us to focus on the bad and become critical or discouraged. Even in circumstances that are less than ideal (Paul was writing from prison), we can find something good, because in times of trouble God is still at work. —JAL

The eyes of faith when fixed on Christ
Give hope for what's ahead,
But focus on life's obstacles
And faith gives way to dread. —D. DeHaan

When your outlook is blurred by problems, focus on Christ.

Old School

READ: 1 Timothy 2:8–10; Romans 12:1–2

I desire . . . that the women adorn themselves in modest apparel. —1 TIMOTHY 2:8–9

As we hurtle through the first part of this new century, we see an increase in people questioning time-honored standards. This was plainly communicated recently by a teen pop star—a girl who professes faith in Jesus.

While discussing standards for modesty in how she dresses, she discounted criticism of her skimpy clothing by saying, "That's so old school."

This young woman is both right and wrong. In a sense, she's right. The standards of dress for Christians are "old school." They were written down more than 2,000 years ago. But her attitude that suggests ancient standards can be set aside is wrong. In the truest sense, the principles in the Bible are not "old" as much as they are timeless. While written ages ago, they are still fresh and applicable.

As to the question of modesty, when the Bible says women should "adorn themselves in modest apparel" (1 Timothy 2:9), it is still true today that we shouldn't dress to draw attention to ourselves. A more general principle, "Do not be conformed to this world, but be transformed" (Romans 12:2), is a timely command that can guide the question of how we dress.

So whether you're a pop star or a pew sitter, don't worry about being "old school" if what you are doing is done according to the Book. —DB

Dear Lord, help us to follow the timeless standards of the Bible in speech, clothing, and other lifestyle matters. May all we say and do bring glory to you.

Do my choices bring glory to God or draw attention to me?

Paul, the Aged

READ: Philemon 1:1–9

Being such a one as Paul, the aged . . . I appeal to you for my son Onesimus. —PHILEMON 1:9–10

Celebrating my sixtieth birthday really changed my perspective on life. I used to think people in their sixties were "old." So when I approached sixty, I started counting the number of productive years I might have left and set the number at ten. I went along with this dead-end kind of thinking until I remembered a very productive coworker who was eighty-five. So I sought him out to ask what life after sixty was like. He told me of some of the wonderful ministry opportunities the Lord had given him over the last twenty-five years.

The apostle Paul, referring to himself as "aged" in Philemon 1:9, really resonates with my own sense of aging: "Being such a one as Paul, the aged . . . I appeal to you for my son Onesimus" (vv. 9–10). Paul was asking Philemon to take back his runaway servant Onesimus. Some scholars believe Paul was in his late forties or early fifties when he wrote this—certainly not a senior citizen by today's standards. But life expectancy in those days was much shorter. Yet despite awareness of his mature years, Paul went on to serve the Lord for several more years.

While we may experience physical or other kinds of limitations, what really matters is that we continue doing what we can for the Lord until He calls us home. —DF

Think not your work of no account
Although it may be small;
The Lord marks well your faithfulness
When you give Him your all. —D. DeHaan

God can use you at any age—if you are willing.

Seeing the Person Inside

READ: 2 Corinthians 5:12–21

From now on, we regard no one according to the flesh. —2 CORINTHIANS 5:16

On February 1, 1960, four students from an all-black college sat down at a "whites only" lunch counter in Greensboro, North Carolina. One of them, Franklin McCain, noticed an older white woman seated nearby looking at them. He was sure that her thoughts were unkind toward them and their protest against segregation. A few minutes later she walked over to them, put her hands on their shoulders, and said, "I am so proud of you."

Recalling the event years later on National Public Radio, McCain said he learned from this never to stereotype anyone. Instead he learned to pause and consider others and seek an opportunity to talk with them.

The first-century church, like ours today, was often fractured by divisions based on race, language, and culture. Paul wrote to the followers of Jesus in Corinth to help them respond to those who were more concerned with outward appearance than with what is in the heart (2 Corinthians. 5:12). Because Christ died for all, Paul said, "From now on, we regard no one according to the flesh" (v. 16).

May we all look closely to see the person inside, for everyone is made in the image of God and can become a new creation in Christ. —DM

First impressions can mislead us
For we do not know the heart;
We can often be mistaken
Since we only know in part. —Fitzhugh

It's what's in the heart that matters.

O. B. Markers

READ: Jeremiah 5:21–31

*I know, O Lord, that Your judgments are right, and that
in faithfulness You have afflicted me.* —PSALM 119:75

In the game of golf, out-of-bounds or O. B. markers designate when a
ball has gone out of play. If a player's ball goes out-of-bounds, a one-
stroke penalty is imposed.

The prophet Jeremiah warned the southern kingdom of Judah about
their persistent rejection of God's boundaries for them. He said that
even the sea knows that the sand on the seashore is its O. B. marker,
"an everlasting barrier it cannot cross" (Jeremiah 5:22 NIV). Yet the
Lord's people had defiant and rebellious hearts (v. 23). There was no
fear of God, who gave them rain for their crops (v. 24). They grew rich
on deceit (v. 27) and ignored the pleas of the disadvantaged (v. 28).

God has given moral boundaries in His Word for us to live within.
He gave them not to frustrate us but so that by keeping within them
we may enjoy His blessings. David wrote: "I know, O Lord, that Your
judgments are right" (Psalm 119:75). God told Israel through Moses, "I
have set before you life and death, blessing and cursing; therefore choose
life" (Deuteronomy 30:19).

Don't test God's boundaries and invite His correction. Make wise
choices to live within His O. B. markers in His Word.   —CPH

The Lord has given us commands,
And told us to obey;
Our own designs are sure to fail,
If we neglect His way! —Bosch

A small step of obedience is a giant step to blessing.

Empty Me

READ: Ephesians 4:17–32

A good man out of the good treasure of his heart brings forth good; and an evil man out of the evil treasure of his heart brings forth evil. —LUKE 6:45

"What a rotten design," I grumbled as I emptied our paper shredder. I was following good advice about shredding personal documents, but I could not empty the container without spilling strips of confetti all over the carpet! One day as I was gathering trash, I debated whether I'd even bother with the shredder since it was only half-full. But when I slipped a small plastic bag over the top and flipped it upside down, I was pleased to see that not a bit of paper had fallen on the floor.

The error had been mine. I had been waiting until the container was filled to the brim before emptying it!

When we allow sin to fill up our hearts, it too will overflow into our life. Luke 6:45 says that "an evil man out of the evil treasure of his heart brings forth evil." It is "out of the abundance of the heart" that we speak.

What if we were to empty our hearts of the rubbish of sin before it started spilling into our interactions with others? To dispose of our bitterness, stubborn pride, seething anger (Ephesians 4:26–32)? First John 1:9 reminds us that "if we confess our sins, He is faithful and just to forgive us our sins and to cleanse us from all unrighteousness."

A paper shredder is designed to be a rubbish receptacle. You and I are not! —CHK

Search me, O God, and know my heart today;
Try me, O Savior, know my thoughts I pray.
See if there be some wicked way in me;
Cleanse me from every sin, and set me free. —Orr

Own up to your sin—you can't hide it from God anyway!

Perfect Fit

READ: Exodus 26:1–11

[Christ], in whom the whole building, being fitted together, grows into a holy temple in the Lord. —EPHESIANS 2:21

Too long. Too short. Too big. Too small. Too tight. Too loose. These words describe most of the clothes I try on. Finding the perfect fit seems impossible.

Finding a church that is a "perfect fit" poses similar problems. Every church has something that's not quite right. Our gifts aren't recognized. Our talents aren't appreciated. Our sense of humor is misunderstood. Certain attitudes, beliefs, people, or programs make us uncomfortable. We feel as if we don't fit. We struggle to find our place.

We know, however, that God wants us to fit together with one another. The apostle Paul said we are being "built together to become a dwelling in which God lives" (Eph. 2:22 NIV).

The believers in the church today, like the tabernacle in the days of Moses (Exodus 26) and the temple in the days of Solomon (1 Kings 6:1–14), are the dwelling place of God on earth. God wants us to fit together—for there to be no divisions in His church. This means that we, the building blocks, are to be "perfectly joined together in the same mind and in the same judgment" (1 Corinthians 1:10).

No church will be a perfect fit, but we can all work at fitting together more perfectly. —JAL

Christ's love creates unity in the midst of diversity.

Sticks and Stones

READ: Psalm 123

Our soul is exceedingly filled with . . . the
contempt of the proud. —PSALM 123:4

The psalmist was fed up with "the contempt of the proud" (Psalm 123:4). Perhaps you are too. People in your neighborhood, office, or classroom may be scornful of your faith and determination to follow Jesus. Sticks and stones do break our bones, but words can wound more deeply. In his commentary on this psalm, Derek Kidner refers to contempt as "cold steel."

We can fend off the jeers of the proud by becoming like them, or we can view their attempt to humiliate us as a badge of honor. We can rejoice that we've been "counted worthy to suffer shame for [Jesus'] name" (Acts 5:41). Better to bear shame for a short time than to endure "everlasting contempt" (Daniel 12:2).

We must not be like the mockers by mocking them in turn, but bless those who persecute us. "Bless and do not curse," Paul reminds us (Romans 12:14). Then God may draw them to faith and repentance, and turn our moments of shame into eternal glory.

Finally, as the psalmist counsels us, we must "look to the Lord our God" (Psalm 123:2). He understands as no other, for He too has endured reproach. He will show compassion to us according to His infinite mercy. —DR

> *When persecution comes your way*
> *And people mock your Lord,*
> *Remember what's in store for those*
> *Who love and trust His Word.* —Sper

When others' treatment of you gets you down, look up to Jesus.

Fear Factor

READ: Genesis 20:1–13

*Abraham said, ". . . surely the fear of God is not in this place;
and they will kill me on account of my wife." —*GENESIS 20:11

If you're a fan of Shakespeare, you know that his heroes always have
a serious character flaw. It makes for a good story and teaches some
important lessons. The same is true of our Bible hero Abraham. His
flaw? Fear.

Twice Abraham succumbed to his fear that a ruler would kill him
and steal his wife (Genesis 12:11–20; 20:2–13). Fearing for his life,
he deceived both Pharaoh and King Abimelech by saying, "She is my
sister"—in essence welcoming the king to take Sarah into his harem
(20:2). With fear dictating his actions, he put at risk God's plan that
through him and Sarah a great nation would arise (12:1–3).

But before we judge Abraham, we should ask ourselves a few questions. For fear of losing our job, would we compromise our integrity?
For fear of appearing old-fashioned, would we set aside our values? For
fear of being ridiculed or misunderstood, would we neglect sharing the
gospel and put someone's eternity at risk? Only one thing will conquer our fears: tenacious faith in God's presence, protection, power,
and promises.

If your fear is putting God's wonderful plans for you at risk, remember that He will never ask you to do anything He can't bring to comple-
tion, even if it requires miraculous intervention on His part.   —JS

> *It often helps in time of trial*
> *When fearful and alone,*
> *To know that every doubt we feel*
> *The greatest saints have known. —D. DeHaan*

Let your faith overcome your fear, and God will turn your worry into worship.

Bedlam

READ: Romans 12:9–21

Those who leave the paths of uprightness . . . rejoice in doing evil, and delight in the perversity of the wicked. —PROVERBS 2:13-14

England's Imperial War Museum is housed in a building in London that was a former location of the Bethlem Royal Hospital, a care center for the mentally ill. The hospital was commonly known as "Bedlam," which gradually became a term used to describe scenes of chaos and madness.

It's ironic that the war museum would occupy Bedlam's former location. As you walk through the museum, in addition to stories of heroism and sacrifice in wartime, you also find bone-chilling accounts of the madness of man's inhumanity to man. From the exhibits about modern genocide and ethnic cleansing to the one on the Holocaust, it is evil on display.

Solomon observed mankind's propensity for evil, describing it as those who "rejoice in doing evil, and delight in the perversity of the wicked" (Proverbs 2:14). While this may describe much of the world around us, followers of Jesus have a refreshingly different way to handle life. Paul challenged us: "Do not be overcome by evil, but overcome evil with good" (Romans 12:21). Christ-centered actions such as living morally (v. 17), making peace (v. 18), and treating our enemies with care (v. 20) will affect the world for good.

If each of us were to live as a reflection of God's love, perhaps there would be a lot less bedlam.   —BC

> *The godless and sinful everywhere*
> *Are objects of God's love and care,*
> *But they will always know hopeless despair*
> *Unless His love with them we share. —D. DeHaan*

A despairing world needs caring Christians.

Life Wish

READ: Acts 20:17–32

None of these things move me; nor do I count my life dear to myself, so that I may finish my race with joy. —ACTS 20:24

A Colorado mountaineer and guide was once asked if he thought climbers had a death wish. He replied, "Actually, they have a life wish—to live life to the fullest." As a careful yet adventurous climber, he explained why he considered the risks worth taking: "When it comes time for me to die," he said, "I do not wish to discover that I have not lived."

As the apostle Paul traveled to Jerusalem, it may have appeared to his closest friends that he had a death wish. At one point, several people warned him of the danger and urged him not to go (Acts 21:4, 12). But Paul had already made up his mind in Ephesus, where he clearly stated that his purpose was to "finish my race with joy, and the ministry which I received from the Lord Jesus, to testify to the gospel of the grace of God" (20:24).

Paul did not take unnecessary risks in his witness as a Christian, but he never shied away from publicly declaring his faith in Jesus Christ. His goal was not to play it safe and protect himself. Instead, he lived to finish his spiritual race with joy and to complete God's task for him.

Paul's courage challenges us to live for Christ with selfless abandon, not apprehension. That's the way to know ultimate fulfillment and joy. Do we share his life wish today?   —DM

Only this hour is mine, Lord—
May it be used for Thee;
May every passing moment
Count for eternity. —*Christiansen*

To find the greatest joy in life, give your life to Christ.

Our Best Defense

READ: John 9:13–25

*Whether He is a sinner or not I do not know. One thing
I know: that though I was blind, now I see.* —JOHN 9:25

Thrown together as seatmates for an eight-hour train ride, a retired
US ambassador and I quickly clashed as he sighed when I pulled
out my Bible.

I took the bait. At first, we traded one-liners aimed at goading the
other or scoring points. Gradually, though, bits and pieces of our respec-
tive life stories started creeping into the discussion. Curiosity got the
better of both of us and we found ourselves asking questions instead of
feuding. A political science major in college and a political junkie by
hobby, I was intrigued with his career, which included two prominent
ambassadorships.

Strangely enough, his questions to me were about my faith. How
I became "a believer" was what interested him most. The train ride
ended amicably, and we even traded business cards. As he left the train,
he turned to me and said, "By the way, the best part of your argument
isn't what you think Jesus can do for me. It's what He's done for you."

In John 9, as on that train, God reminds us that the best story is the
one we know intimately: Our own encounter with Jesus Christ. Practice
telling your story of faith to loved ones and close friends so you'll be able
to tell it clearly to others.   —RK

> *You may be tempted to debate*
> *To change another's view,*
> *But nothing speaks more powerfully*
> *Than what Christ did in you.* —Sper

People know true faith stories when they hear them.

An Amazing View

READ: Psalm 33:13–22

*From the place of His dwelling He looks on all
the inhabitants of the earth.* —PSALM 33:14

From my home in Colorado I recently used Google Maps to "wander around" the neighborhood in Nairobi, Kenya, where my family lived two decades ago. A satellite image on my computer screen enabled me to identify roads, landmarks, and buildings. In some cases, I got a street-level view, as if I were standing on the ground there.

It was quite a view, but only a small taste of how the Lord must see our world.

The psalmist celebrated God's view by writing these words: "The Lord looks from heaven; He sees all the sons of men . . . He considers all their works . . . The eye of the Lord is on those who fear Him, on those who hope in His mercy, to deliver their soul from death, and to keep them alive in famine" (Psalm 33:13–19).

Unlike an unfeeling satellite, the Lord sees with His heart of love as He considers who we are and what we do. The Bible reveals that He longs for us to trust Him and follow His way. We are never out of God's sight, and He keeps a close eye on everyone whose hope is in Him.

For all who know the Lord through faith in Jesus Christ, it's encouraging to realize that every day we're part of His amazing view. —DM

> *Beneath His watchful eye*
> *His saints securely dwell;*
> *That hand which bears all nature up*
> *Shall guard His children well. —Doddridge*

Keep your eyes on God; He never takes His eyes off you.

Stay Close

READ: 1 Peter 4:7-11

Comfort each other and edify one another. —1 THESSALONIANS 5:11

My friend and I were traveling together, and she seemed a bit frazzled. When we got to the airport, she forgot to have her identification readily available and couldn't find her reservation confirmation number. The ticket agent waited patiently, smiled, and then helped her at the "self" check-in. After receiving her ticket, she asked, "Where do we go next?" The agent smiled again, pointed at me, and said to her, "Stay close to your friend."

That can be good advice for all of us when our lives get frazzled—stay close to your friends. Although Jesus is our best friend, we also need relationships with fellow believers to help us survive in this life.

In his first epistle, Peter was writing to believers who needed one another because they were suffering for their faith. In a few short sentences in chapter 4, Peter mentioned the need to receive and give "fervent love," prayer, and hospitality (vv. 7–9). He also included the need for believers to use their spiritual gifts to minister to one another (v. 10). In other passages, we're encouraged to comfort each other with the comfort we've been given by God (2 Corinthians 1:3–4) and to build each other up in love (1 Thessalonians 5:11).

When life gets difficult and we get frazzled, staying close to our Christian friends will help us to get through.   —AC

> *When our friends encounter trials,*
> *We can help them if we're near;*
> *Some may need a word of comfort,*
> *Others just a listening ear.* —Sper

Staying close to godly friends helps us to stay close to God.

The Pleasure Is Mine

READ: Ecclesiastes 2:1–11

I did not withhold my heart from any pleasure . . . All was vanity and grasping for the wind. —ECCLESIASTES 2:10–11

I always look forward to summer. The warm sunshine, baseball, beaches, and barbecues are pleasures that bring joy after a long, cold winter. But pleasure-seeking isn't just seasonal. Don't we all enjoy good food, engaging conversation, and a crackling fire?

The desire for pleasure isn't wrong. God has built us for it. Paul reminds us that God "gives us richly all things to enjoy" (1 Timothy 6:17). Other passages welcome us to the healthy pleasure of food, friends, and the intimacy of a marriage relationship. But thinking that we can find lasting pleasure in people and things is ultimately an empty pursuit.

Ultimate pleasure is not found in the short-lived thrills our world offers, but rather in the long-term joy from a deepening intimacy with our Lord. King Solomon learned this the hard way. "I did not withhold my heart from any pleasure," he admitted (Ecclesiastes 2:10). But after his pleasure-seeking spree, he concluded: "All was vanity and grasping for the wind" (v. 11). It's no wonder he warned, "He who loves pleasure will be a poor man" (Proverbs 21:17).

What we are really looking for is satisfied only in a fulfilling and growing relationship with Jesus. Pursue Him and taste His delights!

—JS

The world is filled with so much good
That brings us joy and pleasure,
But true fulfillment only comes
When Christ we love and treasure. —Sper

Are we living for our own pleasure or living to please our heavenly Father?

Joy in the Morning

READ: Psalm 40:1–5

Weeping may endure for a night, but joy comes in the morning. —PSALM 30:5

Angie could not see through the fogged-up windows in her car. Inadvertently, she pulled out in front of a truck. The accident caused such damage to her brain that she could no longer speak or take care of herself.

Over the years, I have been amazed at the resiliency of Angie's parents. Recently I asked them, "How have you managed to get through this experience?" Her father thoughtfully responded, "In all honesty, the only way we have been able to do this is by drawing close to God. He gives us the strength we need to help us through."

Angie's mother agreed and added that around the time of the accident their grieving was so deep that they wondered if they would ever have joy again. As they both leaned upon God, they experienced countless unexpected provisions for the physical and spiritual care of Angie and their entire family. Although Angie may never regain her ability to speak, she now responds to them with wide smiles and this gives them joy. Her parents' favorite verse continues to be: "Weeping may endure for a night, but joy comes in the morning" (Psalm 30:5).

Have you experienced extreme sorrow? There is the promise of future joy amid your tears as you lean upon our loving Lord.   —DF

> *New mercies every morning,*
> *Grace for every day,*
> *New hope for every trial,*
> *And courage all the way.* —McVeigh

Leave your sorrows with Jesus, the "Man of Sorrows."

Bribery

READ: Deuteronomy 10:12–22

Take no bribe, for a bribe blinds the discerning. —EXODUS 23:8

While traveling in a foreign country, my husband noticed that the paved roads had deep indentations. When he asked about them, our driver explained that they were caused by the tires of trucks carrying illegal, overweight loads. When stopped by police, the drivers paid bribes to avoid being fined. The truckers and police officers came out ahead financially, but other drivers and taxpayers were left with an unfair financial burden and the inconvenience of poor roads.

Not all bribery is overt; some is more subtle. And not all bribes are financial. Flattery is a type of bribe that uses words as currency. If we give people preferential treatment for saying something nice about us, it's similar to taking a bribe. To God, any kind of partiality is an injustice. He even made justice a condition of remaining in the Promised Land. The Israelites were not to pervert justice or show partiality (Deuteronomy 16:19–20).

Bribery deprives others of justice, which is an offense against the character of God, who is "God of gods and Lord of lords, the great God, mighty and awesome, who shows no partiality nor takes a bribe" (10:17).

Thankfully, the Lord treats all of us alike, and He wants us to treat each other the same way. —JAL

> *It matters not what race or gender,*
> *Rich or poor or great or small,*
> *The God who made us is not partial;*
> *He sent Christ to die for all.* —D. DeHaan

Bribery displays partiality; love displays justice.

For the God I Love

READ: Matthew 6:16–18

When you fast, do not be like the hypocrites. —MATTHEW 6:16

A couple of years ago in our church we did a sermon series on the Old Testament tabernacle. Leading up to the message on the table of showbread, I did something I had never done before—I fasted from food for several days. I fasted because I wanted to experience the truth that "man shall not live by bread alone; but man lives by every word that proceeds from the mouth of the Lord" (Deuteronomy 8:3). I wanted to deny myself something I love, food, for the God I love more. As I fasted, I followed Jesus' teaching about fasting in Matthew 6:16–18.

Jesus gave a negative command: "When you fast, do not be like the hypocrites, with a sad countenance" (v. 16). Then He gave a positive command about putting oil on your head and washing your face (v. 17). The two commands taken together meant that they should not draw attention to themselves when they fasted. Jesus was teaching that this was a private act of sacrificial worship that should not provide any room for religious pride. Finally, He gave a promise: Your Father who sees what is done in secret will reward you (v. 18).

Although fasting isn't required, in giving up something we love, we may have a deeper experience of the God we love. He rewards us with himself.
　　　　　　　　　　　　　　　　　　　　　　　　　　—MW

Lord, we desire to walk closely with you every day.
Help us to seek you diligently that we might know
you intimately and follow you obediently.

Moving away from the table can bring us closer to the Father.

The Good Life

READ: Micah 6:6–8

It is good for me to draw near to God. —PSALM 73:28

Philosophers ponder, "What is the good life and who has it?" When I hear that question, I instantly think of my good friend Roy.

Roy was a gentle, quiet man who sought no recognition, who left the care of his life to his heavenly Father, and who occupied himself solely with his Father's will. His was a heavenly perspective. As he often reminded me: "We are but sojourners here."

Roy passed away last fall. At his memorial service, friends reminisced over his influence on their lives. Many spoke of his kindness, selfless giving, humility, and gentle compassion. He was, for many, a visible expression of God's unconditional love.

After the service, Roy's son drove to the assisted-living facility where his father lived out his final days. He gathered up his dad's belongings: two pairs of shoes, a few shirts and pants, and a few odds and ends—the sum of Roy's earthly goods—and delivered them to a local charity.

Roy never had what some would consider the good life, but he was rich toward God in good deeds. George MacDonald wrote, "Which one is the possessor of heaven and earth: He who has a thousand houses, or he who, with no house to call his own, has ten at which his knock arouses instant jubilation?"

Roy's was the good life after all.   —DR

> *Let us be Christ's true disciples*
> *Looking to another's need;*
> *Making stony pathways smoother*
> *By a gentle word or deed.* —Thorson

No one can know the good life without God.

Jupiter Falling

READ: Colossians 1:15–23

In Him all things consist. —COLOSSIANS 1:17

One day I bought an inexpensive model of the solar system for my son. Installing it required me to suspend each planet from the ceiling. After bending up and down several times, I was light-headed and tired. Hours later, we heard a "plink" as Jupiter hit the floor.

Later that night, I thought about how our flimsy replica fell apart, yet Jesus sustains the actual universe. "He is before all things, and in Him all things consist" (Colossians 1:17). The Lord Jesus holds our world together, maintaining the natural laws that rule the galaxy. Our Creator also upholds "all things by the word of His power" (Hebrews 1:3). Jesus is so mighty that He keeps the universe in order simply by commanding it to be so!

As amazing as this is, Jesus is more than a cosmic caretaker. He sustains us too. He "gives life and breath to everything, and He satisfies every need" (Acts 17:25 NLT). While Jesus sometimes provides for us differently than we might expect, our Savior keeps us going whether we are brokenhearted, in need of money, or enduring illness.

Until the day He calls us home, we can trust that the One who keeps Jupiter from falling is the One who holds us up as well.   —JBS

Awesome is our God and King,
Who upholds the stars above;
We now bow before His throne,
Thanking Him for His great love. —D. DeHaan

The God who sustains the universe sustains me.

Free 4 All

READ: Ephesians 1:7–14; 2:8–9

For by grace you have been saved through faith, and that not of yourselves; it is the gift of God. —EPHESIANS 2:8

In an effort to assist people struggling to provide for their families during tough economic times, the church I attend created a program called "Free 4 All." We brought lightly used items to the church and opened the doors to people of the community. They could come and take home anything they needed.

While the day was a huge success as far as the amount of goods people were able to pick up, it was even better for this reason: Six people trusted Jesus Christ as Savior at the event. Indeed, these six new believers took part in the greatest "Free 4 All" of all time—the offer of salvation through Jesus Christ.

The items that were taken to the church on this special day had already been purchased. They were then given without cost to all who simply asked for them. Likewise, eternal forgiveness for our sins has already been purchased. Jesus paid that price when He died on a cross on Golgotha's hill two thousand years ago (Romans 3:23–25). He now offers salvation at no cost to all who simply repent and believe that Jesus has the power to forgive and save (Acts 16:31).

Each of us is needy spiritually, and only Jesus can meet that need. Have you accepted what He offers without cost at the world's biggest "Free 4 All"?   —DB

I know by faith in whom I have believed,
I know that God's free gift I have received,
I know that He will keep me to the end,
My Savior, my Redeemer, and my Friend. —Anonymous

Salvation is free, but you must receive it.

Doing Good

READ: Luke 6:27–36

Jesus of Nazareth . . . went about doing good and healing all who were oppressed by the devil, for God was with Him. —ACTS 10:38

Someone once said, "The good you do today will be forgotten tomorrow. Do good anyway." I like that; it's a great reminder.

In the book of Acts, Luke summarized Jesus' earthly ministry by saying that He "went about doing good" (10:38). But what does the Bible mean when it tells us to "do good"? Jesus did good by teaching, healing, feeding, and comforting people. Using Jesus as the perfect example, His followers are called to meet the needs of others, including those who hate them: "Love your enemies, bless those who curse you, do good to those who hate you" (Matthew 5:44; see also Luke 6:27–35). They are to serve their enemies without expecting anything in return.

Moreover, as opportunity arises, followers of Jesus are to do good especially to fellow believers (Galatians 6:10). They are not to let persecution, selfishness, and busyness cause them to forget to do good and to share what they have with others (Hebrews 13:16).

To be like our Savior and His early followers, we should ask ourselves each day: "What good thing can I do today in Jesus' name?" When we do good, we offer a sacrifice that pleases God and that draws people to Him. —MW

From the example of Jesus,
Who went about doing good,
We are to honor our Savior
By helping wherever He would. —Hess

Imitate Jesus—go about doing good.

Awakened by a Close Friend

READ: John 14:1–7

Where I am, there you may be also. —JOHN 14:3

A few years ago I had some tests to screen for cancer, and I was nervous about the outcome. My anxiety was magnified as I thought about the fact that while the medical personnel were well-trained and extremely competent, they were also strangers who had no relationship with me.

After awakening from the anesthesia, however, I heard the beautiful sound of my wife's voice: "It's great, Honey. They didn't find anything." I looked up at her smiling face and was comforted. I needed the assurance of someone who loved me.

A similar assurance lies ahead for all who have trusted Jesus. Believers can be comforted in knowing that when they wake up in heaven, One who loves them greatly—Jesus—will be there.

The *Book of Common Prayer* expresses this Christian hope: "After my awakening, [my Redeemer] will raise me up; and in my body I shall see God. I myself shall see, and eyes behold Him who is my friend and not a stranger."

Do you have trouble facing your mortality? Jesus promised to be there when we slip from this world into the next. He said, "Where I am [heaven], there you may be also" (John 14:3). What a comfort for believers to know that after death we will be awakened by our closest Friend.   —DF

> *What wonders await us in yonder fair land!*
> *The face of our Savior, the touch of His hand,*
> *No tears and no crying, no sighs or despair,*
> *For Jesus is waiting to welcome us there.* —Kerr

To see Jesus will be heaven's greatest joy.

Mindless Prayer

READ: Joshua 1:1–9

As I was with Moses, so I will be with you. I will
not leave you nor forsake you. —JOSHUA 1:5

Sometimes I am ashamed of my prayers. Too often I hear myself using familiar phrases that are more like mindless filler than thoughtful, intimate interaction. One phrase that annoys me, and that I think might offend God, is "Lord, be with me." In Scripture, God has already promised not to leave me.

God made this promise to Joshua just before he led the Israelites into the Promised Land (Joshua 1:5). The author of Hebrews later claimed it for all believers: "I will never leave you nor forsake you" (13:5). In both cases, the context indicates that God's presence has to do with giving us the power to carry out His will, not our own will, which is generally what I have in mind in my prayers.

Perhaps a better prayer would be something like this: "Lord, thank you for your indwelling Spirit who is willing and able to direct me in the ways you want me to go. May I not take you where you don't want to go. May I not enlist you to do my will, but humbly submit to doing yours."

When we are doing God's will, He will be with us even without our asking. If we're not doing His will, we need to ask for His forgiveness, change our course, and follow Him. —JAL

God himself is with thee—
Thy Savior, Keeper, Friend;
And He will not forsake thee,
Nor leave thee to life's end. —J. D. Smith

May our prayers not be mindless, but instead mindful of God's will.

Sharing the Word

READ: Psalm 19:7–14

*More to be desired are they than gold, yea,
than much fine gold.* —PSALM 19:10

Jerry McMorris began reading the *Wall Street Journal* fifty years ago as a student at the University of Colorado. His appreciation for that publication and for his alma mater led him to donate hundreds of WSJ subscriptions for CU's business school students. McMorris told the *Colorado Springs Gazette*: "The *Journal* gave me a good, broad perspective of what was going on in the business world, and I got into the habit of reading it at the start of my business day. It helps get across to students real business-world issues."

Many people enjoy introducing others to the writings that have shaped their lives. It's not surprising, then, that followers of Christ enjoy sharing God's Word with others. Some support Bible translation and distribution while others invite friends to study the Word with them. There are many ways to pass along God's truth to people hungering for encouragement and help. Our goal is to enable others to experience the great benefit we've found in knowing Christ and being guided by His Word. The psalmist said, "The law of the Lord is perfect, converting the soul; the testimony of the Lord is sure, making wise the simple" (Psalm 19:7).

The Word of God, which guards our hearts and guides our steps, is worth sharing with others. —DM

*As we read your Word, O Lord,
Our spirit will be fed;
We then can share with others
That precious living bread.* —D. DeHaan

The Bible: Know it in your head, stow it in your
heart, show it in your life, sow it in the world.

A Hard Goodbye

READ: Psalm 68:1–10

A father of the fatherless, a defender of widows, is God in His holy habitation. —PSALM 68:5

When our youngest son joined the Army, we knew that challenges lay ahead. We knew that he would face danger and be tested physically, emotionally, and spiritually. We also knew that in some ways our home would never fully be his home again. In the months leading up to his departure, my wife and I steeled ourselves for these challenges.

Then the day came when Mark had to report. We hugged and said our goodbyes, and then he walked into the recruiting station, leaving me with a moment for which I was decidedly unprepared. The pain of that hard goodbye felt unbearable. At the risk of sounding overly dramatic, I can't remember when I have wept as hard as I did that day. The hard goodbye, and the sense of loss it delivered, cut me to the heart.

In such moments, I am thankful to have a heavenly Father who knows what it is to be separated from a beloved Son. I am thankful to have a God who is described as "a father of the fatherless, a defender of widows" (Psalm 68:5). I believe that if He cares for the orphaned and the widows in their loneliness, He will also care for me and comfort me—even in those moments when I face the struggles that accompany hard goodbyes. —BC

When our loved ones say goodbye
And we have to be apart,
God can fill our loneliness
With His presence in our heart. —Sper

Loneliness comes when we forget about the One who is always with us.

The Unexpected

READ: Proverbs 16:1–9

A man's heart plans his way, but the Lord directs his steps. —PROVERBS 16:9

Toni was looking for what wasn't really lost, and she found what she wasn't looking for. As a result, a group of people got a spiritual boost they weren't expecting.

Toni, who conducts a Bible study in a drug and alcohol rehabilitation clinic in Alaska, was looking for her husband's missing driver's license. As she retraced his steps from the previous day, she visited a hospital. The missing license wasn't there, but a Christian high school chorale was, and Toni was touched by their worshipful singing. She asked the director if the teens could sing for her Bible-study group that evening. They could, and they did—bringing hope, joy, and God's love through music and post-concert conversation to some folks trying to put their lives back together.

Oh, and that driver's license? Toni found it on a chair when she got back home. Apparently, the only reason she went out that day was so God could direct her to hear a bunch of teens who could minister to her rehab group.

When God guides us (Proverbs 16:9), He works in ways we can't predict. He can use even our inconveniences to bring honor to His name. When we face a seeming nuisance in our day, perhaps we should look not just for what we think we want but also for what God has for us that day.   —DB

Between the circumstance and me,
A Father's loving hand
Is working all things for my good—
All moves at His command. —*Anonymous*

God is behind the scenes and controls the scenes He stands behind.

Time for the Armor

READ: Ephesians 6:10–18

Take . . . the sword of the Spirit, which is the Word of God. —EPHESIANS 6:17

I discovered rather quickly that a young boy quoting Scripture in a children's program at church didn't know much about the Bible. He was quoting Ephesians 6:17 from our study on spiritual armor: "Take . . . the sword of the Spirit, which is the Word of God." When he tried quoting the reference, he said, "I didn't think I needed to memorize the numbers, since that's just the time of day." That's what he thought the numbers meant since it was close to 6:17 p.m. at the time! I smiled, opened my Bible, and showed him that the numbers refer to the chapter and verse.

While knowing the Bible reference is helpful, hiding God's Word in our hearts is what is truly important (Psalm 119:11). Memorizing Scripture allows us to have it in mind so we can ward off Satan's attacks (Ephesians 6:10–18). For instance, when the Devil tempted Jesus in the wilderness, Christ withstood him by quoting the Scriptures (Matthew 4:1–11). Likewise, when we are tempted to disobey God, we can recall what we've learned and choose to obey. We can also share the teachings of the Word with others to encourage them to trust Him too.

No matter what time of day it is, we should always take the spiritual armor of the Word of God with us.   —AC

For Further Study

What specific temptations do you face? Look in a concordance in the back of a Bible for verses that can guide you in those situations. Review them often.

No evil can penetrate the armor of God.

Fishing Where They Ain't

READ: Luke 7:34–48

One of the Pharisees asked [Jesus] to eat with him. And He went to the Pharisee's house, and sat down to eat. —LUKE 7:36

I have a good friend I fish with now and then. He's a very thoughtful man. After climbing into his waders and boots and gathering up his gear, he sits on the tailgate of his truck and scans the river for fifteen minutes or more, looking for rising fish. "No use fishing where they ain't," he says.

This makes me think of another question: "Do I fish for souls where they ain't?" It was said of Jesus that He was "a friend of tax collectors and sinners" (Luke 7:34). As Christians, we are to be unlike the world in our behavior, but squarely in it as He was. So we have to ask ourselves: Do I, like Jesus, have friends who are sinners? If I have only Christian friends, I may be fishing for souls "where they ain't."

Being with nonbelievers is the first step in "fishing." Then comes love—a heart-kindness that sees beneath the surface of their offhand remarks and listens for the deeper cry of the soul. It asks, "Can you tell me more about that?" and follows up with compassion. "There is much preaching in this friendliness," George Herbert (1593–1633), pastor and poet, said.

Such love is not a natural instinct. It comes solely from God. And so we pray: "Lord, when I am with nonbelievers today, may I become aware of the cheerless voice, the weary countenance, or the downcast eyes that I, in my natural self-preoccupation, could easily overlook. May I have a love that springs from and is rooted in your love. May I listen to others, show your compassion, and speak your truth today." —DR

We are to be channels of God's truth—not reservoirs.

Like a Flock

READ: Psalm 77:11–20

You led Your people like a flock by the
hand of Moses and Aaron. —PSALM 77:20

During a demonstration of sheepherding using a Border Collie, the dog trainer explained that because sheep are highly vulnerable to wild animals, their main defense against predators is to stay together in a tightly knit group. "A sheep alone is a dead sheep," the trainer said. "The dog always keeps the sheep together as it moves them."

The biblical image of God as our shepherd is a powerful reminder of how much we need each other in the community of faith. When writing about the exodus of the Israelites from Egypt, the psalmist said, "[God] made His own people go forth like sheep, and guided them in the wilderness like a flock; and He led them on safely, so that they did not fear" (Psalm 78:52–53).

As part of God's flock, we who have trusted Christ are under His guiding, protecting hand while being surrounded by the shielding presence of others. We are part of a larger body of believers in which there is safety and accountability.

While we don't give up our personal responsibility for thought and action as members of the flock, we are to embrace the concept of "we" rather than "me" in our daily lives. With Christ as our Shepherd and fellow believers around us, we find safety in the flock.   —DM

> *Blest be the tie that binds*
> *Our hearts in Christian love!*
> *The fellowship of kindred minds*
> *Is like to that above.* —Fawcett

As part of God's flock, we're protected by Him and by each other.

Wearing Yourself Out

READ: Exodus 18:13–27

You will surely wear yourselves out. —EXODUS 18:18

My friend Jeff was asked by his daughter to officiate at her wedding. This would be a great joy as they traveled to an exotic and romantic location for the ceremony. But there was one major problem. Because the wedding party was very small, Jeff would have to perform three separate roles that could be in conflict. He would be the officiating minister, the father of the bride, and the wedding photographer!

Have you ever felt as if you were wearing too many hats? Jethro thought his son-in-law Moses was (Exodus 18). Leading the Israelites, arbitrating personal disputes, and handing down legal judgments for a great multitude were taking their toll. Finally, Jethro approached Moses, telling him: "This thing is too much for you; you are not able to perform it by yourself" (v. 18). He wisely counseled Moses to delegate smaller disputes to other advisors and take the more challenging cases himself (v. 22).

Whether you're a mother with small children, an overwhelmed business executive, or an overworked church volunteer, you too can take a lesson from Moses. Why not prayerfully discern if there may be tasks you can delegate to others or even discontinue—so that you don't wear yourself out.   —DF

*Father, we need help with our priorities. Teach us to understand
what's most important and needs to be accomplished, and
to let go of what we can so that we are at our best for you.*

If we don't come apart and rest awhile,
we may just plain come apart! —Havner

Throw the Book at Him

READ: Matthew 4:1–11

Then Jesus was led up by the Spirit into the wilderness to be tempted by the devil. —MATTHEW 4:1

Things were off to a great start for Jesus at the beginning of His ministry. He was baptized and heard the affirming words of His Father, "This is My beloved Son, in whom I am well pleased" (Matthew 3:17). But then things took a turn for the worse.

What happened next—Jesus' temptation in the wilderness—was not a mere coincidence. The Holy Spirit led Him into this face-off between the powers of heaven and hell. Thankfully, Jesus' victory in the face of temptation provides a great example when we find ourselves in the wilderness of Satan's sinister seductions.

Notice that the tempter caught Jesus at a time when He was tired and hungry. Satan uses the same tactic with us. Waiting for those vulnerable moments, he lures us with the bait of seductive suggestions that offer quick relief and opportunities for self-advancement. When facing such challenges, it's important to follow Jesus' example: He responded to temptation by quoting Scripture: "Man shall not live by bread alone, but by every word that proceeds from the mouth of God" (Matthew 4:4; see Deuteronomy 8:3).

The Bible is full of verses about lust, greed, lying, and other sins. If we tuck them away in our memory, we can use them when under attack. Throw "the Book" at Satan!   —JS

> *If we never faced the tempter*
> *With his sharp and fiery sting,*
> *We would never know the victory*
> *That our trust in God can bring.* —Robert

When Satan strikes, strike back with the Word of God.

A New Purpose

READ: Acts 9:1–9

I know the thoughts that I think toward you, says the Lord, thoughts of peace and not of evil, to give you a future and a hope. —JEREMIAH 29:11

A sixty-year-old hotel in Kansas is being renovated into apartments. A rusty ship that is docked in Philadelphia is being restored and may become a hotel or a museum. Hangar 61, an admired piece of architecture at the old Stapleton Airport in Colorado, is being transformed into a church. Each structure had a specific use that is no longer viable. Yet someone was able to see promise and a new purpose in each one.

If structures can find new life and purpose, why not people? Think about these men in the Bible whose lives took an unexpected direction. There was Jacob, who wrestled with the angel of the Lord (Genesis 32); Moses, who talked to a burning bush (Exodus 3); Paul, who was temporarily blinded (Acts 9). Their stories were different, but all had a change of purpose when their encounter with God sent them down a new path.

We too may experience circumstances that change the course of our lives. But God reminds us of this: I loved you before you loved me. I want to give you hope and a future. Give all your worries to me because I care about you (1 John 4:19; Jeremiah 29:11; 1 Peter 5:7; John 10:10).

As you cling to God's promises, ask Him to reveal new direction and purpose for your life. —CHK

God has a purpose for your life,
So what you have to do
Is follow Him, believing that
He'll keep directing you. —Sper

Keep your eyes on the Lord and you won't lose sight of life's purpose.

Master Craftsman

READ: Jeremiah 18:1–10

The vessel that he made of clay was marred in the hand of the potter; so he made it again into another vessel, as it seemed good to the potter. —JEREMIAH 18:4

When Marlene and I were engaged, her dad gave us a special wedding present. As a watchmaker and jeweler, he made our wedding rings. To make my wedding band, Jim used gold scraps left over from resizing other rings. These scraps were seemingly without much value, but in the hands of this craftsman, they became a thing of beauty that I cherish to this day. It is amazing what a master craftsman can do with what others might view as useless.

That is also how God works in our lives. He is the greatest Master Craftsman of all, taking the wasted pieces and broken shards of our lives and restoring them to worth and meaning. The prophet Jeremiah described this when he compared God's work to that of a potter working clay: "The vessel that he made of clay was marred in the hand of the potter; so he made it again into another vessel, as it seemed good to the potter to make" (Jeremiah 18:4).

No matter what messes we have made of our lives, God can remold us into vessels that are good in His eyes. As we confess any sin and submit ourselves in obedience to His Word, we allow the Master to do His redemptive work in our lives (2 Timothy 2:21). That is the only way for the pieces of our brokenness to be made whole and good once again. —BC

Have Thine own way, Lord! Have Thine own way!
Thou art the Potter, I am the clay;
Mold me and make me after Thy will,
While I am waiting, yielded and still. —Pollard

Broken things can become blessed things if you let God do the mending.

Is God Obligated?

READ: Jeremiah 7:1–11

Amend your ways and your doings. —JEREMIAH 7:3

A friend sent me photographs of twenty beautiful churches throughout the world. Located as far apart as Iceland and India, each of them is architecturally unique.

The most beautiful place of worship in Jeremiah's day was the temple in Jerusalem, which King Josiah had recently repaired and restored (2 Chronicles 34–35). The people were fixated on the magnificent building (Jeremiah 7:4), and they foolishly thought that having the temple there meant that God would protect them from their enemies. Instead, Jeremiah pointed out the sin in their lives (vv. 3, 9–10).

God is not impressed by beautiful buildings constructed in His name if there is no inward beauty in the hearts of those who go there. He is not interested in an outward legalistic worship that is not matched by inward holiness. And it is wrong to think that God protects people just because of the religious things they do.

Just because we're reading the Bible, praying, and fellowshiping with other believers doesn't mean that God is somehow then obligated to do something for us. He cannot be manipulated. The purpose of those external activities is to develop our relationship with the Lord and to help us live differently than those in the world around us.   —CPH

Lord, help me to remember that you are most interested in an obedient heart. Change me when I think you're obligated to me because of my religious acts of worship or service. Give me a pure heart.

God cannot and will not be manipulated.

"Embroidery of Earth"

READ: Isaiah 41:17–20

I will plant in the wilderness the cedar and the acacia tree, the myrtle and the oil tree. —ISAIAH 41:19

Near one of the most majestic sites in God's nature is a botanical garden of awe-inspiring beauty. On the Canadian side of Niagara Falls is the Floral Showhouse. Inside the greenhouse is a vast array of beautiful flowers and exotic plants. In addition to the flora my wife and I observed there, something else caught our attention—the wording of a plaque.

It reads: "Enter, friends, and view God's pleasant handiwork, the embroidery of earth." What a marvelous way to describe the way our Creator favored this globe with such jaw-dropping beauty!

The "embroidery of earth" includes such far-ranging God-touches as the verdant rainforests of Brazil, the frigid beauty of Arctic Circle glaciers, the flowing wheat fields of the North American plains, and the sweeping reaches of the fertile Serengeti in Africa. These areas, like those described in Isaiah 41, remind us to praise God for His creative handiwork.

Scripture also reminds us that the wonders of individual plants are part of God's work. From the rose (Isaiah 35:1) to the lily (Matthew 6:28) to the myrtle, cypress, and pine (Isaiah 41:19–20), God colors our world with a splendorous display of beauty.

Enjoy the wonder. And spend some time praising God for the "embroidery of earth." —DB

> *If God's creation helps you see*
> *What wonders He can do,*
> *Then trust the many promises*
> *That He has given you.* —D. DeHaan

Creation is filled with signs that point to the Creator.

Do It Yourself

READ: Mark 6:30–44

*[Jesus] answered and said to them, "You
give them something to eat." —MARK 6:37*

"You give them something to eat." It's easy to miss those words from Jesus. A huge crowd had gathered to hear Him. Late in the day, the disciples got nervous and started pressing Him to send them away. "You give them something to eat," Jesus replied (Mark 6:36–37).

Why would He say that? Did He want to see if they would trust Him to perform a miracle? Maybe, but it seems more likely He wanted His disciples involved in caring for the crowd, to be hands-on in working with and for Him. He then blessed what they brought to Him—five loaves of bread and two fish—and performed the miracle of the feeding of the five thousand.

I think Jesus uses those words with us too. A need presents itself in the lives of those around us, and we bring it to Jesus in prayer. "You do something," Jesus often says. "But, Lord," we object, "we don't have enough time or money or energy." We're wrong, of course. When Jesus asks us to get involved, He already knows how He will accomplish His work through us.

What we need is faith and vision—the ability to see that God wants us to be His instruments and that He will supply what we need. —RK

*God uses us as instruments
To help someone in need,
So we must trust Him to supply
When following His lead. —Sper*

**When God says do it, He's already planned the
resources we need to accomplish the task.**

Friends in the Night

READ: 1 Samuel 20:30–42

The soul of Jonathan was knit to the soul of David, and Jonathan loved him as his own soul. —1 SAMUEL 18:1

Do you have someone you could call in the middle of the night if you needed help? Bible teacher Ray Pritchard calls these people "2 a.m. friends." If you have an emergency, this kind of friend would ask you two questions: "Where are you?" and "What do you need?"

Friends like that are crucial during difficult times. Jonathan was that type of friend for David. Jonathan's father, King Saul—who was filled with envy at David's popularity and God's blessing on him—tried to kill David (1 Samuel 19:9–10). David escaped and asked his friend for help (ch. 20). While David hid in the field, Jonathan sat at dinner with his father and quickly realized that Saul did indeed intend to kill David (vv. 24–34).

Because of their deep friendship, Jonathan "was grieved for David" (v. 34). He warned him of his father's plan and told him he should leave (vv. 41–42). David recognized what a good friend he had in Jonathan. The Bible says they wept together, "but David more so" (v. 41). Their souls were "knit" together.

Do you have loving Christian friends you can count on in a crisis? Are you someone your friends would call a "2 a.m. friend"?   —AC

Thank God for you, good friend of mine,
Seldom is friendship such as thine;
How very much I wish to be
As helpful as you've been to me. —Clark

A true friend stands with us in times of trial.

Promises You Can Bank On

READ: 2 Chronicles 6:1–11

For all the promises of God in [Christ] are Yes, and in Him
Amen, to the glory of God through us. —2 CORINTHIANS 1:20

After a global financial crisis, the US government enacted stricter laws to protect people from questionable banking practices. Banks had to change some of their policies to comply. To notify me of such changes, my bank sent me a letter. But when I got to the end I had more questions than answers. The use of phrases like "we may" and "at our discretion" certainly didn't sound like anything I could depend on!

In contrast, the Old Testament quotes God as saying "I will" numerous times. God promises David: "I will set up your seed after you, who will come from your body, and I will establish his kingdom. He shall build a house for My name, and I will establish the throne of his kingdom forever" (2 Samuel 7:12–13). No uncertainty in those words.

Recognizing God's faithfulness to His promises, King Solomon says in his prayer of dedication for the temple: "You have kept what You promised Your servant David my father; You have both spoken with Your mouth and fulfilled it with Your hand" (2 Chronicles 6:15). Centuries later, the apostle Paul said that all of God's promises are "yes" in Christ (2 Corinthians 1:20).

In a world of uncertainty, our trust is in a faithful God who will always keep His promises. —JAL

Whatever trouble may assail,
Of this we can be sure:
God's promises can never fail,
They always will endure. —Hess

Faith knows that God always performs what He promises.

The Human Camera

READ: 1 John 1:1–5

The Holy Spirit . . . will . . . bring to your remembrance
all things that I said to you. —JOHN 14:26

Steven Wiltshire, who has been called "the human camera," has the amazing ability to recall tiny details about anything he has seen and then reproduce them in drawings. For example, after Steven was flown over the city of Rome, he was asked to draw the city center on blank paper. Astonishingly, he accurately reproduced from memory the winding streets, the buildings, the windows, and other details.

Wiltshire's memory is remarkable. Yet there's another kind of memory that's even more amazing—and much more vital. Before Jesus' return to heaven, He promised His disciples that He would send the Holy Spirit to give them supernatural memory of what they had experienced: "The Helper, the Holy Spirit . . . will . . . bring to your remembrance all things that I said to you" (John 14:26).

The disciples heard Christ's marvelous teachings. They heard Him command the blind to see, the deaf to hear, and the dead to be raised. Yet when the gospel writers recorded these events, their words were not the product of a gifted human memory. Their recollections came from a divine Helper who made sure they compiled a trustworthy record of Christ's life.

Trust the Bible with confidence. It was written with guidance from the "divine camera," the Holy Spirit.   —DF

> *The stories in the Word of God*
> *Are there for us to see*
> *How God has worked in people's lives*
> *Throughout all history.* —Sper

The Spirit of God uses the Word of God to teach the people of God.

An Obstacle Inventory

READ: 2 Corinthians 6:3–10

Let us not judge one another anymore, but rather resolve this, not to put a stumbling block or a cause to fall in our brother's way. —ROMANS 14:13

Faultfinding is a popular pastime, and unfortunately a lot of us find it's easy to join the fun. Concentrating on the warts of others is a great way to feel better about ourselves. And that's just the problem. Avoiding the faults that need to be fixed in our own lives not only stunts our spiritual growth but also obstructs God's work through us. God's effectiveness through our lives is enhanced or hindered by the way we live.

It's no wonder, then, that Paul made a concerted effort to "put no obstacle in anyone's way" (2 Corinthians 6:3 ESV). For him there was nothing more important than his usefulness for Christ in the lives of others. Anything that got in the way of that was dispensable.

If you want to be authentic and useful for God, take an obstacle inventory. Sometimes obstacles are things that in and of themselves may be legitimate, yet in certain contexts may be inappropriate. But sin is clearly obstructive to others. Gossip, slander, boasting, bitterness, greed, abuse, anger, selfishness, and revenge all close the hearts of those around us to the message of God through us.

So, replace your faults with the winsome ways of Jesus. That will enable others to see your "no-fault" Savior more clearly.   —JS

Wherever I am, whatever I do,
O God, please help me to live
In a way that makes me credible
As your representative. —Egner

Followers of Jesus are most effective when
attitudes and actions are aligned with His.

Saints

READ: Colossians 1:1–2

*To the saints and faithful brethren in Christ
who are in Colosse.* —COLOSSIANS 1:2

It's probably not a name we would use for ourselves, but the apostle Paul often called believers "saints" in the New Testament (Ephesians 1:1; Colossians 1:2). Did he call them saints because they were perfect? No. These people were human and therefore sinful. What then did he have in mind? The word *saint* in the New Testament means that one is set apart for God. It describes people who have a spiritual union with Christ (Ephesians 1:3–6). The word is synonymous with individual believers in Jesus (Romans 8:27) and those who make up the church (Acts 9:32).

Saints have a responsibility through the power of the Spirit to live lives worthy of their calling. This includes, but is not limited to, no longer being sexually immoral and using improper speech (Ephesians 5:3–4). We are to put on the new character traits of service to one another (Romans 16:2), humility, gentleness, patience, love, unity of the Spirit in the bond of peace (Ephesians 4:1–3), obedience, and perseverance during hardship and suffering (Revelation 13:10; 14:12). In the Old Testament, the psalmist called saints "the excellent ones, in whom is all my delight" (Psalm 16:3).

Our union with Christ makes us saints, but our obedience to God's Word through the power of the Holy Spirit makes us saintly.   —MW

*Oh, to be filled with His life divine,
Oh, to be clothed with His power and might;
Oh, to reflect my dear Savior sublime,
Always to shine as the saints in light!* —Anonymous

Saints are people whom God's light shines through.

Ponder Your Path

READ: Proverbs 4:14–27

*Keep your heart with all diligence . . . Ponder
the path of your feet.* —PROVERBS 4:23, 26

A forty-seven-year-old Austrian man gave away his entire $4.7 million fortune after concluding that his wealth and lavish spending were keeping him from real life and happiness. Karl Rabeder told the *Daily Telegraph* (London), "I had the feeling I was working as a slave for things I did not wish for or need. It was the biggest shock in my life when I realized how horrible, soulless, and without feeling the 'five-star' lifestyle is." His money now funds charities he set up to help people in Latin America.

Proverbs 4 urges us to consider carefully our own road in life. The passage contrasts the free, unhindered path of the just with the dark, confused way of the wicked (v. 19). "Let your heart retain my words; keep my commands, and live" (v. 4). "Keep your heart with all diligence, for out of it spring the issues of life" (v. 23). "Ponder the path of your feet, and let all your ways be established" (v. 26). Each verse encourages us to evaluate where we are in life.

Most people do not want to go through life on a selfish, heartless road. But it can happen unless we consider where we are going in life and ask the Lord for His direction. May He give us grace today to embrace His Word and follow Him with all our hearts.   —DM

> *If we pursue mere earthly gain,*
> *We choose a path that ends in pain;*
> *But joy remains within the soul*
> *When we pursue a heavenly goal.* —D. DeHaan

You are headed in the right direction when you walk with God.

Joyful Reunion

READ: 2 Timothy 4:1–8

He who testifies to these things says, "Surely I am coming quickly."
Amen. Even so, come, Lord Jesus! —REVELATION 22:20

Some years ago when our children were small, I flew home after a ten-day ministry trip. In those days people were allowed to enter the airport boarding area to greet incoming passengers. When my flight landed, I came out of the jet-bridge and was greeted by our little ones— so happy to see me that they were screaming and crying. I looked at my wife, whose eyes were teary. I couldn't speak. Strangers in the gate area also teared up as our children hugged my legs and cried their greetings. It was a wonderful moment.

The memory of the intensity of that greeting serves as a gentle rebuke to the priorities of my own heart. The apostle John, eagerly desiring Jesus' return, wrote, "He who testifies to these things says, 'Surely I am coming quickly.' Amen. Even so, come, Lord Jesus!" (Revelation 22:20). In another passage, Paul even spoke of a crown awaiting those who have "loved His appearing" (2 Timothy 4:8). Yet sometimes I don't feel as eager for Christ's return as my children were for mine.

Jesus is worthy of the very best of our love and devotion—and nothing on earth should compare to the thought of seeing Him face-to-face. May our love for our Savior deepen as we anticipate our joyful reunion with Him. —BC

And for the hope of His return,
Dear Lord, your name we praise;
With longing hearts we watch and wait
For that great day of days! —Sherwood

Those who belong to Christ should be longing to see Him.

Birds, Lilies, and Me

READ: Luke 12:22–34

Therefore I say to you, do not worry about your life. —LUKE 12:22

In the episodes of an old television show, the veteran police lieutenant always said this to the young officers on their way out to the street for their day's assignments: "Be careful out there!" It was both good advice and a word of compassion because he knew what could happen to them in the line of duty.

Jesus gave His followers a similar warning, but in even stronger terms. Luke 11 ends ominously with these words: "The scribes and the Pharisees began to assail Him vehemently, and to cross-examine Him about many things" (v. 53). In the continuation of this account, Luke says that Jesus compassionately instructed His disciples to "beware" (12:1) but not to worry or be afraid (vv. 4–7, 22).

Jesus was promising to guard, protect, and care for them as they went out into the world. He assured them that because He cared for simple things like birds and lilies, they could be certain that He would take care of His "little flock" of believers (vv. 24–32).

We cannot know the future. But we can know this: No matter what comes, we are under the loving, caring, watchful eye of our Great Shepherd, who also happens to be the Son of God! —DE

> *I walked life's path with worry,*
> *Disturbed and quite unblest,*
> *Until I trusted Jesus;*
> *Now faith has given rest.* —Bosch

If Jesus is concerned about flowers and birds,
He certainly cares about you and me.

Bring It On!

READ: 2 Corinthians 11:22–12:10

Three times I was beaten . . . three times I was shipwrecked . . . in perils . . . in weariness and toil . . . in hunger and thirst. —2 CORINTHIANS 11:25–27

A TV program on the History Channel featured the world's most extreme airports. The one that caught my attention is no longer open, but it is one I had flown into. I agree that Hong Kong's Kai Tak Airport was definitely a thrill ride for passengers and surely a challenge for pilots. If you came in from one direction, you had to fly over skyscrapers and then hope the plane stopped before it plunged into the sea. If you came in the other way, it seemed as if you were going to smack into a mountain.

I found it surprising that a pilot who used to take planeloads of people into Kai Tak said, "I miss flying into that airport." But I think I know what he meant. As a pilot, he relished the challenge. And he had a confidence based on his ability and his reliance on those who guided him into the airport.

Too often, we run from challenges. Yet the people we love to read about in the Bible are impressive because they battled challenges. Consider Paul. With the confidence of God's help, he faced troubles head-on—and conquered them. Christ's promise to Paul and to us is: "My grace is sufficient for you, for My strength is made perfect in weakness" (2 Corinthians 12:9).

In the confidence of God's care we can say to the next challenge: Bring it on! —DB

> *I do not ask for easy paths*
> *Along life's winding roads,*
> *But for the promised grace and strength*
> *To carry all its loads.* —Meadows

If God sends you on stony paths, He will provide you with strong shoes.

The Goodness of the Lord

READ: Psalm 119:97–104

Oh, how I love Your law! —PSALM 119:97

In a short essay written by Sir James Barrie, an English baron, he gives an intimate picture of his mother, who deeply loved God and His Word and who literally read her Bible to pieces. "It is mine now," Sir James wrote, "and to me the black threads with which she stitched it are a part of the contents."

My mother also loved God's Word. She read and pondered it for sixty years or more. I keep her Bible on my bookshelf in a prominent place. It too is tattered and torn, each stained page marked with her comments and reflections. As a boy, I often walked into her room in the morning and found her cradling her Bible in her lap, poring over its words. She did so until the day she could no longer see the words on the page. Even then her Bible was the most precious book in her possession.

When Sir James's mother grew old, she could no longer read the words of her Bible. Yet daily her husband put her Bible in her hands, and she would reverently hold it there.

The psalmist wrote, "How sweet are Your words to my taste, sweeter than honey to my mouth" (Psalm 119:103). Have you tasted the goodness of the Lord? Open your Bible today.   —DR

> *The Bible, the Bible! More precious than gold;*
> *Glad hopes and bright glories its pages unfold;*
> *It speaks of the Father and tells of His love,*
> *And shows us the way to the mansions above.* —Anonymous

A well-read Bible is a sign of a well-fed soul.

A Modest Proposal

READ: Philippians 2:1–11

*[Jesus] humbled Himself . . . to the point of death,
even the death of the cross.* —PHILIPPIANS 2:8

As a college student, I heard countless engagement stories. My starry-eyed friends told about glitzy restaurants, mountaintop sunsets, and rides in horse-drawn carriages. I also recall one story about a young man who simply washed his girlfriend's feet. His "modest proposal" proved he understood that humility is vital for a lifelong commitment.

The apostle Paul also understood the significance of humility and how it holds us together. This is especially important in marriage. Paul said to reject "me-first" urges: "Let nothing be done through selfish ambition" (Philippians 2:3). Instead, we should value our spouses more than ourselves, and look out for their interests.

Humility in action means serving our spouse, and no act of service is too small or too great. After all, Jesus "humbled Himself . . . to the point of death, even the death of the cross" (v. 8). His selflessness showed His love for us.

What can you do today to humbly serve the one you love? Maybe it's as simple as leaving brussels sprouts off the dinner menu or as difficult as helping him or her through a long illness. Whatever it is, placing our spouse's needs before our own confirms our commitment to each other through Christlike humility. —JBS

*In marriage we will honor Christ
By following His lead
Of sacrificial love and care
To meet the other's need.* —Sper

If you think it's possible to love your spouse too
much, you probably haven't loved enough.

Failure to Discipline

READ: 1 Samuel 2:27–36

*No chastening seems to be joyful for the present,
but painful; nevertheless, afterward it yields the
peaceable fruit of righteousness.* —HEBREWS 12:11

We live in the woods, so we get very little prolonged sunlight in the summer. But we love fresh tomatoes, so I decided to try growing them in pots set in a few sunny spots.

The plants started to grow right away and really fast. I was thrilled—until I realized that their fast growth was due to their efforts to reach out to the limited sunlight. By the time I figured out what was happening, the vines were too heavy to support themselves. I found some stakes, lifted the vines carefully, and fastened them in an upright position. Even though I tried to be gentle, one of the twisted vines broke when I tried to straighten it.

This reminded me that discipline must begin before character is permanently bent and twisted.

Eli the priest had two sons whom he failed to discipline. When their wickedness got so bad that he could no longer ignore it, he tried gentle rebuke (1 Samuel 2:24–25). But it was too late, and God announced the dire consequences: "I will judge [Eli's] house forever for the iniquity which he knows, because his sons made themselves vile, and he did not restrain them" (3:13).

Being straightened out is painful, but being left crooked will ultimately hurt even more. —JAL

*Lord, even though it's painful, we're thankful that you,
in love, discipline us as your children. Help us to respond
with repentance and obedience to your ways.*

God's love confronts and corrects.

A Matter of Perspective

READ: Exodus 14:1–14

I will gain honor over Pharaoh and over all his army, that the Egyptians may know that I am the Lord. —EXODUS 14:4

Are you part of the problem or part of the solution? Whether that question is posed during a business meeting, a church council, or a family discussion, it often springs from a sense of exasperation in trying to comprehend why someone has acted in a certain way. More often than not, the answer is a matter of perspective.

If we had been among the Israelites leaving Egypt after four hundred years of slavery, we would likely have seen Pharaoh as part of the problem—and he was. Yet God saw something more.

Inexplicably, the Lord told Moses to take the people back toward Egypt and camp with their backs to the Red Sea so Pharaoh would attack them (Exodus 14:1–3). The Israelites thought they were going to die, but God said that He would gain glory and honor for himself through Pharaoh and all his army, "and the Egyptians shall know that I am the Lord" (vv. 4, 17–18).

When we simply cannot understand why God allows circumstances that threaten to overwhelm us, it's good to remember that He has our good and His glory in mind. If we can say, "Father, please enable me to trust and honor you in this situation," then we will be in concert with His perspective and plan. —DM

Your words of pure, eternal truth
Shall yet unshaken stay,
When all that man has thought or planned,
Like chaff shall pass away. —Anonymous

Faith helps us accept what we cannot understand.

Christ Living in Us

READ: Galatians 2:15–21

I have finished the race, I have kept the faith. Finally, there is laid up for me the crown of righteousness. —2 TIMOTHY 4:7–8

The Ironman Triathlon consists of a 2.4-mile swim, a 112-mile bike ride, and a 26.2-mile run. It is not an easy feat for anyone to accomplish. But Dick Hoyt participated in the race and completed it with his physically disabled son Rick. When Dick swam, he pulled Rick in a small boat. When Dick cycled, Rick was in a seat-pod on the bike. When Dick ran, he pushed Rick along in a wheelchair. Rick was dependent on his dad in order to finish the race. He couldn't do it without him.

We see a parallel between their story and our own Christian life. Just as Rick was dependent on his dad, we are dependent on Christ to complete our Christian race.

As we strive to live a God-pleasing life, we realize that in spite of our best intentions and determination, we often stumble and fall short. By our strength alone, it is impossible. Oh, how we need the Lord's help! And it has been provided. Paul declares it with these insightful words: "It is no longer I who live, but Christ lives in me; and the life which I now live in the flesh I live by faith in the Son of God" (Galatians 2:20).

We cannot finish the Christian race on our own. We have to depend on Jesus living in us. —AL

With longing all my heart is filled
That like Him I may be,
As on the wondrous thought I dwell,
That Christ liveth in me. —Whittle

Faith connects our weakness to God's strength.

A Teachable Spirit

READ: Proverbs 2:1–9

Do not be wise in your own eyes. —PROVERBS 3:7

Just before our church service began, I overheard a young man behind me talking with his mother. They were reading an announcement in the bulletin about a challenge to read one chapter of Proverbs each day for the months of July and August. He asked his mom, "What will we do with chapter 31 in August since there are only thirty days?" She said she thought there were thirty-one days in August. He responded, "No, there are only thirty."

When it was time in the service to greet each other, I turned back toward him and said hello. Then I added, "August does have thirty-one days." He insisted, "No, it doesn't. There can't be two months in a row with thirty-one days." The singing started, so I just smiled.

This brief encounter made me think about our need to develop a teachable spirit, seeking wisdom beyond our own. In Proverbs 3, the attitude the father recommends to the son is one of humility: "Do not be wise in your own eyes; fear the Lord" (v. 7). In chapter 2, he says, "Incline your ear to wisdom . . . search for her as for hidden treasures" (vv. 2, 4).

Having a teachable spirit will help us gain wisdom from God and others. Reading a chapter from Proverbs each day next month may give us a start. —AC

> *Lord, teach us from your holy Word*
> *The truth that we must know,*
> *And help us share the joyous news*
> *Of blessings you bestow.* —D. DeHaan

True wisdom begins and ends with God.

Find the Book

READ: 2 Kings 22:8–23:3

I have found the Book of the Law in the house of the Lord. —2 KINGS 22:8

One Sunday at the church where I pastor, I invited three children to find several scrolls with Bible verses written on them that I had hidden in our worship center. I told them that once they found them and read the words aloud, I would give them a prize. You should have seen those kids! They ran, moved chairs, and looked under plants and in purses (with permission). Their search for the scrolls was intense, but exciting. Their diligent search and subsequent discovery of the scrolls led to joy in the children, affirmation from our congregation, and a renewed sense of the importance of God's Word.

In 2 Kings 22–23 we read how King Josiah and the people of Judah rediscovered the joy and importance of God's Word. During the repairing of the temple, Hilkiah the high priest found the Book of the Law. It must have been lost or hidden during the reign of Manasseh. Then when the scroll was read to King Josiah, he listened and responded to it (vv. 10–11). He sought further understanding of it (vv. 12–20), and he led the people to renew their commitment to its importance in their lives (23:1–4).

Many today have unprecedented access to God's Word. Let's renew our commitment to "find" it every day and by our lives show its prominence. —MW

> *O Book divine, supreme, sublime*
> *Entire, eternal, holy, true;*
> *Sufficient for all men and time—*
> *We pledge our faith to thee anew.* —*Anonymous*

To know Christ, the Living Word, is to love the Bible, the written Word.

Under Surveillance

READ: Amos 9:1–6

*"Can anyone hide himself in secret places, so I shall
not see him?" says the Lord.* —JEREMIAH 23:24

Imagine that you're visiting a foreign country when you realize that you're being followed. Your every move is watched. Your every conversation is monitored. Your hotel room is bugged, and the restaurant tables are electronically rigged to pick up every word you speak. It's as if at all times someone wants to know what you are doing, saying, thinking, and planning. You are constantly under the scrutiny of another, and it seems there is no place to hide.

Fortunately, most of us don't know what it's like to live under that kind of surveillance. Yet, in reality, we do live every moment of every day under the watchful eyes of the Lord. He sees everything we do; He hears everything we say; He knows every thought we think.

For those who love and trust the Lord, this is an awesome yet comforting truth. But for those who are determined to resist Him, it's a different story. Amos told Israel that God was pleading with them to turn from their sins (Amos 5:4–15), and he warned them that there would be no hiding place for those who refused to repent (9:1–6).

Father, have mercy on us when we are rebellious. We lift our heart to you in behalf of all who think they can somehow elude your constant surveillance and final judgment. —MD

> *They shall not stand the judgment test*
> *Who live for self today,*
> *For God sees all and He will judge*
> *The evildoer's way!* —Bosch

Live today as you will wish you had lived when you stand before God.

The Need for Tears

READ: Luke 19:37–44

As He drew near, He saw the city and wept over it. —LUKE 19:41

Following the 2010 earthquake in Haiti, we were overwhelmed by the images of devastation and hardship endured by the people of that tiny nation. Of the many heartbreaking pictures, one captured my attention. It showed a woman staring at the massive destruction and weeping. Her mind could not process the suffering of her people, and as her heart was crushed, tears poured from her eyes. Her reaction was understandable. Sometimes crying is the only appropriate response to the suffering we encounter.

As I examined that picture, I thought of the compassion of our Lord. Jesus understood the need for tears, and He too wept. But He wept over a different kind of devastation—the destruction brought on by sin. As He approached Jerusalem, marked by corruption and injustice and the pain they create, His response was tears. "Now as He drew near, He saw the city and wept over it" (Luke 19:41). Jesus wept out of compassion and grief.

As we encounter the inhumanity, suffering, and sin that wreak havoc in our world, how do we respond? If the heart of Christ breaks over the broken condition of our world, shouldn't ours? And shouldn't we then do everything we can to make a difference for those in need, both spiritually and physically?　　　　　　　　　　　　　　—BC

> *Lord, when I learn that someone is hurting,*
> *Help me know what to do and to say;*
> *Speak to my heart and give me compassion,*
> *Let your great love flow through me today.* —K. DeHaan

Compassion offers whatever is necessary to heal the hurts of others.

Ant World

READ: 2 Timothy 4:9–18

Demas has forsaken me, having loved this present world. —2 TIMOTHY 4:10

One of the highlights of my work as a college president is commencement. One year, while walking to the graduation ceremony, I was excited by the thought that our graduates were ready to go out to engage the world with the transforming power of the kingdom of Christ. On my way, I noticed some industrious ants busily going about their routine. I thought, *There are much greater things happening than the building of sand piles!*

It's easy for us to get lost in "ant world"—to be so busy with our routines that we miss the joy of personally embracing the bigger picture of God's great work around the world. The work of the Spirit is sweeping across South America; thousands in Africa are coming to know Christ daily; persecuted Christians are thriving; and the Asian Rim is throbbing with the pulse of the gospel! Do those thoughts ever capture your heart? Your prayer life? Your checkbook?

Our preoccupation with lesser things reminds me of Paul's report that "Demas has forsaken me, having loved this present world" (2 Timothy 4:10). I wonder if Demas regretted abandoning the gospel for the sand piles of this world?

Let's get out of "ant world" and engage our hearts and lives in spreading the gospel of Jesus Christ. —JS

Lord, I love you and want to be a part of your work around the world. Give me an open heart to know which opportunities you want me to be a part of and wisdom in knowing how to carry that out.

Don't let smaller things distract you from
the bigger work of God around the world.

The Goodness of Work

READ: Genesis 1:26–31

God said, "Let Us make man in Our image,
*according to Our likeness." —*GENESIS 1:26

Some Christians grow up believing work is bad—that it's a curse brought about by Adam and Eve's sin. Left uncorrected, this mistaken belief can cause people to feel that what they do in their jobs every day isn't important to God—or, at the very least, isn't as important as the work of missionaries and pastors. This is not true, as Genesis 1:26–31 teaches us.

First, we learn that God himself works, as evidenced by the labor involved in creation and by the fact that He rested on the seventh day. Then we discover that we were made in His image (v. 26) and that we were granted dominion over creation. This implies that we are to work to tend creation. Clearly, the tending of God's creation is work—noble work, for God looked upon His labors and declared them "very good" (v. 31).

It mustn't escape our notice either that work was declared good before sin entered the picture. In other words, work didn't result from the fall and therefore is not a curse. We see this idea again in Genesis 2, when God "took the man and put him in the garden of Eden to tend and keep it" (v. 15).

Let's approach each day's labor—whether at a job or doing another activity to help our family—with an awareness of the dignity and nobility God granted it in creation. —RK

> *Our daily work is used by God*
> *To help us care for daily needs;*
> *And work that's done as to the Lord*
> *Gives witness to our words and deeds. —D. DeHaan*

God, give me work till my life shall end—and life till my work is done.

Measuring Growth

READ: Ephesians 4:1–16

Till we all come to the unity of the faith and . . . to the measure of the stature of the fullness of Christ. —EPHESIANS 4:13

When a high school student tried using a thermometer to measure a table, his teacher was dumbfounded. In fifteen years of teaching Dave had seen many sad and shocking situations. But even he was amazed that a student could make it to high school without knowing the difference between a ruler and a thermometer.

When a friend told me this story, my heart broke for that student and others like him who have fallen so far behind in their education. They can't move forward because they haven't yet learned basic lessons of everyday life.

But then a sobering thought came to me: Don't we sometimes do the same thing when we use wrong spiritual measuring devices? For example, do we assume that churches with the most resources are the most blessed by God? And do we ever think that popular preachers are more godly than those with few followers?

The proper measure of our spiritual condition is the quality of our lives, which is measured by such attributes as lowliness, gentleness, and longsuffering (Ephesians 4:2). "Bearing with one another in love" (v. 2) is a good indication that we are moving toward God's goal for us: "the measure of . . . the fullness of Christ" (v. 13). —JAL

Our love for God can be measured by our love for others.

A Focus on Fairness

READ: Proverbs 1:1–9

Hate evil, love good; establish justice in the gate. —AMOS 5:15

During the past 135 years of Major League Baseball, only twenty pitchers have thrown a perfect game. On June 2, 2010, Armando Galarraga of the Detroit Tigers would have been number twenty-one, but an umpire's mistake denied him what every pitcher dreams of. The video replay showed the truth. Even though the umpire later acknowledged his error and apologized to Galarraga, the call made on the field could not be changed.

Through it all, Galarraga remained calm, expressed sympathy for the umpire, and never criticized him. Armando's refusal to retaliate amazed fans, players, and sportswriters alike.

If we insist on fair treatment for ourselves, we can become angry and frustrated. But when we embrace the Bible's wisdom, we will seek the welfare of others. Proverbs calls us "to perceive the words of understanding, to receive the instruction of wisdom, justice, judgment, and equity" (1:2–3). Oswald Chambers said of our personal dealings with others: "Never look for justice, but never cease to give it; and never allow anything you meet with to sour your relationship to men through Jesus Christ."

When we experience unfairness, it is our privilege and responsibility as followers of Christ to respond with honesty and integrity, doing what is right, just, and fair. —DM

> *How others handle justice*
> *May not be up to me;*
> *But when I react to others,*
> *I must show integrity.* —Branon

Life is not fair, but God is always faithful.

Grandfather's Clock

READ: Psalm 90:1–12

Teach us to number our days, that we may gain a heart of wisdom. —PSALM 90:12

In 1876, Henry Clay Work wrote the song "My Grandfather's Clock." The song describes a grandfather's clock that faithfully ticks its way through its owner's life. Childhood, adulthood, and old age are all viewed in relationship to his beloved timepiece. The refrain says:

Ninety years without slumbering,
Tick, tock, tick, tock,
His life's seconds numbering,
Tick, tock, tick, tock,
But it stopped, short,
Never to go again,
When the old man died.

The relentless ticking of the clock reminds us that our time on earth is limited. Despite the joys and pains of life, time always marches on. And for the believer, our time on earth is an opportunity for gaining wisdom. The psalmist writes, "Teach us to number our days, that we may gain a heart of wisdom" (Psalm 90:12).

One way of numbering our days is to ask ourselves these kinds of questions: How can I become more like Christ? Am I reading the Word regularly? Am I devoting time to prayer? Am I meeting together with other believers? The way we answer these questions is an indicator of the progress we're making in gaining wisdom and becoming more like Christ.

No matter the phase of life—childhood, youth, middle age, or our senior years—life always affords us opportunities to grow in faith and wisdom. Numbering our days is the wise response to life's inevitable progress.

How are you progressing on your journey?   —DF

Don't spend your time—invest it.

You Never Know

READ: Mark 4:26–32

For the earth yields crops by itself. —MARK 4:28

During my seminary years I directed a summer day camp for boys and girls at the YMCA. Each morning I began the day with a brief story in which I tried to incorporate an element of the gospel.

To help illustrate that becoming a Christian means to become a new creation in Christ, I told a story about a moose that wanted to be a horse. The moose had seen a herd of wild horses, thought them elegant creatures, and wanted to be like them. So he taught himself to act like a horse. However, he was never accepted as a horse because he was . . . well, a moose. How can a moose become a horse? Only by being born a horse, of course. And then I would explain how we can all be born again by believing in Jesus.

One summer I had a staff counselor named Henry who was hostile to the faith. I could do nothing but love him and pray for him, but he left at the end of the summer hardened in unbelief. That was more than fifty years ago. A few years ago I received a letter from Henry. The first sentence said: "I write to tell that I have been born again and now, at last, I am a 'horse.'" This confirmed to me that we need to keep praying and planting the seed of the Word (Mark 4:26) so that it may bear fruit one day. —DR

> *You think your word or deed is very small,*
> *That what you say will hardly count at all;*
> *But God can take the seed that you have sown*
> *And nourish it until it's fully grown.* —Hess

We sow the seed; God produces the harvest.

Good Neighbors

READ: Hebrews 13:1–6

Be merciful, just as your Father also is merciful. —LUKE 6:36

When US airspace was closed after the September 11, 2001, attacks, planes had to land at the closest airport available. Nearly forty planes landed in Gander, Newfoundland. Suddenly this small Canadian community almost doubled in size when thousands of frightened passengers arrived. People opened their homes, and officials converted high schools, lodges, churches, and meeting halls into places to stay. Stranded passengers were overwhelmed with neighborly generosity and kindness.

The people of Gander showed the kind of love described in Hebrews 13: "Do not forget to entertain strangers, for by so doing some have unwittingly entertained angels" (v. 2). This is probably referring to Abraham when he entertained three men who came to tell him that he would soon have a son (Genesis 18:1–16). Two of the "men" were angels, and one was the Angel of the Lord. Bible commentator F. F. Bruce says about Abraham, "Among the Jews, Abraham was regarded as outstanding for his hospitality as [he was] for his other virtues; a true son of Abraham must be hospitable too."

God calls believers to show their love and gratefulness for Him in their good works of hospitality and compassion. How will you answer His call today?　　　　　　　　　　　　　　　　　　　　—AC

How many lives shall I touch today?
How many neighbors will pass my way?
I can bless so many and help so much,
If I meet each one with a Christlike touch. —Jones

Christlike love is seen in good works.

The Mercy of God

READ: Psalm 31:9–15

Have mercy on me, O Lord, for I am in trouble; my eye wastes away with grief, yes, my soul and my body! —PSALM 31:9

Today marks the anniversary of the terrorist attacks in the US on September 11, 2001. It's hard to think about that date without mental images of the destruction, grief, and loss that swept over America and the world following those tragic events. The loss of thousands of lives was compounded by the depth of loss felt corporately—a lost sense of security as a country. The sorrow of loss, personal and corporate, will always accompany the memory of the events of that day.

Those horrific events are not the only painful memories of September 11. It also marks the anniversary of my father-in-law's death. Jim's loss is felt deeply within our family and his circle of friends.

No matter what kind of sorrow we experience, there is only one real comfort—the mercy of God. David, in his own heartache, cried to his heavenly Father, "Have mercy on me, O Lord, for I am in trouble; my eye wastes away with grief, yes, my soul and my body!" (Psalm 31:9). Only in the mercy of God can we find comfort for our pain and peace for our troubled hearts.

In all losses, we can turn to the true Shepherd, Jesus Christ, who alone can heal our brokenness and grief.   —BC

When God permits suffering, He also provides comfort.

Blessed Assurance

READ: 2 Corinthians 5:1–10

We are confident, yes, well pleased rather to be absent from the body and to be present with the Lord. —2 CORINTHIANS 5:8

As I was talking with a gentleman whose wife had died, he shared with me that a friend said to him, "I'm sorry you lost your wife." His reply? "Oh, I haven't lost her; I know exactly where she is!"

To some this may seem like a rather bold or even flippant assertion. With so many after-death theories, one might wonder how we can be really sure where our loved ones go after death, let alone where we ourselves will end up.

Yet confidence is appropriate for followers of Jesus Christ. We have the assurance from God's Word that when we die we will immediately be with our Lord (2 Corinthians 5:8). Thankfully, this is more than just wishful thinking. It is grounded in the historic reality of Jesus, who came and died to cancel our penalty for sin so that we could receive eternal life (Romans 6:23). He then proved that there is life after death by exiting His grave and ascending into heaven where, as He promised, He is preparing a place for us (John 14:2).

So, rejoice! Since the benefits of this reality are out of this world, we can boldly say with Paul that "we are confident, yes, well pleased rather to be absent from the body and to be present with the Lord" (2 Corinthians 5:8). —JS

Lord, when I take my final breath
And see you face to face in death,
Then shall my heart forever sing
The heavenly praises of my King. —Raniville

For the follower of Jesus, death means heaven, happiness, and Him.

Character Amnesia

READ: Job 1:13–22

There was a man . . . whose name was Job; and that man was blameless and upright, and one who feared God and shunned evil. —JOB 1:1

It seems that young people in China are beginning to forget how to write the characters that comprise the beautiful calligraphy of their traditional language. Some are calling the phenomenon "character amnesia." Heavy usage of computers and smart phones often means that writing is neglected, and some can no longer remember the characters they learned in childhood. One young man said, "People don't write anything by hand anymore except for [their] name and address."

Some people appear to have "character amnesia" of a different sort. When faced with a dilemma, they seem to "forget" the right thing to do and instead choose the easy way out.

God called Job "a blameless and upright man, one who fears God and shuns evil" (Job 1:8). God allowed Satan to take everything Job had—his children, his wealth, and his health. But despite his heart-wrenching circumstances, Job refused to curse God. "In all this Job did not sin nor charge God with wrong" (v. 22). Satan had challenged God's assertion of Job's blameless character, but he was proven wrong.

Character amnesia? No. Character is who we are; it's not something we "forget." Those who have a loss of character make a choice. —CHK

> *It isn't the tranquil and placid seas*
> *That bring out the sailor's skill;*
> *It's the wind and waves that pound his ship*
> *And toss it about at will.* —Ritter

When wealth is gone, little is lost; when health is gone, something is lost; but when character is gone, all is lost!

Rising to the Top

READ: 1 Samuel 15:17–30

Let nothing be done through selfish ambition or conceit.
—PHILIPPIANS 2:3

L acks ambition." That is not a phrase you want to see on your performance review. When it comes to work, employees who lack ambition
seldom rise to the top of an organization. Without a strong desire to
achieve something, nothing is accomplished. Ambition, however, has a
dark side. It often has more to do with elevating self than with accom-
plishing something noble for others.

This was the case with many of the kings of Israel, including the
first one. Saul started out with humility, but he gradually came to consider his position as something that belonged to him. He forgot that he
had a special assignment from God to lead His chosen people in a way
that would show other nations the way to God. When God relieved him
of duty, Saul's only concern was for himself (1 Samuel 15:30).

In a world where ambition often compels people to do whatever
it takes to rise to positions of power over others, God calls His people
to a new way of living. We are to do nothing out of selfish ambition
(Philippians 2:3), and we are to lay aside the weight of sin that ensnares
us (Hebrews 12:1).

If you want to be someone who truly "rises up," make it your ambition to humbly love and serve God with all your heart, soul, mind, and
strength (Mark 12:30).   —JAL

Ambition is shortsighted if our focus is not on God.

Heavy Lifting

READ: Matthew 11:25–30

Come to Me, all you who labor and are heavy laden.
—MATTHEW 11:28

One day I found my son straining to lift a pair of four-pound barbells over his head—an ambitious feat for a toddler. He had raised them only a few inches off the ground, but his eyes were determined and his face was pink with effort. I offered to help, and together we heaved the weight up toward the ceiling. The heavy lifting that was so hard for him was easy for me.

Jesus has this perspective on the stuff that's hard for us to manage. When life seems like a carousel of catastrophes, Jesus isn't fazed by a fender-bender, troubled by a toothache, or harassed by a heated argument—even if it all happens in one day! He can handle anything, and that is why He said, "Come to Me, all you who labor and are heavy laden" (Matthew 11:28).

Are you worn out from ongoing problems? Are you weighed down with stress and worry? Jesus is the only real solution. Approaching the Lord in prayer allows us to cast our burdens on Him so that He can sustain us (Psalm 55:22). Today, ask Him to assist you with everything. By helping you with your burdens, He can supply rest for your soul, for His yoke is easy and His burden is light (Matthew 11:29–30).   —JBS

> *O what peace we often forfeit,*
> *O what needless pain we bear,*
> *All because we do not carry*
> *Everything to God in prayer. —Scriven*

Prayer is the place where burdens change shoulders.

Be an Armor-Bearer

READ: 1 Samuel 14:1–14

Do all that is in your heart. Go then;
here I am with you. —1 SAMUEL 14:7

The Israelites and the Philistines were at war. While Saul relaxed under a pomegranate tree with his men, Jonathan and his armor-bearer left camp quietly to see if the Lord would work on their behalf, believing that "nothing restrains the Lord from saving by many or by few" (1 Samuel 14:6).

Jonathan and his helper were about to cross a path between two high cliffs. Armed enemy soldiers were stationed above them on both sides. They were two men against who knows how many. When Jonathan suggested they climb up after them, the armor-bearer never flinched. "Do all that is in your heart," he told Jonathan. "I am with you, according to your heart" (v. 7). So the two climbed the cliff, and with God's help they overcame the enemy (vv. 8–14). We have to admire this courageous young armor-bearer. He lugged the armor up that cliff and stayed with Jonathan as they battled the enemy together.

The church needs strong leaders to face our spiritual foes, but they must not be left to face them alone. They need the help and support of everyone in the congregation—loyal "armor-bearers" like you and me who are willing to join them in battle against the "enemy of our souls." —DE

We give the help that pastors need
For burdens they must bear
When we entrust them to the Lord
And hold them up in prayer. —D. DeHaan

We stand strong when we stand together.

No Reverse

READ: Exodus 16:1–12

You shall know that the Lord has brought you out of the land of Egypt. —EXODUS 16:6

The first time I saw her, I fell in love. She was a beauty. Sleek. Clean. Radiant. As soon as I spied the 1962 Ford Thunderbird at the used-car lot, her shiny exterior and killer interior beckoned me. I knew this was the car for me. So I plunked down $800 and purchased my very first car.

But there was a problem lurking inside my prized possession. A few months after I bought my T-Bird, it suddenly became particular about which way I could go. It allowed me to go forward, but I couldn't go backward. It had no reverse.

Although not having reverse is a problem in a car, sometimes it's good for us to be a little like my old T-Bird. We need to keep going forward—without the possibility of putting life into reverse. In our walk with Jesus, we need to refuse to go backward. Paul said it simply: We need to "press toward the goal" (Philippians 3:14).

Perhaps the children of Israel could have used my T-Bird's transmission. We read in Exodus 16 that they were in danger of putting life into reverse. Despite the many miracles God had performed, they longed for Egypt and failed to trust that He could guide them forward.

We need to keep moving ahead in our walk with God. Don't back up. Look forward. Press on. —DB

> *When long and steep the path appears*
> *Or heavy is the task,*
> *Our Father says, "Press on, my child;*
> *One step is all I ask." —D. DeHaan*

When facing a crisis, trust God and move forward.

Daddy!

READ: 2 Kings 19:10–19

*Incline Your ear, O Lord, and hear; open
Your eyes, O Lord, and see.* —2 KINGS 19:16

Twenty-month-old James was leading his family confidently through the hallways of their large church. His daddy kept an eye on him the whole time as James toddled his way through the crowd of "giants." Suddenly the little boy panicked because he could not see his dad. He stopped, looked around, and started to cry, "Daddy, Daddy!" His dad quickly caught up with him and little James reached up his hand, which Daddy strongly clasped. Immediately James was at peace.

Second Kings tells the story of King Hezekiah who reached up to God for help (19:15). Sennacherib, the king of Assyria, had made threats against Hezekiah and the people of Judah, saying, "Do not let your God in whom you trust deceive you . . . You have heard what the kings of Assyria have done to all lands by utterly destroying them; and shall you be delivered?" (vv. 10–11). King Hezekiah went to the Lord and prayed for deliverance so "that all the kingdoms of the earth may know that You are the Lord God" (vv. 14–19). In answer to his prayer, the angel of the Lord struck down the enemy, and Sennacherib withdrew (vv. 20–36).

If you're in a situation where you need God's help, reach up your hand to Him in prayer. He has promised His comfort and help (2 Corinthians 1:3–4; Hebrews 4:16). —AC

> *When you're serving the Lord and you lose your way,*
> *Just hold out your hand and let Jesus lead;*
> *He'll come to your aid, and you'll hear Him say,*
> *I'll show you the way and meet every need.* —Hess

God's dawn of deliverance often comes when the hour of trial is darkest.

Seasons of Ups and Downs

READ: Ecclesiastes 3:1–8

A time to weep, and a time to laugh; a time to mourn, and a time to dance. —ECCLESIASTES 3:4

Most of us would agree that life has its ups and downs. Wise King Solomon believed this and reflected on our responses to fluctuating circumstances. He wrote: "To everything there is a season, a time for every purpose under heaven . . . a time to weep, and a time to laugh; a time to mourn, and a time to dance" (Ecclesiastes 3:1–4).

Solomon's father, David, was called "a man after [God's] own heart" (1 Samuel 13:14; Acts 13:22). Yet David's life illustrates how life is filled with seasons of ups and downs. David wept over his and Bathsheba's first child who was fatally ill (2 Samuel 12:22). Yet he also wrote songs of praise and joyous laughter (Psalm 126:1–3). With the death of his rebellious son Absalom, David experienced a time of deep mourning (2 Samuel 18:33). And when the ark was brought to Jerusalem, David, in spiritual ecstasy, danced before the Lord (2 Samuel 6:12–15).

We do a disservice to ourselves and others when we portray the Christian life as peaceful and happy all the time. Instead, the Bible portrays the believer's life as consisting of seasons of ups and downs. In what season are you? Whether a time of joy or sadness, each season should motivate us to seek the Lord and trust Him.   —DF

Dear Lord, help us to turn to you not only in sadness but also in joy. We know you give us both good times and bad to draw us to you and help us grow. May we learn to trust you in all seasons of life.

Every season needs faith to get us through it.

Are You Ready?

READ: 2 Peter 3:1–13

The Lord is not slack concerning His promise. —2 PETER 3:9

Many will remember the fall season of 2008 as the beginning of the worst financial crisis since the Great Depression of 1929. In the months to follow, many lost their jobs, homes, and investments. In a BBC interview a year later, Alan Greenspan, former head of the US Federal Reserve, indicated that the average person doesn't believe it will happen again. He said, "That is the unquenchable capability of human beings when confronted with long periods of prosperity to presume that it will continue."

Assuming that things will continue as they always have is not just 21st-century-type thinking. In the first century, Peter wrote of people who thought that life would continue as it was and that Jesus would not return. He said, "Since the fathers fell asleep, all things continue as they were from the beginning of creation" (2 Peter 3:4). Jesus said He would come back, but the people continued to live in disobedience as though He would never return. But His delay is only because of God's patience with us, for He is "not willing that any should perish but that all should come to repentance" (v. 9).

Paul tells us that Christians ought to live "soberly, righteously, and godly" in the light of Christ's certain return (Titus 2:12). Are you ready to meet Him? —CPH

> *Faithful and true would He find us here*
> *If He should come today?*
> *Watching in gladness and not in fear,*
> *If He should come today?* —Morris

Jesus may come any time, so we should be ready all the time.

A Lesson in Crying

READ: Revelation 21:1–7

Blessed are those who mourn, for they shall be comforted. —MATTHEW 5:4

Has your heart ever been broken? What broke it? Cruelty? Failure? Unfaithfulness? Loss? Perhaps you've crept into the darkness to cry.

It's good to cry. "Tears are the only cure for weeping," said Scottish preacher George MacDonald. A little crying does one good.

Our tears attract our Lord's lovingkindness and tender care. He knows our troubled, sleepless nights. His heart aches for us when we mourn. He is the "God of all comfort, who comforts us in all our tribulation" (2 Corinthians 1:3–4). And He uses His people to comfort one another.

But tears and our need for comfort come back all too frequently in this life. Present comfort is not the final answer. There is a future day when there will be no death, no sorrow, no crying, for all these things will "have passed away" (Revelation 21:4). There in heaven God will wipe away every tear. We are so dear to our Father that He will be the one who wipes the tears away from our eyes; He loves us so deeply and personally.

Remember, "Blessed are those who mourn, for they shall be comforted."

—DR

Think of a land of no sorrow,
Think of a land of no fears,
Think of no death and no sickness,
Think of a land of no tears. —Anonymous

God cares and shares in our sorrow.

Beyond the Status Quo

READ: John 5:35–47

But you are not willing to come to Me
that you may have life. —JOHN 5:40

Dr. Jack Mezirow, professor emeritus at Columbia Teachers College, believes that an essential element in adult learning is to challenge our own ingrained perceptions and examine our insights critically. Dr. Mezirow says that adults learn best when faced with what he calls a "disorienting dilemma"—something that "helps you critically reflect on the assumptions you've acquired." This is the opposite of saying, "My mind is made up—don't confuse me with the facts."

When Jesus healed on the Sabbath, He challenged the deeply held beliefs of many religious leaders, and they sought to silence Him (John 5:16–18). Jesus said to them: "You search the Scriptures, for in them you think you have eternal life; and these are they which testify of Me. But you are not willing to come to Me that you may have life" (vv. 39–40).

Oswald Chambers observed, "God has a way of bringing in facts which upset a man's doctrines if these stand in the way of God getting at his soul."

Unsettling experiences that cause us to question our assumptions about the Lord can also lead us to a deeper understanding and trust in Him—if we're willing to think it through and come to Him.   —DM

> *My mind cries its questions,*
> *My longing heart, joining.*
> *O Father, please hear me!*
> *O Spirit, keep teaching! —Verway*

The unexamined life is not worth living. —Socrates

Serious Business

READS: Psalm 96

The Lord reigns; the world also is firmly established, it shall not be moved; He shall judge the peoples righteously. —PSALM 96:10

Recently I was called for jury duty. It meant extraordinary inconvenience and lots of lost time, but it was also serious business. During the first day's orientation, the judge lectured us on the responsibility of sitting on a jury and the important nature of the task. We were going to sit in judgment of people who either had disputes (civil court) or were charged with crimes (criminal court). As I listened, I felt a great sense of inadequacy. Passing judgment on another person, with serious life consequences riding on the decision, is not a simple thing. Because we're flawed human beings, we may not always make the right judgments.

While the justice systems of our world might struggle and falter because of the inherent failings of the humans that manage them, we can always trust our God to excel in wisdom and fairness. The psalmist sang, "The Lord reigns; the world also is firmly established, it shall not be moved; He shall judge the peoples righteously" (Psalm 96:10). God judges according to righteousness—defined by His own perfect justice and flawless character.

We can trust God now when life seems unfair, knowing that He will one day make all things right in His final court (2 Corinthians 5:10).

—BC

The best of judges on this earth
Aren't always right or fair;
But God, the righteous Judge of all,
Wrongs no one in His care. —Egner

One day God will right every wrong.

From Bad to Worse

READ: Exodus 5:1–14, 22–23

I am the Lord; I will bring you out from under the burdens of the Egyptians . . . and I will redeem you with an outstretched arm. —EXODUS 6:6

It happened again. I got the urge to clean my office. Before I could resist, I had created an even bigger mess than I started with. One pile turned into many piles when I started sorting books, papers, and magazines. As the mess mushroomed, I lamented that I had started. But there was no going back.

When God recruited Moses to rescue the Hebrews from slavery, their situation went from bad to worse as well. There was no doubt that the job needed to be done. The people had been crying out to God to help them (Exodus 2:23). Reluctantly, very reluctantly, Moses agreed to appeal to Pharaoh on behalf of the Hebrews. The encounter did not go well. Instead of releasing the people, Pharaoh increased his unreasonable demands. Moses questioned whether he should have ever even approached Pharaoh (5:22–23). Only after a lot more trouble for a lot of people did Pharaoh let the people leave.

Whenever we set out to do something good, even when we're certain that God wants us to do it, we shouldn't be surprised when the situation gets worse before it gets better. This doesn't prove that we're doing the wrong thing; it just reminds us that we need God to accomplish everything.   —JAL

*There is only One who knows
All the answers to my woes;
He will all my needs supply
When in faith to Him I cry.* —Morgan

The supreme need in every hour of
difficulty is a vision of God. —G. C. Morgan

Ash-Heap Christians

READ: 1 Corinthians 3:5–15

Each one's work will become clear; for the Day will declare it . . . the fire will test each one's work, of what sort it is. —1 CORINTHIANS 3:13

Someone once asked me why she should be like Jesus now since she would become like Him when she got to heaven (1 John 3:1–3). Great question! Especially when it's easier to just be yourself.

Actually, there are several reasons why becoming like Him now is important, but one is near the top. When we stand before Him, we will give an account as to whether or not we lived in ways that were consistent with His will. Or, as Paul put it, whether or not we have built on Him as our foundation with "gold, silver, precious stones, wood, hay, [or] straw" (1 Corinthians 3:12–13).

All that we do to advance His kingdom—things like contribute to the strength of His church, serve the poor and needy, and promote righteousness and justice as He did—builds with essential materials that will survive the fire of His judgment. But living to advance ourselves and our earthly desires builds with things that will turn into a pile of ashes before the consuming fire of His glory.

I don't know about you, but I'd rather love Jesus enough to live like Him now, for the thought of standing before Him in a heap of ashes is an unthinkable alternative.   —JS

Father, thank you for the Spirit,
Fill us with His love and power;
Change us into Christ's own image
Day by day and hour by hour. —*Anonymous*

Build your life with commodities that will stand the test of God's judgment.

A FIRM Foundation

READ: Deuteronomy 6:1–9

These words which I command you . . . you shall teach
them diligently to your children. —DEUTERONOMY 6:6–7

Before she was two years old, my granddaughter Katie did something that would make any grandpa proud: She began to recognize cars by make and year. This all started when she and her daddy began spending time together playing with his old collection of toy cars. Daddy would say, "Katie, get the 1957 Chevy," and she would pick it out of the hundreds of tiny cars. And once, while he was reading a Curious George book to her, she climbed down from his lap and ran to get a miniature Rolls Royce—an exact replica of the car pictured in the book.

If a two-year-old child can make such connections, doesn't that show the importance of teaching children the right things early on? We can do this by using what I call the FIRM principle: Familiarity, Interest, Recognition, and Modeling. This follows Moses' pattern in Deuteronomy 6 of taking every opportunity to teach biblical truths so that children become familiar with them and make them a part of their lives. Using their interests as teaching opportunities, we repeat Bible stories so they become recognizable, while modeling a godly life before them.

Let's give the children in our lives a FIRM foundation by teaching them about God's love, Christ's salvation, and the importance of godly living.   —DB

O give us homes built firm upon the Savior,
Where Christ is Head and Counselor and Guide,
Where every child is taught His love and favor
And gives his heart to Christ, the crucified. —Hart

Build your children's lives on the firm foundation of the Word.

The Tales of Two Sticks

READ: Exodus 4:1–9, 17

You shall take this rod in your hand, with
which you shall do the signs. —EXODUS 4:17

Conventional wisdom questions how much can be accomplished with little. We tend to believe that a lot more can be done if we have large financial resources, talented manpower, and innovative ideas. But these things don't matter to God. Consider just a couple of examples:

In Judges 3:31, a relatively unknown man named Shamgar delivered Israel from the Philistines single-handedly. How? He won a great victory by killing six hundred Philistines with nothing more than an oxgoad (a stick sharpened on one end to drive slow-moving animals).

In Exodus, when God asked Moses to lead the people of Israel out of Egypt, Moses was afraid the people wouldn't listen to him or follow him. So God said, "What is that in your hand?" (4:2). Moses replied, "A rod." God went on to use that rod in Moses' hand to convince the people to follow him, to turn the Nile River into blood, to bring great plagues on Egypt, to part the Red Sea, and to perform miracles in the wilderness.

Moses' rod and Shamgar's oxgoad, when dedicated to God, became mighty tools. This helps us see that God can use what little we have, when surrendered to Him, to do great things. God is not looking for people with great abilities, but for those who are dedicated to following and obeying Him. —AL

If you use what little you may have
To serve the Lord with all your heart
You will find that He can do great things
When you begin to do your part. —Sper

Little is much when God is in it.

Not at This Time

READ: Romans 11:33–12:2

Be transformed by the renewing of your mind. —ROMANS 12:2

It can be quite discouraging for wannabe writers to get their work rejected time after time. When they send in a manuscript to a publisher, they'll often hear back in a letter with these words: "Thank you. But your submission does not meet our needs at this time." Sometimes this really means "not at this time—or ever." So they try the next publisher and the next.

I've found that the phrase *This does not meet our needs at this time— or ever* can be a helpful saying in my Christian walk to renew my mind and refocus my thoughts on the Lord.

Here's what I mean. When starting to worry, we can remind ourselves: "Worry does not meet my needs at this time—or ever. My heart's need is to trust God. I will 'be anxious for nothing' " (Philippians 4:6).

When we envy what another person has or does, we can reinforce the truth: "Envy does not meet my needs at this time—or ever. My need is to give thanks to God. His Word says, 'Envy is rottenness to the bones' (Proverbs 14:30), and 'In everything give thanks' " (1 Thessalonians 5:18).

We can't renew our minds by ourselves (Romans 12:2); it's the transforming work of the Holy Spirit who lives in us. Yet speaking the truth in our thoughts can help us submit to the Spirit's work within.   —AC

—————— FOR FURTHER THOUGHT ——————

What are some areas you struggle with in your heart?
Ask God to renew your mind that it might think like His.
Then keep reminding yourself of the truth.

The Spirit of God renews our minds when we review the Word of God.

The Story of a Wall

READ: Ephesians 2:11–22

He Himself is our peace, who has made both one, and has broken down the middle wall of separation. —EPHESIANS 2:14

While visiting the ruins of Hadrian's Wall in Northern England, I reflected on the fact that this may be the most remembered achievement of the Roman emperor who came to power in AD 117. As many as 18,000 Roman soldiers manned this eighty-mile-long barrier, built to keep the northern barbarians from invading the south.

Hadrian is remembered for building a physical wall to keep people out. In contrast, Jesus Christ is remembered for tearing down a spiritual wall to let people in.

When the early church experienced tension between believers of Jewish and non-Jewish birth, Paul told them that, through Christ, they stood equally in the family of God. "For He Himself is our peace, who has broken down the middle wall of separation . . . so as to create in Himself one new man from the two, thus making peace . . . For through Him we both have access by one Spirit to the Father" (Ephesians 2:14–15, 18).

One of the most beautiful aspects of the Christian faith is the unity among those who follow Jesus. Through His death on the cross, Christ has removed the barriers that so often separate people and has drawn us together in true friendship and love. —DM

God's people have so much to do
In serving Christ today
That they should use their precious time
To share, to love, to pray. —Branon

Christian unity begins at the cross.

1,000th Birthday

READ: Amos 4:7–13

Prepare to meet your God! —AMOS 4:12

In his book *Long for This World*, Jonathan Weiner writes about science's promise to radically extend how long we live. At the center of the book is English scientist Aubrey de Grey, who predicts that science will one day offer us 1,000-year life spans. Aubrey claims that molecular biology has finally placed a cure for aging within our reach.

But what difference does it make if, after living 1,000 years, we will eventually die anyway? De Grey's prediction only postpones facing the ultimate question of what happens when we die. It does not answer it.

The Scriptures tell us that death is not the end of our existence. Instead, we are assured that everyone will stand before Christ—believers for their works and nonbelievers for their rejection of Him (John 5:25–29; Revelation 20:11–15). All of us are sinners and in need of forgiveness. And only Christ's death on the cross has provided forgiveness for all who believe (Romans 3:23; 6:23). The Bible says, "It is appointed for men to die once, but after this the judgment" (Hebrews 9:27).

Our appointed face-to-face encounter with God puts everything in perspective. So whether we live seventy years or 1,000, the issue of eternity is the same: "Prepare to meet your God!" (Amos 4:12).   —DF

Only those who have placed their faith in
Christ are prepared to meet their Maker.

Tone Check

READ: Colossians 4:2–6

Let your speech always be with grace, seasoned with salt, that you may know how you ought to answer each one. —COLOSSIANS 4:6

Driving home from work, I heard a radio advertisement that got my attention. It was for a computer program that checks e-mails as they are written. I was familiar with "spell check" and "grammar check" programs, but this was different. This was "tone check." The software monitors the tone and wording of e-mails to make certain they are not overly aggressive, unkind, or mean-spirited.

As I listened to the announcer describe the features of this software, I wondered what it would be like to have something like that for my mouth. How many times have I reacted harshly and later regretted the words I spoke? Certainly a tone check would have protected me from responding so foolishly.

Paul saw the need for us as believers to check our speech—especially when talking to those who are not Christians. He said, "Let your speech always be with grace, seasoned with salt, that you may know how you ought to answer each one" (Colossians 4:6). His concern was that our speech be graceful, reflecting the beauty of our Savior. And it must be inviting to others. Talking with the right tone to unbelievers is vital to our ability to witness to them. Colossians 4:6 can be our tone check.   —BC

Tone of voice can be effective
If our spirit's calm and meek;
Let us watch our words and actions,
Always careful how we speak. —Hess

Every time we speak, our heart is on parade.

In Search of Silence

READ: Mark 1:35–45

I have calmed and quieted my soul. —PSALM 131:2

My next record should be forty-five minutes of silence," said singer Meg Hutchinson, "because that's what we're missing most in society."

Silence is indeed hard to find. Cities are notoriously noisy due to the high concentration of traffic and people. There seems to be no escape from loud music, loud machines, and loud voices. But the kind of noise that endangers our spiritual well-being is not the noise we can't escape but the noise we invite into our lives. Some of us use noise as a way of shutting out loneliness: voices of TV and radio personalities give us the illusion of companionship. Some of us use it as a way of shutting out our own thoughts: other voices and opinions keep us from having to think for ourselves. Some of us use noise as a way of shutting out the voice of God: constant chatter, even when we're talking about God, keeps us from hearing what God has to say.

But Jesus, even during His busiest times, made a point of seeking out places of solitude where He could carry on a conversation with God (Mark 1:35).

Even if we can't find a place that is perfectly quiet, we need to find a place to quiet our souls (Psalm 131:2), a place where God has our full attention. —JAL

Don't let the noise of the world keep you from hearing the voice of the Lord.

Healing from Heaven

READ: 2 Corinthians 1:1–10

Blessed be . . . the Father of mercies and God of all comfort.
—2 CORINTHIANS 1:3

Thomas Moore (1779–1852) was an Irish songwriter, singer, and poet. His talents brought joy to many who saw him perform or who sang his music. Yet, tragically, his personal life was troubled by repeated heartaches, including the death of all five of his children during his lifetime. Moore's personal wounds make these words of his all the more meaningful: "Here bring your wounded hearts, here tell your anguish; earth hath no sorrow that heaven cannot heal." This moving statement reminds us that meeting with God in prayer can bring healing to the troubled soul.

The apostle Paul also saw how our heavenly Father can provide solace to the hurting heart. To the believers at Corinth he wrote: "Blessed be the God and Father of our Lord Jesus Christ, the Father of mercies and God of all comfort, who comforts us in all our tribulation" (2 Corinthians 1:3–4). Sometimes, though, we can be so preoccupied with an inner sorrow that we isolate ourselves from the One who can offer consolation. We need to be reminded that God's comfort and healing come through prayer.

As we confide in our Father, we can experience peace and the beginning of healing for our wounded hearts. For truly "earth hath no sorrow that heaven cannot heal." —DF

Under His wings, what a refuge in sorrow!
How the heart yearningly turns to His rest!
Often when earth has no balm for my healing,
There I find comfort, and there I am blessed. —*Cushing*

Prayer is the soil in which hope and healing grow best.

No Authority?

READ: Proverbs 6:6–11

Consider [the ant's] ways and be wise, which, having no . . . ruler, provides her supplies . . . and gathers her food. —PROVERBS 6:6–8

When the deck behind our house began caving in, I knew its repair would exceed my abilities. So I made some calls, got some bids, and picked a builder to construct a new deck.

Once the contractor was done, I took a close look at his work and noticed some problems. Seeking a second opinion, I called the local building inspector and got a surprise. The deck guy had not obtained a building permit. Working without official oversight, he had violated many points of the building code.

This incident reminded me of an important truth (other than asking to see the building permit): We often do less than our best if we don't have any accountability to the authority over us.

In Scripture, we see this principle explained in two of Jesus' parables (Matthew 24:45–51; 25:14–30). In both cases, at least one unsupervised worker failed when the master was gone. But then we see a different approach in Proverbs 6. We see the example of the ant, which does good work without a visible supervisor. It intrinsically does its work without being monitored.

What about us? Do we do good work only when someone is watching? Or do we recognize that all our service is for God, and so do our best at all times—even when no human authority is watching?   —DB

God sees and knows the work we do:
Our faithfulness He will reward;
With His authority in view,
Let's do our best for Christ the Lord. —Hess

No matter who your boss is, you are really working for God.

Location, Location, Location

READ: Colossians 1:3–14

He has delivered us from the power of darkness and conveyed us into the kingdom of the Son. —COLOSSIANS 1:13

Buying and selling real estate in the US is tricky business these days. Housing prices have dropped significantly, and if you're trying to unload commercial property, it's even more difficult. So in the game of real estate, it remains important to keep this old adage in mind: "The three most important things to know about buying and selling property are location, location, location!"

The same is true of living for Jesus. Knowing our location spiritually is critical if we are to succeed in navigating through the greatly devalued territory of our world. Paul reminds us that we have a new location in Christ, having been delivered "from the power of darkness and conveyed . . . into the kingdom of the Son" (Colossians 1:13). Knowing that we have been relocated by His amazing grace into the kingdom of Jesus makes a difference. Jesus now reigns as King in our hearts and minds, and we are His grateful subjects. His will is our will and His ways become patterns for all of life and behavior. And when we are forced to make a choice, our allegiance is to Him.

So when the temptations and the seductions of the darkness from which you have been removed threaten His reign in your heart, remember your new postal code: Colossians 1:13! —JS

> *Where Jesus reigns there is no fear,*
> *No restless doubt, no hopeless tear,*
> *No raging sea nor tempest dread,*
> *But quietness and calm instead.* —*Anonymous*

The subjects of the kingdom should display the manners of the court.

Shine On!

READ: Matthew 5:14–16; 1 Peter 2:9–10

Let your light so shine before men, that they may see your good works and glorify your Father in heaven. —MATTHEW 5:16

I was frustrated that, despite my repeated calls, the streetlight in front of my house was still out. Because we don't have sidewalks and there is such a large distance between the streetlights, it's important that each light is functional to illuminate the darkness. I worried that I might hit one of the school kids as I pulled out of my driveway in the early morning hours.

The idea of light is used frequently in the Bible. Jesus said that He is the Light of the world (John 9:5). We are told to "put on the armor of light" by clothing ourselves with the Lord (Romans 13:12–14). And Matthew 5:16 instructs that we should "let [our] light so shine before men, that they may see [our] good works and glorify [our] Father in heaven."

A light that doesn't shine has lost its usefulness. Jesus said that no one hides a light under a basket but puts it on a lampstand to illuminate everything around it (Matthew 5:15). Our light (our actions) should point people to the One who is the Light. We don't have any light in ourselves, but we shine with the reflection of Christ (Ephesians 5:8).

God has placed each of us in a specific environment that will best allow us to shine with His light. Don't be like a burned-out streetlight. Shine on!   —CHK

> Lord, help us always put you first
> In everything we say and do
> So that your light will shine through us
> And show to all their need of you. —Sper

Whether you're a candle in a corner or a beacon on a hill, let your light shine.

A No-Smiling Policy

READ: John 13:31–35

By this all will know that you are My disciples,
if you have love for one another. —JOHN 13:35

Usually we're told to smile before someone takes our picture. But in some parts of the US, a no-smiling policy is enforced when getting your photo taken for a driver's license. Because of identity theft, these motor vehicle departments carefully check new photos that are taken to be sure they don't match photos already in the system. If someone gets a picture taken under a false name, an alarm is sent to the operator. From 1999 to 2009, one state stopped 6,000 people from getting fraudulent licenses. But why no smiling? Because the technology recognizes a face more easily if the person has a neutral facial expression.

Jesus prescribed a good way to recognize a Christian. He told His disciples, "By this all will know that you are My disciples, if you have love for one another" (John 13:35). The ways to show love to fellow believers are as endless as there are people with needs: a note of encouragement, a visit, a meal, a gentle rebuke, a prayer, a Bible verse, a listening ear, even just a friendly smile.

The apostle John wrote, "We know that we have passed from death to life, because we love the brethren" (1 John 3:14). Can others recognize, by our care for fellow Christians, that we know and love the Lord?   —AC

One measure of our love for God is how much we show love to His children.

Free to Choose

READ: Daniel 6:1–10

He knelt down on his knees three times that day,
and prayed and gave thanks before his God, as
was his custom since early days. —DANIEL 6:10

When it was learned that the biggest football game of the 2011 season was scheduled to be played on Yom Kippur, the student government at the University of Texas petitioned school officials to change the date. They said it was unfair to make Jewish students choose between the classic football rivalry with Oklahoma and observing their most important and sacred holy day of the year. But the date was not changed. Even in societies where people have religious freedom, difficult choices are still required of every person of faith.

Daniel demonstrated the courage to obey God no matter what the consequences. When his political rivals set a trap to eliminate him from their path to power (Daniel 6:1–9), he didn't challenge the law or complain that he had been wronged. "When Daniel knew that the writing was signed, he went home. And in his upper room, with his windows open toward Jerusalem, he knelt down on his knees three times that day, and prayed and gave thanks before his God, as was his custom since early days" (v. 10).

Daniel didn't know if God would save him from the lions' den, but it didn't matter. He chose to honor God in his life whatever the outcome. Like Daniel, we are free to choose to follow the Lord. —DM

What freedom lies with all who choose
To live for God each day!
But chains of bondage shackle those
Who choose some other way. —D. DeHaan

You can never go wrong when you choose to follow Christ.

The Cost of Fighting

READ: James 4:1–10

Where do wars and fights come from among you? Do they not come from your desires for pleasure that war in your members? —JAMES 4:1

During a documentary on World War I, the narrator said that if Britain's casualties in "the war to end all wars" were marched four abreast past London's war monument, the processional would take seven days to complete. This staggering word picture set my mind spinning at the awful cost of war. While those costs include monetary expense, destruction of property, and economic interruption, none of these compare to the human cost. Both soldiers and civilians pay the ultimate price, multiplied exponentially by the grief of the survivors. War is costly.

When believers go to war with one another, the cost is also high. James wrote, "Where do wars and fights come from among you? Do they not come from your desires for pleasure that war in your members?" (James 4:1). In our own selfish pursuits, we sometimes battle without considering the price exacted on our witness to the world or our relationships with one another. Perhaps that is why James preceded these words with the challenge, "Now the fruit of righteousness is sown in peace by those who make peace" (3:18).

If we are to represent the Prince of Peace in our world, believers need to stop fighting with one another and practice peace.   —BC

The wars and fights within the church
Disrupt our unity and peace;
How can we show the peace of Christ
Unless our conflicts cease? —Sper

When Christians are at peace with one another,
the world can more clearly see the Prince of Peace.

The Joy of Remembering

READ: Psalm 103:1–14

Bless the Lord, O my soul, and forget not all His benefits.
—Psalm 103:2

A longtime friend described the days surrounding his 90th birthday as "a time . . . to do a little reflecting, looking in the rearview mirror of my life, and spending many hours in what I call 'The Grace of Remembrance.' It's so easy to forget all the ways that the Lord has led! 'Forget not all His benefits'" (Psalm 103:2).

This was typical of the person I've known and admired for more than fifty years. Rather than reviewing disappointments, his letter was filled with thankfulness and praise to God.

First, he recalled the Lord's temporal mercies—his good health, the enjoyment of his wife and children, the joy and success of work, his enriching friendships, and the opportunities he'd had to serve God. He considered them all gifts—none deserved, but all gratefully received.

Next, he reviewed God's spiritual mercies—the influence of Christian parents and the experience of God's forgiveness when he accepted Christ as a teenager. He concluded with the encouragement he'd received from churches, schools, and Christian men who cared and prayed for each other.

It's a model we should follow on a regular basis—the joy of remembering. "Bless the Lord, O my soul; and all that is within me, bless His holy name!" (v. 1). —DM

He knoweth best! His will for me
Is better than my plans.
Do not all good and perfect gifts
Come from my Father's hand? —Doonan

Give loving thanks for the Lord's lavish gifts.

The Forgotten God

READ: 1 Corinthians 2:6–16

No one knows the things of God except the Spirit of God.
—1 CORINTHIANS 2:11

When we quote The Apostles' Creed, we say, "I believe in the Holy Spirit." Author J. B. Phillips said, "Every time we say [this] we mean that we believe that [the Spirit] is a living God able and willing to enter human personality and change it."

Sometimes we forget that the Holy Spirit is not an impersonal force. The Bible describes Him as God. He possesses the attributes of God: He is present everywhere (Psalm 139:7–8), He knows all things (1 Corinthians 2:10–11), and He has infinite power (Luke 1:35). He also does things that only God can do: create (Genesis 1:2) and give life (Romans 8:2). He is equal in every way with the other Persons of the Trinity—the Father and the Son.

The Holy Spirit is a Person who engages in personal ways with us. He grieves when we sin (Ephesians 4:30). He teaches us (1 Corinthians 2:13), prays for us (Romans 8:26), guides us (John 16:13), gives us spiritual gifts (1 Corinthians 12:11), and assures us of salvation (Romans 8:16).

The Holy Spirit indwells us if we have received forgiveness of sin through Jesus. He desires to transform us so that we become more and more like Jesus. Let's cooperate with the Spirit by reading God's Word and relying on His power to obey what we learn.　　—MW

> *God's guidance and help that we need day to day*
> *Is given to all who believe;*
> *The Spirit has sealed us—He's God's guarantee*
> *Of power that we can receive.* —Branon

The Christian who neglects the Holy Spirit is like a lamp that's not plugged in.

Drained of All Strength

READ: Isaiah 40:25–31

He gives power to the weak, and to those who have no might He increases strength. —ISAIAH 40:29

When I was a teenager, my dad and I went on many hunting and fishing trips together. Most became happy memories, but one fishing expedition was nearly a disaster. We drove up into a high mountain range and set up camp in a remote area. Then Dad and I trudged a long way down the mountain to get to a stream to fish. After a long day fishing in the hot sun, it was time to return to camp. But as we began to head back, Dad's face grew pale. He was dizzy and nauseated, and he had almost no strength.

Trying not to panic, I had him sit down and drink liquids. Then I prayed aloud to God for help. Bolstered by prayer, rest, and nourishment, Dad improved, and we began to go slowly back up the mountain. He held on to my loosened belt as I crawled upward, leading the way back to camp.

Sometimes we find ourselves in what feels like a hopeless valley without the strength to go on. When this happens, it's important to recall God's promise: "He gives power to the weak, and to those who have no might He increases strength" (Isaiah 40:29).

Do you feel drained? Exhausted? Ask God for help. Depend on Him for the power to go on and the strength to make it through the valley. —DF

When circumstances overwhelm
And seem too much to bear,
Depend upon the Lord for strength
And trust His tender care. —Sper

When we have nothing left but God, we discover that God is enough.

Too Busy to Know God?

READ: Luke 10:38–42

She had a sister called Mary, who also sat at
Jesus' feet and heard His word. —LUKE 10:39

One day when I was waiting to board a plane, a stranger who had overheard me mention that I was a chaplain began to describe to me his life before he met Christ. He said it was marked by "sin and self-absorption. Then I met Jesus."

I listened with interest to a list of changes he had made to his life and good deeds he had done. But because everything he told me was about his busyness for God and not his fellowship with God, I wasn't surprised when he added, "Frankly, chaplain, I thought I'd feel better about myself by now."

I think the New Testament character Martha would have understood that stranger's observation. Having invited Jesus to be a guest in her home, she set about doing what she thought were the important things. But this meant she couldn't focus on Jesus. Because her sister Mary wasn't helping, Martha felt justified asking Jesus to chide her. It's a mistake many of us make: We're so busy doing good that we don't spend time getting to know God better.

My advice to my new airplane friend came from the core of Jesus' words to Martha in Luke 10:41–42. I said to him: "Slow down and invest yourself in knowing God; let His Word reveal Him to you."

If we're too busy to spend time with God, we're simply too busy.

—RK

Savior, let me walk beside Thee,
Let me feel my hand in Thine;
Let me know the joy of walking
In Thy strength and not in mine. —Sidebotham

Our heavenly Father longs to spend time with His children.

The Way We Walk

READ: Deuteronomy 11:13–23

Just as Christ was raised from the dead by the glory of the Father, even so we also should walk in newness of life. —ROMANS 6:4

A television program that I enjoy watching has a segment called Ambush Makeover. Two women are chosen to undergo three hours of pampering to update their hair, makeup, and wardrobe. The change is often dramatic. When the women step from behind a curtain, the audience gasps. Friends and family members sometimes start to cry. After all of this, the person with the new look finally gets to see herself. Some are so shocked that they keep looking in the mirror as if to find proof that it's really them.

As the women walk across the set to join their companions, however, the former self becomes evident. Most do not know how to walk in their new shoes. Although they look chic, their clumsy walk gives them away. Their transformation is incomplete.

This is true in our Christian lives as well. God does the work in us to give us a new start, but to walk in the way of the Lord (Deuteronomy 11:22) requires time, effort, and lots of practice. If we just stand still and smile, we can pass as being transformed. But the way we walk tells how far along we are in living out that transformation. Being changed means giving up our previous way of life and learning a new way to walk (Romans 6:4).   —JAL

The new life in Christ has begun—
The past with its darkness is gone;
Look closer to see what the Savior has done,
For change is beginning to dawn. —Hess

A change in behavior begins with a change in the heart.

A Debt of Gratitude

READ: Romans 16:1–16

[They] risked their own necks for my life, to whom not only I give thanks, but also all the churches of the Gentiles. —ROMANS 16:4

Dave Randlett was someone of whom I can say, "Because of him, my life will never be the same." Dave, who went to heaven in October 2010, became a mentor to me when I was a new follower of Jesus in my college years. He not only invested time in me, but he took risks by giving me opportunities to learn and grow in ministry. Dave was God's instrument to give me the opportunity to be a student preacher and travel with a college music team. As a result, he helped shape and prepare me for a life of teaching God's Word. I'm glad I was able to express thanks to him on a number of occasions.

Just as I am thankful for Dave's influence in my life, the apostle Paul was grateful for Aquila and Priscilla, who served the Lord with him. He said they "risked their own necks for my life." In gratitude, he thanked them, as did "all the churches of the Gentiles" (Romans 16:4).

You too may have people in your life who have taken risks by giving you opportunities to serve or who have greatly influenced you spiritually. Perhaps pastors, ministry leaders, friends, or family members have given of themselves to move you further along for Christ. The question is, have you thanked them? —BC

> Consider what the Lord has done
> Through those who've shown you love;
> And thank Him for each faithful one—
> A blessing from above. —Sper

For those who have helped you, take time to give them thanks.

The Wooden Rule

READ: 1 Corinthians 12:14–26

The body is not one member but many. —1 CORINTHIANS 12:14

Legendary UCLA basketball coach John Wooden had an interesting rule for his teams. Whenever a player scored, he was to acknowledge the person on the team who had assisted. When he was coaching high school, one of his players asked, "Coach, won't that take up too much time?" Wooden replied, "I'm not asking you to run over there and give him a big hug. A nod will do."

To achieve victory on the basketball court, Wooden saw the importance of teaching his players that they were a team—not "just a bunch of independent operators." Each person contributed to the success of everyone else.

That reminds me of the way the body of Christ should work. According to 1 Corinthians 12:19–20, each of us is a separate part of one body. "If they were all one member, where would the body be? But . . . there are many members, yet one body." Is the success of a pastor, a Bible study, or a church program based solely on one person's accomplishments? How many people contribute to the smooth operation of a church, a Christian organization, a family?

Coach Wooden's rule and 1 Corinthians 12 are both rooted in the principle of seeing our need for one another. Let's use our gifts within the body of Christ to build up, strengthen, and help to carry out God's purposes (vv. 1–11). —CHK

> *All Christians have been gifted*
> *By grace from God above,*
> *Equipped to build and strengthen*
> *The church in faith and love.* —Fitzhugh

There are no unimportant people in the body of Christ.

Character at Play

READ: 2 Peter 1:1–11

His divine power has given to us all things that pertain to life and godliness. —2 PETER 1:3

A college football coach in the Bronx (New York) built his team around good character qualities. Instead of displaying their names on the back of their jerseys, the Maritime College players displayed words like *family*, *respect*, *accountability*, and *character*. Before each game, Coach Clayton Kendrick-Holmes reminded his team to play by those principles on the field.

The apostle Peter had his own list of Christian qualities (2 Peter 1:5–7) that he encouraged believers to add to their life of faith:

Virtue: Fulfilling God's design for a life with moral excellence.

Knowledge: Studying God's Word to gain wisdom to combat falsehood.

Self-control: Revering God so much that we choose godly behavior.

Perseverance: Having a hopeful attitude even in difficulties, because we're confident in God's character.

Godliness: Honoring the Lord in every relationship in life.

Brotherly kindness: Displaying warmhearted affection for fellow believers.

Love: Sacrificing for the good of others.

Let's develop these qualities in increasing measure and integrate them into every part of our life.   —AC

Just as the body grows in strength
With exercise each day,
Our spirit grows in godliness
By living life God's way. —D. DeHaan

Godly exercise is the key to godly character.

Papa Didn't Say "Oh!"

READ: Ephesians 5:1–10

The Lord is gracious and full of compassion. —PSALM 145:8

I have a friend who was working in his home office one evening, trying to get some necessary paperwork done. His little girl, who was about four years old at the time, was playing around his desk, puttering about, moving objects here and there, pulling out drawers, and making a good deal of noise.

My friend endured the distraction with stoic patience until the child slammed a drawer on one of her fingers and screamed in pain. Reacting in exasperation he shouted, "That's it!" as he escorted her out of the room and shut the door.

Later, her mother found her weeping in her bedroom and tried to comfort her. "Does your finger still hurt?" she asked. "No," the little girl sniffled. "Then why are you crying?" her mother asked. "'Cause," she whimpered, "when I pinched my finger, Papa didn't say, 'Oh!'"

Sometimes that's all we need, isn't it? Someone who cares and who will respond with kindness and compassion. Someone who will say, "Oh!"

Thankfully, we have One named Jesus who does that for us. Jesus loves us, understands our sorrows, and gave himself for us (Ephesians 5:2). Now we are to "walk in love" and imitate Him.   —DR

> *Knowing God—what comfort there,*
> *Drawn by His eternal care;*
> *Love from God—what joy we share,*
> *Drawn into His mercies rare.* —Branon

God's whisper of comfort quiets the noise of our trials.

Investing in the Future

READK: Matthew 6:19–24

Lay up for yourselves treasures in heaven, where neither moth nor rust destroys and where thieves do not break in and steal. —MATTHEW 6:20

Jason Bohn was a college student when he made a hole-in-one golf shot that won him a million dollars. While others may have squandered that money, Bohn had a plan. Wanting to be a pro golfer, he used the money as a living-and-training fund to improve his golf skills. The cash became an investment in his future—an investment that paid off when Bohn won the PGA Tour's 2005 B.C. Open. Bohn's decision to invest in the future instead of living for the moment was a wise one indeed.

In a sense, that is what Jesus calls us to do. We have been entrusted with resources—time, ability, opportunity— and we decide how to use them. Our challenge is to see those resources as an opportunity to invest long-term. "Lay up for yourselves treasures in heaven" is how Jesus put it in Matthew 6:20. Those protected treasures cannot be destroyed nor taken away, Jesus assures us.

Think of your resources: talent, time, knowledge. These are temporal and limited. But if you invest them with an eye toward eternity, these temporary things can have enduring impact. What is your focus? Now or forever? Invest in the future. It will not only have an eternal impact, but it will also change the way you view life each day.   —BC

Whatever is done in love for Christ
Will one day have heaven's reward;
Today let's do what we can for Him,
Our loving Savior and Lord. —Hess

The richest people on earth are those who invest their lives in heaven.

My Fingernails or His Hand?

READ: Psalm 37:23–26

The Lord upholds him with His hand. —PSALM 37:24

Tough times can cause us to get our perspective turned around. I was reminded of this recently as I talked to a fellow griever—another parent who, like Sue and me, lost a teenage daughter to death suddenly and without warning. She told me she had been missing her daughter terribly, and she told God she felt as if she were hanging on by her fingernails. Then she felt as if God reminded her that His hand of protection was there to hold her up—that she could let go, and He would catch her.

That's a better perspective, isn't it? This picture reminds us that when troubles come and we feel least able to hold on to our faith, it's not up to us. It's up to God to support us with His mighty hand.

Psalm 37:23–24 says: "The steps of a good man are ordered by the Lord . . . Though he fall, he shall not be utterly cast down; for the Lord upholds him with His hand." And Psalm 63:8 tells us: "My soul follows close behind You; Your right hand upholds me."

In tough times, we can become so preoccupied with our role in "clinging to God" that we forget about His promised protection. It's not our fingernails that sustain us—it's His loving, upholding hand. —DB

> God's hand that holds the ocean's depths
> Can hold my small affairs;
> His hand that guides the universe,
> Can carry all my cares. —Anonymous

No one is more secure than the one who is held in God's hand.

One Heart at a Time

READ: Philemon 1:12-22

No longer as a slave but more than a slave—
a beloved brother. —PHILEMON 1:16

Quaker John Woolman was an itinerant preacher who waged his own personal campaign to end slavery in colonial America. Woolman met with slaveholders to speak of the injustice of holding other human beings as property. Although Woolman did not eradicate slavery completely, he did persuade many masters to free their slaves. His success was due to individual, personal persuasion.

The book of Philemon contains a similar one-on-one appeal. Onesimus was a runaway slave who had escaped from his Christian master, Philemon. Onesimus had come to faith through Paul's ministry, and now Paul was sending him back to Philemon with these words: "Perhaps he departed for a while for this purpose, that you might receive him forever, no longer as a slave but more than a slave—a beloved brother" (vv. 15-16). Although we don't know if Onesimus was set free from slavery, his new faith in Jesus had changed his relationship with his Christian master. He was now also a brother in Christ. Paul was influencing his world one heart at a time.

By the transforming power of the gospel, people and situations can change. Like Woolman and like Paul, let's seek to influence our world one heart at a time. —DF

If I can help some wounded heart,
If I can by my love impart
Some blessing that will help more now—
Lord, just show me how. —Brandt

The kindest thing you can do for another is to show him the truth.

So Long

READ: 1 Thessalonians 4:13–18

[Do not] sorrow as others who have no hope.
—1 THESSALONIANS 4:13

My grandfather refused to say "goodbye." He felt the word was too final. So when we would drive away after family visits, his farewell ritual was always the same. Standing in front of the green ferns that lined his house, he would wave and call out, "So long!"

As believers, we never have to say "goodbye" to the ones we love, as long as they have placed their trust in Jesus as Savior. The Bible promises that we will see them again.

The apostle Paul said that we should not "sorrow as others who have no hope" (1 Thessalonians 4:13), because when Jesus returns, the Christians who have died will rise from their graves and—together with the believers who are still alive—will meet the Lord in the air (vv. 15–17). We have confidence that one day in heaven there will be "no more death, nor sorrow, nor crying" (Revelation 21:4). It's in that wonderful place that "we shall always be with the Lord" (1 Thessalonians 4:17).

Christians have the hope of an eternal reunion with Christ and with believing loved ones who have passed away. That's why Paul exhorted us to "comfort one another with these words" (v. 18). Today, encourage someone with the hope that allows us to say "so long," instead of "goodbye." —JBS

Beyond the sunset, O glad reunion
With our dear loved ones who've gone before;
In that fair homeland we'll know no parting—
Beyond the sunset forevermore. —Brock

At death, God's people don't say "Goodbye," but "We'll see you later."

He Guards Me Well

READ: John 10:7–15

I lay down My life for the sheep. —JOHN 10:15

During the quiet moments before a Sunday morning service, the organist played a hymn that was new to me. I turned to the page noted in the hymnal and read the words of the song "The Lord My Shepherd Guards Me Well," a beautiful paraphrase of Psalm 23:

The Lord my Shepherd guards me well,
And all my wants are fed:
Amid green pastures made to lie,
Beside still waters led.
My care-worn soul grows strong and whole
When God's true path I tread.

No matter how often we read or hear the familiar Psalm 23, it seems to come with a fresh message of God's care for us. The shepherd and sheep image was familiar to the people who heard Jesus say, "I am the good shepherd. The good shepherd gives His life for the sheep" (John 10:11). Unlike a hired person who runs away from danger, the true shepherd stays with the sheep to protect them. "But a hireling, he who is not the shepherd . . . sees the wolf coming and leaves the sheep and flees . . . I am the good shepherd; and I know My sheep" (vv. 12–14).

No matter what you're facing today, Jesus knows your name, He knows the danger, and He will not leave your side. You can say with confidence: The Lord my Shepherd guards me well!　　　—DM

The Lamb who died to save us is the Shepherd who lives to lead us.

Stuck in the Mire

READ: Jeremiah 20:7–13

His word was in my heart like a burning fire shut up in my bones; I was weary of holding it back. —JEREMIAH 20:9

Jeremiah has been called "the weeping prophet." He may have had a sensitive and melancholic disposition that was compounded by his heartbreak over God's judgment on disobedient Israel. His capacity for sorrow is amazing: "Oh, that my head were waters, and my eyes a fountain of tears, that I might weep day and night!" (Jeremiah 9:1).

As if sorrow for his nation were not enough, Jeremiah was persecuted for his prophetic message of judgment. In one instance, he was imprisoned in a cistern filled with mire (38:6). Opposition to his ministry had gotten the great prophet stuck in a place of despair.

Sometimes in our attempts to serve the Lord, we can feel stuck in painful circumstances and surprising heartache. But the prophet's resilience should inspire us to persevere. Jeremiah's sense of divine call was so strong that he could not be deterred from serving the Lord. "But His word was in my heart like a burning fire shut up in my bones; I was weary of holding it back, and I could not" (20:9).

Have the results of your service for the Lord been disappointing? Ask Him to renew your heart by His Spirit, and continue to serve God despite your setbacks. —DF

> *Be not weary in your serving;*
> *Do your best for those in need;*
> *Kindnesses will be rewarded*
> *By the Lord who prompts the deed. —Anonymous*

No service for Christ is insignificant.

Poetic Justice

READ: Esther 3:1–11; 7:1–10

"Vengeance is Mine, I will repay," says the Lord. —ROMANS 12:19

For nearly a year, a former publishing colleague lived under a cloud of fear that he would be fired. A new boss in the department, for reasons unknown, began filling his personnel file with negative comments. Then, on the day my friend expected to lose his job, the new boss was fired instead.

When the Israelites were taken as captives to Babylon, a Jew named Mordecai found himself in this kind of situation. Haman, the highest noble of King Xerxes, expected every royal official to kneel down and honor him, but Mordecai refused to bow to anyone but God (Esther 3:1–2). This outraged Haman, and he set out to destroy not only Mordecai but every Jew in the whole Persian Empire (vv. 5–6). Haman convinced Xerxes to sign a decree authorizing the destruction of all Jews and started building a gallows for the execution of Mordecai (5:14). But, in a startling turn of events, Haman was executed on the gallows he had built for Mordecai, and the Jewish people were spared (7:9–10; 8).

In literature this is called poetic justice. Not everyone gets justice in such dramatic fashion, but Scripture promises that God will one day avenge all injustice (Romans 12:19). While we wait, we are to do what we can to work for justice and leave the results in God's hands. —JAL

> *The call for justice must be strong*
> *To show what's right, to thwart what's wrong,*
> *But let's reject the smallest part*
> *Of vengeance harbored in the heart.* —D. DeHaan

The scales of divine justice always balance—if not here, then hereafter.

Divine Appointments

READ: Acts 16:9–31

Paul and Silas were praying and singing hymns to God,
and the prisoners were listening to them. —ACTS 16:25

Have you ever been stuck in an airport? For twenty-four hours? In a city where you can't speak the language? Four thousand miles from home?

It happened to a friend recently, and we can learn from his response. While most of us would find such an inconvenience intolerable, my friend John saw God's hand in his delay. As he waited out his forced stay, he looked for opportunities to connect with fellow passengers. He "happened" to find some fellow Christians from India, and in talking to them he heard about a ministry they were involved with. In fact, because John's interests matched his new friends' ministry, they invited him to India to participate in a short-term project.

How often do we treat a delay, a change of plans, or a redirection as an intrusion? Instead, it could be that God is detouring us so we can do something different or new for Him. Consider Paul's trip to Philippi in Acts 16. He had gone to Macedonia because of a God-directed vision (vv. 9–10). How could he know that he would end up in prison there? But even that trip to jail was God-led, because He used Paul to bring salvation to a jailer and his family (vv. 25–34).

God can use inconveniences in our lives if we look at them as divine appointments.   —DB

> *"Disappointment—His appointment,"*
> *Change one letter, then I see*
> *That the thwarting of my purpose*
> *Is God's better choice for me.* —Young

God can turn obstacles into opportunities.

Zero Tolerance

READ: Leviticus 19:11–18

You shall not go about as a talebearer among your people.
—LEVITICUS 19:16

When Shayla McKnight applied for a job for an online printing company, she was surprised to learn that they had a zero-tolerance policy for gossip. If employees are caught gossiping, they are reprimanded; and if they continue, they are fired.

Long before this kind of policy was ever implemented by a company, God spoke of His own zero-tolerance policy for gossip and slander among His people (Leviticus 19:16). Idle talk that foolishly or maliciously spread rumors or facts about another person was forbidden.

Solomon said that speaking badly of others could have disastrous effects. It betrays confidence (Proverbs 11:13), separates close friends (16:28; 17:9), shames and saddles you with a bad reputation (25:9–10), and perpetually fuels the embers of a quarrel (26:20–22). People rarely can undo the damage their untrue words have done to a neighbor.

Let's ask the Lord to help us not to engage in harmful talk about others. He wants us to set a guard over our mouths so that we'll instead speak all the good we know about everybody.　　　　—MW

Many things that others say
Are not for us to tell;
Help us, Lord, to watch our tongue—
We need to guard it well. —Branon

Destroy gossip by ignoring it.

Why Me?

READ: Psalm 131

The secret things belong to the Lord our God. —DEUTERONOMY 29:29

Recently I read Psalm 131, one of my favorite psalms. In the past I viewed it as an encouragement to understand that mystery is one of the hallmarks of God's character. It challenged me to let my mind be at rest, since I am unable to understand all that God is doing in His universe.

But then I saw another side of David's calm spirit: I am unable to understand all that God is doing in me, and it is impossible to try.

David draws a comparison between a weaned child that no longer frets for what it once demanded, and a soul that has learned the same lesson. It is a call to learn humility, patient endurance, and contentment in all my circumstances—whatever they are—though I do not understand God's reasons. Divine logic is beyond the grasp of my mind.

I ask, "Why this affliction? Why this anguish?"

The Father answers, "Hush, child. You wouldn't understand if I explained it to you. Just trust me!"

So I turn from contemplating David's example to ask myself: Can I, in my circumstances, "hope in the Lord"? (v. 3). Can I wait in faith and patience without fretting and without questioning God's wisdom? Can I trust Him while He works in me His good, acceptable, and perfect will?

—DR

> *It may not be for me to see*
> *The meaning and the mystery*
> *Of all that God has planned for me*
> *Till "afterward"!* —*Anonymous*

In a world of mystery, it's a comfort to know the God who knows all things.

The Right Ingredients

READ: Matthew 22:34–39; 28:16–20

Always be ready to give a defense . . . with meekness. —1 PETER 3:15

Although my culinary skills remain undeveloped, occasionally I use a box of premixed ingredients to make a cake. After adding eggs, vegetable oil, and water, I stir it all together. To bake a palate-pleasing cake, it's vital to have the correct balance of the right ingredients. That helps me picture the relationship of the greatest commandment (Matthew 22:36–38) and the Great Commission (28:19–20) as we spread the gospel.

When Jesus told His followers to go and make disciples of all nations, He did not give them permission to be rude and uncaring as they did so. His own citing of the "first and great commandment"—to love God with all your heart, soul, and mind—was quickly followed by the call to "love your neighbor as yourself" (Matthew 22:37–39). Throughout the New Testament, we find this model of compassionate, respectful living restated many places, including "the love chapter" (1 Corinthians 13) and Peter's instruction to give a reason for the hope within us "with gentleness and respect" (1 Peter 3:15 NIV).

In our eagerness to share Christ with others, we must always include a healthy balance of those two ingredients—the true gospel and godly love. This wonderfully sweet cake bakes best in the warmth of God's love. —DM

> *Lord, help me to love with both words and deeds,*
> *To reach out to sinners and meet their needs;*
> *Lord, burden my heart for those lost in sin,*
> *With mercy and love that flows from within.* —Fitzhugh

They witness best who witness with their lives.

Father of Lies

READ: John 8:37–47

When [the devil] speaks a lie, he speaks from his own resources, for he is a liar and the father of it. —JOHN 8:44

Satan's sway over mankind began when he turned the minds of Adam and Eve against God. In order to pull it off, he had to lie to them about God—and they had to fall for it. In that defining moment, he lied to them about God's goodness, God's Word, and God's intentions (Genesis 3:1–6).

Satan is still up to his old tricks. Jesus said that when the Devil "speaks a lie, he speaks from his own resources, for he is a liar" (John 8:44). It should not be surprising, then, that when trouble interrupts our lives, the Father of Lies whispers in our ears and suddenly we are questioning God's goodness. When we are told to follow His commands, we wonder if His Word is really true in the first place. When Jesus tells us things like "Do not lay up for yourselves treasures on earth" (Matthew 6:19), Satan tells us that the good life is about piling up things here, causing us to doubt God's good intentions.

Our problem is that we, like Adam and Eve, believe Satan's lies. And when we do, our loyalty to God is compromised. Then our enemy slithers off to his next assignment, leaving us alone to face our regrets and the realization that his lies have seduced us away from our truest and dearest Friend.

Who have you been listening to lately?   —JS

> *Satan can catch you by surprise*
> *And stop you in your tracks,*
> *So keep on guard and trust God's Word,*
> *Resist his strong attacks.* —Branon

The power of Satan is no match for the power of God's Word.

Surprise!

READ: John 1:6-13

*Behold! The Lamb of God who takes
away the sin of the world!* —JOHN 1:29

A writer for the *Washington Post* conducted an experiment to test people's perception. He asked a famous violinist to perform incognito at a train station in the nation's capital one January morning. Thousands of people walked by as he played, but only a few stopped to listen. After forty-five minutes, just $32 had been dropped into the virtuoso's open violin case. Two days earlier, this man—Joshua Bell—had used the same $3.5 million Stradivarius for a sold-out concert where people paid $100 a seat to hear him perform.

The idea of a person not being recognized for his greatness isn't new. It happened to Jesus. "He was in the world," John said, ". . . and the world did not know Him" (John 1:10). Why did people who had been expecting the Messiah give Jesus such a cold reception? One reason is that they were surprised. Just as people today don't expect famous musicians to play in railway stations, the people in Jesus' day didn't expect Messiah to be born in a stable. They also expected Him to be a political king, not the head of a spiritual kingdom.

The people in the first century were blinded to God's purpose in sending Jesus to this world. He came to save people from their sins (John 1:29). Receive God's surprising gift of salvation that He offers freely to you today.   —CPH

> *Amazing thought! That God in flesh*
> *Would take my place and bear my sin;*
> *That I, a guilty, death-doomed soul,*
> *Eternal life might win!* —*Anonymous*

God broke into human history to offer us the gift of eternal life.

Staying Clean

READ: Psalm 119:9–16

Your Word I have hidden in my heart, that I might not sin against You. —PSALM 119:11

During a business trip to Philadelphia, I walked down Broad Street toward City Hall each morning to catch the subway. Each day I passed a long line of people waiting for something. They were a cross-section of humanity in age, ethnic origin, and appearance. After wondering about it for three days, I asked a man on the sidewalk why all those people were standing in line. He told me that they were on probation or parole after breaking the law and had to take a daily drug test to show that they were staying clean.

This struck me as a vivid illustration of my need to stay spiritually clean before God. When the psalmist pondered how he could live a pure life, he concluded that the key was to consider and obey God's teaching. "Your Word I have hidden in my heart, that I might not sin against You. Blessed are You, O Lord! Teach me Your statutes . . . I will delight myself in Your statutes; I will not forget Your Word" (Psalm 119:11–12, 16).

In the light of God's Word we see our sin, but we also see God's love in Christ. "If we confess our sins, He is faithful and just to forgive us our sins and to cleanse us from all unrighteousness" (1 John 1:9).

By His grace . . . staying clean.   —DM

> *Lord, grant that we may hear you speak*
> *As truth within your Word we seek;*
> *And may it show us all our sin*
> *And make us clean without, within.* —D. DeHaan

Read the Bible to be wise, believe it to be safe, practice it to be holy.

Mouth Guard

READ: Proverbs 15:1–7

The tongue of the wise uses knowledge rightly, but the mouth of fools pours forth foolishness. —PROVERBS 15:2

I was walking in a subway in Minsk, Belarus, with my friend Yuliya and her daughter Anastasia when I suddenly fell face-first onto the dirty concrete floor. I don't remember the fall, but I do remember suddenly having a mouth filled with sand, gravel, and grit. Ugh! I couldn't get that stuff out of my mouth quickly enough!

I didn't enjoy what went into my mouth on that embarrassing occasion. But Scripture teaches that it's more important to guard what comes out of our mouths. When the writer of Proverbs 15 said that "the mouth of fools pours forth foolishness" (v. 2), the word translated *pours forth* literally means "explodes out." Rash accusations, angry words, and verbal abuse can do immeasurable and lifelong harm. The apostle Paul spoke bluntly about this: "Let no corrupt word proceed out of your mouth" (Ephesians 4:29)—no dirty talk. He also said to "[put] away lying" and to "speak truth" (v. 25)—no lies. And later, "Let all bitterness, wrath, anger, clamor, and evil speaking be put away from you" (v. 31)—no character assassination. What comes out of our mouths should be wholesome and uplifting.

We guard carefully what goes into our mouths, and rightly so. To honor God, let's also keep tight control on the words that come out of our mouths.   —DE

Lord, help us to control our tongues,
To clean up what we say,
To use words that will edify,
To honor you today. —Sper

Be careful of your thoughts; they may become words at any time.

Looking for Water

READ: John 4:1–15

Whoever drinks of the water that I shall give him will never thirst. —JOHN 4:14

The United States has spent millions of dollars looking for water on Mars. A few years ago, NASA sent twin robots, Opportunity and Spirit, to the red planet to see if water was present or had been present at one time. Why did the US do this? The scientists who are poring over data sent back from those two little Martian rovers are trying to figure out if life ever existed on Mars. And for that to have happened, there had to be water. No water, no life.

Two thousand years ago a couple of "rovers" set out across the countryside of an Earth-outpost called Samaria looking for water. One was a woman who lived nearby. The other was a man from Galilee. They ended up meeting at a well near the village of Sychar. When they did, Jesus found the water He was looking for, and the woman found the water she didn't know she needed (John 4:5–15).

Water is essential for both physical and spiritual life. Jesus had a surprise for the woman at the well. He offered her the Water of Life—himself. He is the refreshing, renewing "fountain of water springing up into everlasting life" (John 4:14).

Do you know anyone looking for water? Someone who is spiritually thirsty? Introduce that person to Jesus, the Living Water. It's the greatest discovery of all time. —DB

> *Gracious and Almighty Savior,*
> *Source of all that shall endure,*
> *Quench my thirst with living water,*
> *Living water, clear and pure.* —Vinal

Only Jesus, the Living Water, can satisfy the thirsty soul.

Lambs May Wade

READ: 2 Timothy 3:13–17

All Scripture . . . is profitable. —2 TIMOTHY 3:16

Author C. S. Lewis says that religious concepts are like soups: some are thick and some are clear. There are indeed "thick" concepts in the Bible: mysteries, subtleties, and complexities that challenge the most accomplished mind. For example, "[God] has mercy on whom He wills, and whom He wills He hardens" (Romans 9:18). And yet in the same volume there are thoughts that are crystal "clear": simple, attainable, and easily grasped. What could ever surpass the simplicity of the clear affirmation in 1 John 4:16: "God is love"?

John Cameron, a fifteenth-century writer, suggests, "In the same meadow, the ox may lick up grass . . . the bird may pick up seeds . . . and a man finds a pearl; so in one and the same Scripture are varieties to be found for all sorts of conditions. In them, the lamb may wade, and the elephant swim, children may be fed with milk, and meat may be had for stronger men."

All the treasures of wisdom and knowledge are found in God's Book, the Bible—ocean depths that can stir the most sophisticated mind, and clear streams that can be negotiated by any simple, honest soul.

Why hesitate? "All Scripture . . . is profitable" (2 Timothy 3:16). Jump in! —DR

> *Thy Word is like a deep, deep mine,*
> *And jewels rich and rare*
> *Are hidden in its mighty depths*
> *For every searcher there.* —Hodder

God speaks through His Word—take time to listen.

Peace in Crisis

READ: John 14:19–27

Peace I leave with you. —JOHN 14:27

Ted, one of the elders in our church, used to be a police officer. One day after he responded to a report of violence, the situation turned life-threatening. A man had stabbed someone and then menacingly turned the blade toward Ted. A fellow officer fired his weapon at the assailant as he attacked Ted. The criminal was subdued, but Ted was shot in the cross fire. As he was driven by ambulance to the hospital, he felt deep waves of peace flowing over his soul from the Holy Spirit. Ted felt so tranquil that he was able to offer words of comfort to his fellow officer who was emotionally distraught over the crisis.

The Lord Jesus promised us peace in crisis. Just hours before His own crucifixion, Christ comforted His disciples with these words: "Peace I leave with you, My peace I give to you; not as the world gives do I give to you. Let not your heart be troubled, neither let it be afraid" (John 14:27).

What is your worst fear? If you should have to face it, Christ will be there with you. Trusting Him through prayer makes available "the peace of God, which surpasses all understanding," and it "will guard your hearts and minds through Christ Jesus" (Philippians 4:7). —DF

> *O the blessedness to nestle*
> *Like a child upon His breast;*
> *Finding ever, as He promised*
> *Perfect comfort, peace, and rest.* —Hennessay

The secret of peace is to give every anxious care to God.

Mighty Waters

READp: Revelation 1:9–17

His feet were like fine brass, as if refined in a furnace, and His voice as the sound of many waters. —REVELATION 1:15

While in Brazil, I went to see Iguazu Falls, one of the greatest waterfalls in the world. The massive falls are breathtaking, but what impressed me most at Iguazu was not the sight of the falls or the spray of the water. It was the sound. The sound was beyond deafening—I felt as if I was actually inside the sound itself. It was an overwhelming experience that reminded me how small I am by comparison.

Later, with this scene in mind, I couldn't help but think about John in Revelation 1:15. While on the island of Patmos, he saw a vision of the risen Christ. The apostle described Jesus in the glory of His resurrection, noting both His clothing and His physical qualities. Then John described Christ's voice "as the sound of many waters" (v. 15). I didn't fully appreciate what that meant until I visited Iguazu and was overwhelmed by the thundering sound of the falls. As those mighty waters reminded me of my own smallness, I better understood why John fell at the feet of Christ as if dead (v. 17).

Perhaps that description will help you grasp the awesomeness of Jesus' presence and prompt you to follow John's example of worshiping the Savior. —BC

Pay honor to our marvelous Savior—
Daily His wonders proclaim;
Dwell always in the presence of Jesus,
And worship His holy name. —Branon

True worship of Christ changes admiration into adoration.

Plowing Straight Lines

READ: Philippians 3:8–17

I press toward the goal for the prize of the upward call of God in Christ Jesus. —PHILIPPIANS 3:14

It's my first day on the tractor! A crisp morning breeze brushes across the field. Crickets and country silence yield to the roar of the engine. Dropping the plow into the soil, I head out across the field. I look down at the gauges and gearshift, squeeze the cold steel of the steering wheel, and admire the power at my disposal. Finally, I look back to view the results. Instead of the ramrod straight line I was expecting, I see what looks like a slithering snake, with more bends and curves than the Indianapolis Motor Speedway.

I knew better. "Plow with your eye on the fence post straight ahead," I'd been told. By staying focused on a fixed point across the field, a person plowing is assured of a straight line. On the return I complied, with telling results: The line was straight. The row was messed up only when I didn't have a focus point.

Paul had similar wisdom when he wrote of having his focus on Jesus Christ and the impact it had on him. Not only did he ignore distractions (Philippians 3:8, 13), but he set the focus (vv. 8, 14), noted the result (vv. 9–11), and observed the pattern it set for others (vv. 16–17).

Like Paul, if we focus on Christ, we will plow a straight path and accomplish God's purpose in our lives.   —RK

> *Lord, help us keep our eyes on you*
> *And focused on the task*
> *Of bringing glory to your name*
> *By doing what you ask.* —Sper

When you keep your eyes on Christ, everything will come into focus.

What a Great Neighborhood

READ: Romans 14:13–19

For the kingdom of God is not eating and drinking, but righteousness and peace and joy in the Holy Spirit. —ROMANS 14:17

Where you live has a way of making certain demands on how you live. In my neighborhood, the garbage collector comes on Tuesday mornings, so it's my responsibility to get our garbage can out to the curb the night before. Letting the trash pile up on the curb for days before doesn't make for happy neighbors. And we have lots of children playing outside, so signs are posted everywhere reminding drivers to slow down. That means I drive slowly and watch for little ones who, without looking, chase wayward balls into the street.

It's important to remember that God has placed us into "the kingdom of the Son" (Colossians 1:13). Living in His neighborhood means there are life-transforming behavior patterns that should clearly reflect our spiritual location. This is why Paul reminds us that God's kingdom is not about arguing and bickering over earthly stuff but about "righteousness and peace and joy" (Romans 14:17). Living by God's right standards, living to be a peacemaker, and living to be a source of joy in our relationships are what kingdom life is all about. And when we live like this, our lives please God and bless others (v. 18).

Sounds like the kind of neighborhood anyone would love to live in!

—JS

The world gets a glimpse of God
When those who claim to be
The followers of Jesus Christ
Are living righteously. —Sper

If you're part of the kingdom of God, it will make a difference in how you live.

Waiting

READ: Luke 2:22–38

Blessed are all those who wait for Him. —Isaiah 30:18

Autumn is hunting season here in Michigan. For a few weeks every year, licensed hunters are allowed to go out into the woods and hunt for various species of wildlife. Some hunters build elaborate tree stands high above the ground where they sit quietly for hours waiting for a deer to wander within rifle range.

When I think of hunters who are so patient when it comes to waiting for deer, I think of how impatient we can be when we have to wait for God. We often equate "wait" with "waste." If we're waiting for something (or someone), we think we are doing nothing, which, in an accomplishment-crazed culture, seems like a waste of time.

But waiting serves many purposes. In particular, it proves our faith. Those whose faith is weak are often the first to give up waiting, while those with the strongest faith are willing to wait indefinitely.

When we read the Christmas story in Luke 2, we learn of two people who proved their faith by their willingness to wait. Simeon and Anna waited long, but their time wasn't wasted; it put them in a place where they could witness the coming of Messiah (vv. 22–38).

Not receiving an immediate answer to prayer is no reason to give up faith. —JAL

Not ours to know the reason why
Unanswered is our prayer,
But ours to wait for God's own time
To lift the cross we bear. —Anonymous

Waiting for God is never a waste of time.

It's All About Him

READ: John 3:22–36

He must increase, but I must decrease. —JOHN 3:30

When Sheri got engaged, her single friend Amy celebrated with her. She planned a bridal shower, helped pick out her wedding dress, walked down the aisle just before her, and stood by her side during the ceremony. When Sheri and her husband had children, Amy gave baby showers and rejoiced in her friend's blessings.

Sheri told Amy later, "You've comforted me during hard times, but the way I especially know you love me is that you rejoice with me in my good times. You haven't let any jealousy hold you back from celebrating with me."

When John's disciples heard that a new rabbi named Jesus was gaining followers, they thought John might be jealous (John 3:26). They came to him and said, "He is baptizing, and all are coming to Him!" But John celebrated Jesus' ministry. He said, "I have been sent before Him . . . The friend of the bridegroom, who stands and hears him, rejoices greatly because of the bridegroom's voice. Therefore this joy of mine is fulfilled" (vv. 28–29).

An attitude of humility should also characterize us. Rather than desiring attention for ourselves, everything we do should bring glory to our Savior. "He must increase, but I must decrease" (v. 30).　　—AC

> *Not I but Christ be honored, loved, exalted;*
> *Not I but Christ be seen, be known, be heard;*
> *Not I but Christ in every look and action;*
> *Not I but Christ in every thought and word.* —Whiddington

If we want an increase of Christ, there must be a decrease of self.

True Security

READ: Romans 8:31–39

In all these things we are more than conquerors through Him who loved us. —ROMANS 8:37

During the Cold War—a period of unrest between major world powers in the last half of the twentieth century—Americans lived under the threat of nuclear war. I recall that during the 1962 Cuban Missile Crisis we seemed to be a heartbeat away from annihilation. It was heady stuff for a sixth-grader.

One of my strangest memories of those turbulent times was the school safety drill. An alarm would sound, and we would hide under our desks—for protection from atomic bombs. Looking back, I realize this may have given us a false sense of security. I'm certain hiding under our desks wouldn't have saved us in the event of a nuclear holocaust.

In our world today there are still many dangers that scare us—and some of them are spiritual. Ephesians 6:12 reminds us that our battles are "against principalities, against powers, against the rulers of the darkness of this age, against spiritual hosts of wickedness in the heavenly places." These are mighty foes indeed, but God has given us His protective love (Romans 8:35, 38–39) and the spiritual resources of His armor (Ephesians 6:13–17).

The result? While we face powerful enemies, "we are more than conquerors through Him who loved us" (Romans 8:37). In our heavenly Father, we have true security. —BC

Though danger lurks on every side,
In Christ our Lord we will abide;
Our God is strong, our hope is sure—
In Him alone we are secure! —Fitzhugh

Safety is not found in the absence of danger but in the presence of God.

The Road to Blessing

READ: Exodus 15:22–27

So [Moses] cried out to the Lord, and the Lord showed him a tree.
—EXODUS 15:25

Robyn and Steve have a counseling ministry that provides very little income. Recently a family crisis forced them to embark on a 5,000-mile round trip in their well-used minivan. After attending to the crisis, they started back to Michigan. While about 2,000 miles from home, their van began to sputter and stall. A mechanic looked at it and told them, "It's done. You need a new engine."

Unable to afford one, they had no choice but to coax the van home. Three days, a case of oil, and a lot of prayers later, they miraculously limped into their driveway. Then they heard of a "car missionary" who assisted people in ministry. Amazed that the van had made it, he offered to replace the engine free of charge. If Steve had gotten the van fixed en route, it would have cost him thousands of dollars he didn't have.

When the Israelites fled from Egypt, they were led by God into the desert. Three days into their journey, they ran out of water. But God knew about the problem. In fact, a solution awaited them in Marah and Elim (Exodus 15:25, 27). God not only solved their water problem but also provided a place to rest.

Even when our situation looks difficult, we can trust that God is leading. He already knows what we'll need when we get there.   —DB

> *I know not by what methods rare*
> *The Lord provides for me;*
> *I only know that all my needs*
> *He meets so graciously. —Adams*

Facing an impossibility gives us the opportunity to trust God.

Be Who You Are

READ: 1 Peter 3:8–17

Even if you should suffer for righteousness' sake, you are blessed.
—1 PETER 3:14

While awaiting a routine medical procedure in a local hospital, I noticed a wall plaque showing Christ on a cross. Later, a nurse asked me several administrative questions, including, "Do you have any spiritual needs you'd like to discuss with a chaplain?" I said that I appreciated her asking that question, which I found unusual in today's world. She replied with a smile that they are a faith-based hospital and "that's part of our mission." I was impressed that the people were not afraid to be who they are in an increasingly secular and pluralistic society.

Peter urged the first-century believers who had been scattered by persecution and were living in a hostile world to consider it a blessing to suffer for the sake of what is right. "But even if you suffer for doing what is right, God will reward you for it. So don't worry or be afraid of their threats. Instead, you must worship Christ as Lord of your life. And if someone asks about your Christian hope, always be ready to explain it" (1 Peter 3:14–15 NLT).

Just as the woman at the hospital freely stated their faith, so we can express ours. And if we are criticized or treated unfairly because of our belief in Christ, we should respond with gentleness and respect. We should never be afraid to be who we are in Him.   —DM

> *Whenever people judge and say*
> *They don't like what we believe,*
> *We need to show a Christlike grace—*
> *Then our Lord they might receive. —Branon*

It's better to suffer for the cause of Christ than for the cause of Christ to suffer.

Grieving from A to Z

READ: Lamentations 3:25–33

Though He causes grief, yet He will show compassion.
—LAMENTATIONS 3:32

Jerusalem was engulfed in flames, and the prophet Jeremiah wept. His prediction of divine judgment had largely gone unheeded. Now his terrible prophecy had come to pass with horrifying vividness. The short book of Lamentations records the prophet's grieving process over the destruction of Jerusalem.

Jeremiah organized the book around the twenty-two letters of the Hebrew alphabet, using a technique of alphabetic acrostics to aid the reader in memorizing the passages more easily. But using this technique also shows that he didn't cut short his grieving process. He took deliberate and intentional time to reflect upon and even to write down his heartbreak. You might say he was learning to grieve from A to Z.

In the midst of his grief, the comfort of God surfaced. Reminders of God's sovereignty and goodness gave the prophet hope as he faced the future: "The Lord will not cast off forever. Though He causes grief, yet He will show compassion according to the multitude of His mercies" (Lamentations 3:31–32).

If you've recently experienced a painful loss, remember to take adequate time to grieve and to reflect upon God's goodness. Then you will be able to experience His comfort and hope for the future.   —DF

> *To experience God's comfort*
> *While you're suffering with grief,*
> *Try to focus on God's goodness,*
> *And He'll bring your heart relief.* —Sper

God allows sorrows and tears today to open our hearts to the joys of tomorrow.

Baby Food

READ: Hebrews 5:12–6:2

Solid food belongs to those who are of full age, that is, those who by reason of use have their senses exercised to discern both good and evil. —HEBREWS 5:14

Have you ever tasted baby food? I have. It's terribly bland. But babies have no other choice without teeth. They certainly can't eat a nice, juicy steak!

Sadly, some Christians are content with spiritual baby food. They are happy to go over and over the simple truths of the Scriptures and don't move beyond the basics of the gospel (Hebrews 6:1–2). By not sinking their teeth into deeper truths and more difficult Bible passages, they lack biblical understanding and convictions to make right choices (5:13). They may have been Christians for many years, but their spiritual abilities remain underdeveloped. They remain babies.

As children grow physically, they learn to eat solid food that gives them strength and vitality. In the same way, believers need to take on the responsibility to feed themselves on solid spiritual food. To fail to do this is to remain spiritually weak and undernourished.

You can roughly tell the physical age of people by how they look. Their spiritual age is revealed by their ability to distinguish good from evil and by their personal character that's shown day by day.

Is this spiritual discernment evident in your life? Or are you still on spiritual baby food? —CPH

To handle the Word of truth
Takes diligence and care,
So make the time to study it
And then that truth declare. —Hess

Apply yourself to the Scriptures and the Scriptures to yourself.

Beware!

READ: 1 John 2:18–27

You have heard that the Antichrist is coming, even now many antichrists have come, by which we know that it is the last hour.
—1 JOHN 2:18

When Secret Service agents train bank tellers to identify counterfeit bills, they show them both fake money and real money, and they study both. To detect a counterfeit problem, they must look for the differences in the genuine bill compared to the counterfeit—and not the similarities.

In 1 John 2, the apostle John helps to protect believers from heresy by showing them examples of counterfeit Christians and teachers. One of the signs of the last days is the coming of antichrists (1 John 2:18). Antichrists are those who claim to have His power and authority but don't, or those who reject and oppose Him and His teachings.

John gave three marks of false teachers who are controlled by the spirit of the antichrists: They depart from the fellowship (v. 19), they deny Jesus as the Messiah (v. 22), and they draw the faithful away from Jesus (v. 26). He encouraged believers to protect themselves against the spirit of the antichrists by depending on the indwelling presence of the Spirit, knowing the truth, and remaining in fellowship with Jesus.

We can protect ourselves from error and deception by knowing the false but relying on the Truth—Jesus Christ.   —MW

Beware: The devil may add a few grains of truth to what is false.

A Companion on the Road

READ: Matthew 4:18–22

Jesus, walking by the Sea of Galilee, saw two brothers . . .
Then He said to them, "Follow Me." —MATTHEW 4:18-19

I love to walk Idaho's paths and trails and enjoy its grandeur and pictur-esque beauty. I'm often reminded that these treks are symbolic of our spiritual journey, for the Christian life is simply walking—with Jesus alongside as our companion and guide. He walked through the land of Israel from one end to the other, gathering disciples, saying to them, "Follow Me" (Matthew 4:19).

The journey is not always easy. Sometimes giving up seems easier than going on, but when things get difficult, we can rest awhile and renew our strength. In *Pilgrim's Progress*, John Bunyan describes the arbor on Hill Difficulty where Christian caught his breath before con-tinuing the climb. His scroll provided comfort, reminding him of the Lord's continual presence and sustaining power. He got a second wind so he could walk a few more miles.

Only God knows where the path will take us, but we have our Lord's assurance, "I am with you always" (Matthew 28:20). This is not a metaphor or other figure of speech. He is real company. There is not one hour without His presence, not one mile without His companion-ship. Knowing He's with us makes the journey lighter. —DR

When life becomes a heavy load
An upward climb, a winding road,
In daily tasks, Lord, let me see
That with me you will always be. —D. DeHaan

As you travel life's weary road, let Jesus lift your heavy load.

Becoming Bilingual

READ: Acts 17:19–31

In Him we live and move and have our being, as also some of your own poets have said, "For we are also His offspring." —ACTS 17:28

I s it possible—in a society that seems increasingly indifferent to the gospel—to communicate the good news to people who don't share our faith?

One way to connect with people who are unfamiliar with the things of Christ is to become "culturally bilingual." We do this by communicating in ways people can easily relate to. Knowing about and discussing music, film, sports, and television, for example, can offer just such an opportunity. If people hear us "speak their language," without endorsing or condoning the media or events we refer to, it could open the door to sharing the timeless message of Christ.

Paul gave us an example of this in Acts 17. While visiting the Areopagus in Athens, he spoke to a thoroughly secular culture by quoting pagan Greek poets as a point of reference for the spiritual values he sought to communicate. He said, "In Him we live and move and have our being, as also some of your own poets have said, 'For we are also His offspring'" (Acts 17:28). Just as Paul addressed that culture by knowing what they were reading, we may have greater impact for the gospel by relating it to people in terms they can readily embrace.

Are you trying to reach a neighbor or a coworker with the gospel? Try becoming bilingual. —BC

> To earn your neighbor's ear
> And prove you really care,
> Use terms he understands
> To show you are aware. —Branon

The content of the Bible must be brought into contact with the world.

When God Cleans House

READ: Jonah 1

*Let all bitterness, wrath, anger, clamor, and evil speaking
be put away from you, with all malice.* —EPHESIANS 4:31

God did some fall housecleaning this week. He sent a mighty wind through our neighborhood that made the trees tremble and shake loose their dead branches. When it finished, I had a mess to clean up.

In my own life, God sometimes works in a similar way. He will send or allow stormy circumstances that shake loose the "lifeless branches" I've been refusing to release. Sometimes it's something that once was good, like an area of ministry, but is no longer bearing fruit. More often it's something that's not good, like a bad habit I've slid into or a stubborn attitude that prevents new growth.

The Old Testament prophet Jonah discovered what can happen when one refuses to get rid of a stubborn attitude. His hatred for the Ninevites was stronger than his love for God, so God sent a great storm that landed Jonah in a giant fish (Jonah 1:4, 17). God preserved the reluctant prophet in that unlikely place and gave him a second chance to obey (2:10; 3:1–3).

The lifeless limbs in my yard caused me to think of attitudes that God expects me to dispose of. Paul's letter to the Ephesians lists some of them: bitterness, anger, and evil speech (4:31). When God shakes things up, we need to get rid of what He shakes loose. —JAL

*Lord, give me a listening heart and help me to cooperate
with you when you point out changes that need to be made
in my life. I want to honor you and please you.*

Christ's cleansing power can remove the most stubborn stain of sin.

A Family Trait

READ: Matthew 5:9, 38–48

Blessed are the peacemakers, for they shall be called sons of God. —MATTHEW 5:9

There's an old Sunday school song that periodically comes back to my mind. Its words testify to the blessing of the peace that Jesus so generously gives: "I have the peace that passes understanding down in my heart—down in my heart to stay!"

There is something missing in that well-intentioned song, however. The peace of God is truly a gift we enjoy in our hearts as we fellowship in His presence (John 14:27; 16:33). But He never intended for us to keep all of that peace to ourselves. Peace is a gift to be shared with those around us. As Christians, it should mark our relationships and characterize the environment of our churches.

In His Sermon on the Mount, Jesus said, "Blessed are the peacemakers" (Matthew 5:9), which indicates that we are to be intentional about bringing peace to our relationships. Since we are prone to be troublemakers instead of peacemakers, this is important advice. So, what does peacemaking look like? Peacemakers are those who turn the other cheek (v. 39), go the extra mile (v. 41), and love their enemies while praying for those who persecute them (v. 44).

Why should we do this? Because God is a peacemaker, and when we make peace, we are "called sons of God" (v. 9). Peacemaking is a family trait. —JS

Lord, thank you for the peace we have down in our hearts. And that we can be peacemakers with others through our attitude, words, and deeds. Help me to show your mercy and peace.

Because of the peace of God and peace with God, we can be peacemakers for God.

The Craftsman's Touch

READ: Exodus 31:1–5

We are His workmanship, created in Christ Jesus for good works. —EPHESIANS 2:10

I recently saw a documentary about the making of a Steinway piano. It traced the meticulous care that goes into crafting this fine instrument. From the cutting of trees until the piano appears on a showroom floor, it goes through countless delicate adjustments by skilled craftsmen. When the year-long process is complete, accomplished musicians play the piano and often comment on how the same rich sounds could never be produced by a computerized assembly line. The secret to the final product is the craftsman's touch.

God also values the craftsman's touch. When the tabernacle was built, He chose the craftsman Bezalel and said of him: "I have filled him with the Spirit of God, in wisdom, in understanding, in knowledge, and in all manner of workmanship, to design artistic works, to work in gold, in silver, in bronze, in cutting jewels for setting, in carving wood" (Exodus 31:3–5).

Today God dwells in the hearts of believers. Yet the call to craftsmanship has not ended. Now each individual believer is God's "workmanship" (Ephesians 2:10). The Master Craftsman is the Holy Spirit, who chips away at flaws in our character to make each of us like Jesus (Romans 8:28–29). And as we yield to His workmanship, we will find that the secret to the final product is the Craftsman's touch.   —DF

The Spirit is the Craftsman
Who makes us like the Son;
He'll mold and shape our being
Until His work is done. —Sper

The Father gave us the Spirit to make us like His Son.

Unexpressed Gratitude

READ: Psalm 107:31–43

*Give thanks to the Lord, for He is good! . . . Let
the redeemed of the Lord say so.* —PSALM 107:1–2

The whole reason for saying thanks is to let the giver of a gift know how much you appreciate something. Author G. B. Stern once said, "Silent gratitude isn't much use to anyone."

When our son was young, he sometimes needed to be reminded that avoiding eye contact, looking down at his feet, and mumbling some unintelligible words was not an acceptable "thank you." And after many years of marriage, my husband and I are still learning that it's important for us to continually express our gratitude to each other. When one of us feels appreciative, we try to verbalize it—even if we've said it many times before about the same thing. William Arthur Ward said, "Feeling gratitude and not expressing it is like wrapping a present and not giving it."

Showing our gratitude is obviously important in human relationships, but it's even more essential in our relationship with God. As we think about the many blessings we have received, do we express our thanks to Him throughout the day? And when we think of the amazing gift of His death and resurrection for forgiveness of our sins, do our hearts bubble over with awe and thanksgiving? (Romans 6:23; 2 Corinthians 9:15).

Take the reminder in Psalm 107:1 to heart each day: "Give thanks to the Lord, for He is good!" —CHK

> *How great should be our gratitude*
> *To God our unseen Friend!*
> *The volume of His gifts to us*
> *We cannot comprehend.* —Hess

God's highest Gift should awaken our deepest gratitude.

The World of More

READ: Romans 5:1–11

Eye has not seen . . . the things which God has prepared for those who love Him. —1 CORINTHIANS 2:9

My cable company sent a postcard inviting me to check out its latest improvements in TV channels. The card indicated that I needed to contact the company to get the necessary new digital equipment and explained how to hook it up and activate it. After that, the ad said, I was just to "sit back and enjoy the World of More."

The card made me think of the "World of More" that Christians are privileged to live in. When God transports people from the darkness of sin "into His marvelous light" (1 Peter 2:9), a whole new life opens up.

Romans 5 tells us some of the *more* that we have in Christ: We have been "reconciled to God through the death of His Son" (v. 10) and therefore have "peace with God through our Lord Jesus Christ" (v. 1). We have access to God and His grace (v. 2). Rejoicing in trouble is now possible because we understand that it's an opportunity to grow in our character through trusting Him (vv. 3–4). Additionally, the Holy Spirit, who has been given to live in us, pours the love of God into our hearts (v. 5). And sin no longer has the same hold on us (6:18).

As Christians, we have unlimited access to a real "World of More." Wouldn't it be selfish not to invite others to join us in that special world?
—AC

> The world seeks fulfillment in
> The pleasures they adore;
> But those who follow Jesus Christ
> Are given so much more. —Sper

Belonging to God brings boundless blessings.

Thanksgiving Pardon

READ: 1 John 1:1–10

The blood of Jesus Christ [God's] Son
*cleanses us from all sin. —*1 JOHN 1:7

Each year at the end of November, the President of the United States issues an official pardon for the National Thanksgiving Turkey. During this lighthearted ceremony, one president remarked: "Our guest of honor looks a little nervous. Nobody's told him yet that I'm going to give him a pardon." The poor turkey had a good reason to be uneasy—without an acquittal, he was doomed to be Thanksgiving dinner.

We are in a similar situation when it comes to our sin. Without God's pardon, we're on our way to certain demise. This condition is a direct result of our own wrongdoing. The Bible says, "The wages of sin is death" (Romans 6:23). However, we can be set free from this death sentence because God's Son bore our sin in His body on the cross, "that we, having died to sins, might live for righteousness—by whose stripes you were healed" (1 Peter 2:24). First John 1:7 tells us that Jesus' blood "cleanses us from all sin."

We can accept God's pardon for our sin and receive eternal life when we confess that Jesus Christ is Lord and believe that God raised Him from the dead (Romans 10:9). Today, consider how you will respond to God's offer of forgiveness. —JBS

Pardon for sin and a peace that endureth,
Thine own dear presence to cheer and to guide.
Strength for today and bright hope for tomorrow—
Blessings all mine, with ten thousand beside! —Chisholm

Through faith in Christ, we receive God's pardon and escape sin's penalty.

Finding Hope

READ: Psalm 42:1–11

Why are you cast down, O my soul? . . . Hope in
God, for I shall yet praise Him. —PSALM 42:5

A study conducted by researchers at the University of Minnesota found that almost 15 percent of American teenagers felt it was "highly likely" that they would die before their 35th birthday. Those with this pessimistic outlook were more likely to engage in reckless behavior. Dr. Iris Borowsky, author of the study published in *Pediatrics* magazine, said: "These youth may take risks because they feel hopeless and figure that not much is at stake."

No one is immune to feelings of despair. The Psalms express repeated pleas for help when life seems dark. "Why are you in despair, O my soul? And why have you become disturbed within me? Hope in God, for I shall again praise Him for the help of His presence" (Psalm 42:5 NASB). In a defiant step of faith, the psalmist tells himself not to forget about God, who will never forsake him.

Curtis Almquist has written: "Hope is fueled by the presence of God . . . [It] is also fueled by the future of God in our lives." We can say with the psalmist, "I shall yet praise Him" (v. 5).

No follower of Christ should feel reluctant to seek counsel for depression. Nor should we feel that faith and prayer are too simplistic to help. There is always hope in God!   —DM

> *My sheep I know, they are my own,*
> *I leave them not in trials alone;*
> *I will be with them to the end,*
> *Their Hope, their Joy, their dearest Friend.* —*Anonymous*

Hope for the Christian is a certainty because its basis is Christ.

Singing Bowl

READ: Deuteronomy 4:32–40

We therefore ought to . . . become fellow workers for the truth.
—3 JOHN 1:8

Artist and scientist Michael Flynn designed a singing bowl for display in ArtPrize, an international art competition held in Grand Rapids, Michigan. The bowl requires no electricity but it does require something that is in short supply: cooperation.

As I observed people trying to make the bowl sing, I was surprised that none of them bothered to read the directions about rocking it gently. Instead, impatient to make music, they kept trying their own ideas. After a few minutes they walked away frustrated and disappointed, as if the bowl was defective.

How many times, I wonder, do we become frustrated that life isn't working the way we think it should? We keep trying ways that seem right, but things keep turning out wrong. Instead of following God's Word, we continue trying to find our own way.

The singing bowl reminds us that we can't expect life to go well if we ignore the instructions of the Designer (Deuteronomy 4:40). Failing to obey divides us from one another and separates us from God. To fulfill His plan for the world and make the way of salvation known (Psalm 67:2), we need to follow His instructions about living and working peacefully together. When life doesn't go well, it may be that we've stopped following God's plan.   —JAL

Sure it takes a lot of courage to put things in God's hands,
To give ourselves completely, our lives, our hopes, our plans;
To follow where He leads us and make His will our own;
But all it takes is foolishness to go the way alone! —Kline

Life is a beautiful song that God is teaching us to sing.

Feeling Poor?

READ: Psalm 86

I am poor and needy. —PSALM 86:1

In one way or another, we can all relate to Psalm 86:1 where David says, "I am poor and needy." Even the richest among us should understand that poverty and need relate more to the spirit than to the wallet. When billionaire Rich DeVos speaks to groups, he often says, "I'm just a sinner saved by grace."

Psalm 86 tells us that the help God provides is not measured by a monetary ledger sheet. When we acknowledge that we are poor and needy, it's not so God will lavish material riches on us. No, we do so to open the door to other, more valuable treasures.

Here's what God does for the poor and needy. He will "preserve" our lives and "save" all those who trust in Him (v. 2). He will be "merciful" and "ready to forgive" (vv. 3, 5). He will listen to and answer prayer (vv. 6–7).

But we're not to take God's blessings without giving back. We have a responsibility to learn God's ways, walk in His truth, "fear [God's] name," praise the Lord, and "glorify [His] name" (vv. 11–12).

Do you consider yourself among the "poor and needy"? If so, welcome to the club. Let's not forget all the spiritual blessings God has for us and the godly response we should have toward His generosity.   —DB

We're thankful for the blessings, Lord,
You give us day by day;
Now help us show our gratitude
By walking in your way. —Sper

The poorest man is he whose only wealth is money.

Just Do What's Right

READ: Philippians 2:12–18

That you may become . . . children of God without fault in the midst of a crooked and perverse generation. —PHILIPPIANS 2:15

On a trip out of the country I happened to meet an attorney who was from my hometown in New Jersey. We were surprised at how much we had in common. In the course of the conversation, he asked, "Did you say your name was Stillwell?" I said, "No, it's Stowell." He then mentioned that he had a client named Stillwell. "Is it Art Stillwell?" I asked, and, to my surprise, he said yes. Art Stillwell attended my church and was an influential businessman in the community.

The attorney admitted that he had no client quite like Art. He explained that most of his clients want him to do whatever it takes to get them out of their problems, but Art was different. Whenever he asked Art what to do in any given situation, Art always replied, "Just do what's right!" Obviously it had made an impression on the attorney.

Yielding to Christ in all of our desires and decisions, regardless of the outcome, is what sets us apart in a world full of people consumed by their own interests. When we live blameless lives "without fault"— courageously reflecting the integrity, love, and grace of Jesus—we clearly "shine as lights in the world" (Philippians 2:15).

So, if you want to light up your world in a compelling way, just do what's right!　　　　　　　　　　　　　　　　　　　　　　　　—JS

Dim not, little candle,
Show Jesus through me!
Glow brightly till others
The Light clearly see! —Adams

Light up your world by reflecting the light of Jesus.

Honoring Your Parents

READ: Exodus 20:1–17

Honor your father and mother. —EPHESIANS 6:2

My dad recently turned ninety years old and his physical capabilities are fading. He can still move around with his walker, but he needs someone to cook his meals and help him with other tasks.

My older brother Steve and his wife Judy lived close to Dad, so they decided to move in with him to care for him. Wanting to help in some way, my wife and I flew across the country to help out a bit by watching Dad while my brother and his wife had some time away together. We enjoyed our time with my father and were glad to ease Steve and Judy's load, even if it was only for a few days.

The Bible says to "honor your father and mother" (Ephesians 6:2). One New Testament commentary says that to honor someone is to "treat him with the deference, respect, reverence, kindness, courtesy, and obedience which his station in life . . . demands."

For young children, this means obeying parents. For teenagers, it indicates showing respect for Mom and Dad, even if you think you know more than they do. For young adults, this means including your parents in your life. And for those in middle age and beyond, it means making sure that parents are cared for as they move into old age or their health declines.

How can you honor your parents this week? —DF

> *Don't miss the opportunity*
> *To honor and obey*
> *The parents God has given you—*
> *For they'll be gone someday.* —Sper

Honoring our parents has no age limit.

Actions and Results

READ: Romans 5:12–19

*If by the one man's offense many died, much more
the grace of God and the gift by the grace of the one Man,
Jesus Christ, abounded to many.* —ROMANS 5:15

On November 24, 1971, a man known today as D. B. Cooper hijacked a commercial flight between Portland and Seattle by threatening to blow up the plane unless he received $200,000. After landing to receive the ransom money, he ordered the plane back into the air. Then he lowered the rear stairs of the 727 aircraft and parachuted into the night. He was never captured, and the case is still unsolved. This act hastened the age of airport security in which trust and confidence have been replaced by suspicion and fear. What he did affected us all.

The Bible describes two actions that changed the world in a far more significant way. Through Adam's choice, sin and death entered the world, "and thus death spread to all men, because all sinned" (Romans 5:12). But through Christ's sacrifice on the cross, God provided a remedy for the results of sin. "Through one man's [Adam's] offense judgment came to all men, resulting in condemnation, even so through one Man's [Christ's] righteous act the free gift came to all men, resulting in justification of life" (v. 18).

Christ did what no one else could do when He broke the power of sin and death by His resurrection. He offers forgiveness and eternal life to all who will accept His gift. And for that we thank Him with all our hearts.   —DM

> *When Adam sinned, death spread to all—*
> *One act condemned the human race;*
> *But Jesus' death upon the cross*
> *Provides mankind God's saving grace.* —Sper

The cross of Christ can cure the condemnation of Adam's choice.

Advent Themes

READ: 1 Peter 1:3–5, 13–21

*Rest your hope fully upon the grace that is to be brought
to you at the revelation of Jesus Christ.* —1 PETER 1:13

I believe that all Scripture is related and all Scripture is relevant. Nevertheless, I was surprised when my November reading in the book of 1 Peter touched on all four themes of Advent—that period of time on the church calendar when many Christians prepare to celebrate the first coming of Christ while looking forward to His second coming. During Advent, we emphasize hope, peace, joy, and love, which God sent with Christ.

HOPE. We have an inheritance reserved in heaven, a living hope through the resurrection of Christ from the dead (1 Peter 1:3–5).

PEACE. We will love life and see good days if we turn from evil and do good and if we seek peace, for the Lord watches over the righteous and hears their prayers (3:10–12).

JOY. We have inexpressible joy even though we have trials because our faith is being tested and proven genuine. The end of this faith is the salvation of our souls (1:6–9).

LOVE. We can love one another with a pure heart because we have been born again through the Word of God which lives and abides forever (1:22–23).

Because Christ came the first time, we can live with hope, peace, joy, and love till He comes again. —JAL

*The hope we have in Jesus Christ
Brings joy into our heart;
And when we know the love of God,
His peace He will impart.* —Sper

**If you're looking for hope, peace, joy, and
love this Christmas season, look to God.**

Never Too Busy

READ: Psalm 145:8–21

The Lord is near to all who call upon Him, to
all who call upon Him in truth. —PSALM 145:18

College students rent a house from my sister and her husband. One night, a thief attempted to break in. When the young woman living there called the police to tell them that a break-in was in progress, the operator responded in an unusual way: "You'll have to call back in the morning. We're just too busy right now." That response was very disturbing! The young woman had done the right thing by calling the police, but for some reason her plea for help was disregarded. That kind of indifference is upsetting.

But indifference never happens when we go to God in prayer. We may not always feel that God is listening, but He is. He cares, and He will respond. The Bible reminds us that we can take comfort in the fact that our God is deeply concerned with what concerns our hearts: "The Lord is near to all who call upon Him, to all who call upon Him in truth" (Psalm 145:18). When we call out to Him, we will never get a disinterested response.

Rather than distancing himself from us when we cry to Him, our heavenly Father draws close to us in our time of need. He is never too busy for His child's prayers. He hears us when we call. —BC

For answered prayer we thank you, Lord,
We know you're always there
To hear us when we call on you;
We're grateful for your care. —Branon

You'll never get a busy signal on the prayer line to heaven.

Sandcastles

READ: Luke 12:22–34

Where your treasure is, there your heart will be also. —LUKE 12:34

When our kids were young, my wife Martie and I enjoyed family vacations in Florida visiting our parents. It was especially wonderful to be there in the warmth for a brief respite from the Michigan windchill factor. I couldn't wait to just relax on the beach with a good book.

But my kids had other ideas. They wanted my help building sandcastles. Reluctantly, I'd get up to help, only to be quickly consumed by the project. Before I knew it, I had spent hours creating an impressive castle—not thinking that it was only a matter of time until the tide would wash away all my hard work.

We often make the same mistake in life, spending lots of time and energy building our own little "castles" of stuff and basking in our accomplishments. It all may seem worthwhile, but in the end it's worthless.

In Luke 12, Jesus challenged His followers to sell their possessions and give to the poor, "For where your treasure is, there your heart will be also" (v. 34). In other words, the way we spend our time and resources says a lot about our eternal perspective. As the old hymn goes, "Only one life, 'twill soon be past; only what's done for Christ will last." So what have you done today that will last for eternity?   —JS

> *Who measures how we've done in life*
> *And judges our success?*
> *Our God, who gives rewards to those*
> *Who live in righteousness.* —Branon

God wants you to spend your time and treasure
building His kingdom, not your own.

Peace

READ: Colossians 1:19–29

You, who once were alienated . . . now He has reconciled. —COLOSSIANS 1:21

In the days of Adam and Eve, peace was lost. As soon as they ate the forbidden fruit and realized their nakedness, they started blaming each other and introduced conflict to God's peaceful planet (Genesis 3:12–13). Sadly, all of their descendants, including us, have followed their bad example. We blame others for our own bad choices and become angry when no one will accept the guilt. Blaming others for our unhappiness breaks apart families, churches, communities, and nations. We can't make peace because we're preoccupied with placing the blame.

Christmas is the season of peace. The Old Testament tells the story of how God set the stage to introduce the Prince of Peace (Isaiah 9:6). Jesus came to break the cycle of sin and blame by making peace for us with God "through the blood of His cross" (Colossians 1:20). Instead of blaming us for all the trouble we cause, He bore the blame for all of us. He is now recruiting followers who, having received His forgiveness, want others to receive it as well.

When we accept forgiveness from God, we lose our desire to withhold it from others. And when we live in peace with God, we are eager to make peace with others. We can both give and receive the gift of peace this Christmas. —JAL

At Christmastime we celebrate
The coming of the Prince of Peace;
Though now our world is locked in strife,
One day He'll make all conflict cease. —Sper

Jesus took our place to give us His peace.

Well-Loved

READ: 1 John 4:7–21

We love Him because He first loved us. —1 JOHN 4:19

A friend described his grandmother as one of the greatest influences in his life. Throughout his adult years he has kept her portrait next to his desk to remind him of her unconditional love. "I really do believe," he said, "that she helped me learn how to love."

Not everyone has had a similar taste of human love, but through Christ each of us can experience being well-loved by God. In 1 John 4 the word *love* occurs twenty-seven times, and God's love through Christ is cited as the source of our love for God and for others. "In this is love, not that we loved God, but that He loved us and sent His Son to be the propitiation for our sins" (v. 10). "We have known and believed the love that God has for us" (v. 16). "We love Him because He first loved us" (v. 19).

God's love is not a slowly dripping faucet or a well we must dig for ourselves. It is a rushing stream that flows from His heart into ours. Whatever our family background or experiences in life—whether we feel well-loved by others or not—we can know love. We can draw from the Lord's inexhaustible source to know His loving care for us, and we can pass it on to others.

In Christ our Savior we are well-loved. —DM

> *Loved with everlasting love,*
> *Led by grace that love to know—*
> *Spirit, breathing from above,*
> *Thou hast taught me it is so! —Robinson*

Nothing is more powerful than God's love.

Fret-Free Living

READ: Psalm 37:1–11

Do not fret—it only causes harm. —PSALM 37:8

Does it bother you to see how much attention is paid in today's culture to people who stand for all the wrong things? Perhaps it is entertainment stars who get the headlines while espousing immoral philosophies in their music, movies, or programs. Or it could be leaders who openly thumb their noses at right-living standards.

It would be easy to fret about this and wring our hands in despair, but Psalm 37 suggests a better way. Listen to David's wise advice: "Do not fret because of evildoers, nor be envious of the workers of iniquity" (v. 1).

While it is right to be "salt and light" (Matthew 5:13–14) in this tasteless, dark world—attempting to counter sin by reflecting Jesus' light wherever possible—we cannot let negative forces cause us to live in anger and wrath (Psalm 37:8). Instead, we must rely on God to have the ultimate say about evildoers: "They shall soon be cut down like the grass" (v. 2). Beyond that, we should take David's approach: (1) "Trust in the Lord, and do good." (2) "Feed on His faithfulness." (3) "Delight yourself also in the Lord." (4) "Commit your way to the Lord." (5) "Rest in the Lord" (vv. 3-7).

We may not like what we see and hear from some aspects of society, but remember this: God is in control. Trust Him to do what is right. And don't fret. —DB

> *When tragedy, heartache, and sorrow abound,*
> *When evil appears to have conquered the right,*
> *We center our heart on our Father's great love,*
> *For He will bring hope in the darkest of night.* —D. DeHaan

Don't despair because of evil; God will have the last word.

This Do in Remembrance

READ: 1 Corinthians 11:23–34

When [Jesus] had given thanks, He broke it and said, "Take, eat; this is My body which is broken for you." —1 CORINTHIANS 11:24

When a US Navy vessel arrives or departs from the military bases in Pearl Harbor, the crew of that ship lines up in dress uniform. They stand at attention at arm's length on the outer edges of the deck, in salute to the soldiers, sailors, and civilians who died on December 7, 1941. It is a stirring sight, and participants often list it among the most memorable moments of their military career.

Even for spectators on shore, the salute triggers an incredible emotional connection, but especially between the servants of today and the servants of yesterday. It grants nobility to the work of today's sailor, while giving dignity to the sacrifice of those from the past.

When Jesus instituted the Lord's Supper (Matthew 26:26–29), it was surely with an eye toward creating this same kind of emotional bond. Our participation in the Lord's Table honors His sacrifice while also granting us a connection to Him unlike any other act of remembrance.

Just as the Navy carefully prescribes the way it salutes the fallen, so too Scripture teaches us how to remember Jesus' sacrifice (1 Corinthians 11:26–28). These acts of reverence and thanksgiving serve to honor past action while giving purpose to present service. —RK

Read with fresh eyes the detailed instructions Scripture offers for the Lord's Supper in 1 Corinthians 11, and experience anew its power in your spiritual journey.

The Lord's Supper—Christ's memorial that He left for us.

Only a Sketch

READ: 1 Corinthians 13:8–12

Now we see in a mirror, dimly, but then face to face. Now I know in part, but then I shall know just as I also am known. —1 CORINTHIANS 13:12

In *The Weight of Glory*, C. S. Lewis tells the story of a woman who gave birth to a son while confined as a prisoner in a dungeon. Since the boy had never seen the outside world, his mother tried to describe it by making pencil drawings. Later when he and his mother were released from prison, the simple pencil sketches were replaced by the actual images of our beautiful world.

In a similar way, the inspired picture the Bible gives us of heaven will someday be replaced by joyful, direct experience. Paul understood that our perception of heaven is limited until one day in the future when we will be in Christ's presence. "Now we see in a mirror, dimly, but then face to face. Now I know in part, but then I shall know just as I also am known" (1 Corinthians 13:12). Yet Paul's confidence in future glory gave him strength in the midst of trial: "I consider that the sufferings of this present time are not worthy to be compared with the glory which shall be revealed in us" (Romans 8:18).

Our current idea of the glories of heaven is only a simple sketch. But we can be completely confident in Jesus' claim that He has gone to prepare a place for us (John 14:1–3). The best is yet to come!   —DF

Sometimes I grow homesick for heaven
And the glories I there shall behold;
What a joy that will be when my Savior I see
In that beautiful city of gold! —Anonymous

Now we see Jesus in the Bible, but one day we'll see Him face-to-face.

What Shall I Give You?

READ: 1 Kings 3:1–9

God said, "Ask! What shall I give you?" —1 KINGS 3:5

I've been told that "three-wish stories" occur in almost every culture, all following a similar theme: A benefactor appears and offers to grant three wishes to an unsuspecting beneficiary. The fact that the stories so often occur suggests we all want something we cannot get on our own.

There's even a "wish story" in the Bible. It happened one night when the Lord appeared to Solomon in a dream and said to him, "Ask! What shall I give you?" (1 Kings 3:5). Solomon could have asked for anything—riches, honor, fame, or power. But he asked for none of these things. He requested "an understanding heart" (v. 9), or a "hearing heart," a humble heart to listen and learn from God's Word. The young, inexperienced king, weighed down with the responsibilities of ruling a vast nation, needed the Lord's wisdom to govern well.

Am I that wise? If God spoke to me directly and asked what He could do for me, what would I ask for? Would I ask for health, wealth, youth, power, or prestige? Or would I ask for wisdom, holiness, and love? Would I be wise or foolish?

Suppose God asked you what He could give to you. What would you ask for? —DR

True wisdom is in leaning
On Jesus Christ, our Lord;
True wisdom is in trusting
His own life-giving Word. —Anonymous

God's wisdom is given to those who humbly ask Him for it.

Risky Business

READ: Matthew 1:18–25

Then Joseph . . . did as the angel of the
Lord commanded him. —MATTHEW 1:24

On some of the Christmas cards you will receive this year no doubt there will be a man standing in the background looking over the shoulder of Mary, who will be prominently displayed caring for the baby Jesus. His name is Joseph. And after the nativity narratives, he isn't heard from much again. If we didn't know better, we would think Joseph was an insignificant bystander or, at best, a mere necessity to undergird Jesus' claim to the throne of David.

But, in fact, the role that Joseph played was strategically important. If he had disobeyed the angel's command to take Mary as his wife (Matthew 1:20), he would have, from a human perspective, put the entire mission of Jesus at risk. Taking Mary as his wife was a risky assignment. Public perception that he was the baby's father put him in serious violation of Jewish law and made him a public disgrace. Yet today all of us are thankful that he was willing to risk his reputation to participate in and facilitate God's unfolding drama.

Most of us are insignificant compared to the major players in this world. But all of us are called to obey. Who knows what God has in store when we are willing to surrender to God's will—even when it puts us at risk! —JS

When we walk with the Lord in the light of His Word,
What a glory He sheds on our way!
While we do His good will, He abides with us still,
And with all who will trust and obey. —Sammis

It's no small thing to trust and obey.

Breathtaking

READ: Ecclesiastes 2:1–11

A man has nothing better under the sun than to eat, drink, and be merry; for this will remain with him in his labor all the days of his life. —ECCLESIASTES 8:15

Life is not measured by the number of breaths we take, but by the moments that take our breath away." I see that popular slogan everywhere, on everything from T-shirts to pieces of art. It's a catchy phrase, but I think it's misleading.

If we measure life by breathtaking moments, we miss the wonder of ordinary moments. Eating, sleeping, and breathing seem "ordinary" in that we do them every day, usually without much thought. But they are not ordinary at all. Every bite and every breath are miracles. In fact, having breath is more miraculous than anything that takes our breath away.

King Solomon may have had more breathtaking moments than anyone. He said, "I did not withhold my heart from any pleasure" (Ecclesiastes 2:10). But he expressed cynicism about it by saying, "All of it is meaningless" (v. 17 NIV).

Solomon's life reminds us that it's important to find joy in "ordinary" things, for they are indeed wonderful. Bigger is not always better. More is not always an improvement. Busier doesn't make us more important.

Rather than look for meaning in breathtaking moments, we should find meaning in every breath we take, and make every breath meaningful. —JAL

All that I want is in Jesus;
He satisfies, joy He supplies;
Life would be worthless without Him,
All things in Jesus I find. —Loes

Breathing is more miraculous than anything that takes our breath away.

A Growing Belligerence

READ: Philippians 4:4–9

If it is possible, as much as depends on you,
live peaceably with all men. —ROMANS 12:18

On a recent trip, the flight attendant asked if I flew very often. When I said I did, he asked, "Have you noticed people on planes becoming increasingly more belligerent and aggressive in recent months?" I said, yes, I had noticed that. We then began talking about what might be contributing to it—things like increased airport security, higher costs, fewer services, and a general dissatisfaction with travel. As if to prove the point, our conversation was interrupted by a passenger who refused to sit in his assigned seat because he liked someone else's seat assignment better!

When we encounter anger and belligerence, as followers of Christ we can be peacemakers. Paul wrote to the church at Rome with this challenge: "If it is possible, as much as depends on you, live peaceably with all men" (Romans 12:18). What does that mean? For one thing, it means that we must control what we can control. We can't control the attitudes of others, but we can control our response.

When we see angry or hostile attitudes displayed around us, we can show the heart of the Prince of Peace by responding graciously in a peaceful manner. In this way we will demonstrate the attitude of our Savior in a world filled with a growing belligerence.   —BC

Sometimes in a conversation
Words of anger can be heard;
If in peace we can defuse it,
We are living by God's Word. —Hess

The world needs a peace that passes all misunderstanding.

Free Pizza!

READ: John 6:25–41

*I am the bread which came down from heaven. —*JOHN 6:41

Money is tight when you're a college student. So when free food is available, students will show up anytime, anywhere. If a company wants to recruit new employees, it will entice young people on college campuses to come to a presentation by offering free pizza. Some students attend presentation after presentation—just for the pizza. The food in the present seems to be more important than the job for the future.

Jesus fed a crowd of five thousand, and the next day many searched for Him (John 6:10–11, 24–25). He challenged them: "You seek Me, not because you saw the signs, but because you ate of the loaves and were filled" (v. 26). It seems that, to some of the people, the food was more important than the everlasting life Jesus offered. He told them He was "the bread of God . . . who comes down from heaven and gives life to the world" (v. 33). Some didn't believe, wouldn't accept His teaching, and "walked with Him no more" (v. 66). They had wanted the food, but they didn't want Him and what would be required of them to follow Him.

Jesus calls us today to come to Him—not for the blessings from His hand but to receive the eternal life He offers and to follow Him, "the bread of God." —AC

> *Examining our motives*
> *For following the Lord*
> *Will show if we're authentically*
> *Believing in His Word. —Sper*

Only Christ the Living Bread can satisfy our spiritual hunger.

The Horse and Her Boy

READ: Colossians 3:12–17

[We are] strengthened with all might, according to His glorious power, for all patience. —COLOSSIANS 1:11

When I was about five years old, my father decided that I needed a horse of my own to care for. So he bought an old bay mare and brought her home to me. I named her Dixie.

Dixie was a formidable beast for me at my age and small stature. No saddle was small enough, no stirrups short enough for my legs, so I rode bareback most of the time.

Dixie was plump, which meant that my feet stuck straight out, making it difficult to stay astride. But whenever I fell off, Dixie would simply stop, look at me, and wait while I tried to climb on her back again. This leads me to Dixie's most admirable trait: She was wonderfully patient.

I, on the other hand, was less than patient with Dixie. Yet she bore my childish tantrums with stoic patience, never once retaliating. I wish I could be more like Dixie, having patience that overlooks a multitude of offenses. I have to ask myself, "How do I react when others aggravate me?" Do I respond with humility, meekness, and patience (Colossians 3:12)? Or with intolerance and indignation?

To overlook an offense. To forgive seventy times seven. To bear with human frailty and failure. To show mercy and kindness to those who exasperate us. To gain such control over our souls—this is the work of God.   —DR

God of grace and God of goodness,
Teach me to be ever kind,
Always gentle and forgiving
With the Savior first in mind. —Brandt

Love that is born at Calvary bears and forbears, gives and forgives.

A Supporting Role

READ: Romans 12:9–21

Be kindly affectionate to one another with brotherly love,
in honor giving preference to one another. —ROMANS 12:10

After the American TV personality Ed McMahon died in 2009, one newspaper headline read, "When it came to being the No. 2 man, he was No. 1." Best known for his thirty-year tenure as Johnny Carson's late-night sidekick, McMahon excelled at helping Carson succeed in the spotlight. While most entertainers strive for top billing, McMahon was content with a supporting role.

When the apostle Paul gave instructions about how to exercise our gifts as members of the body of Christ, he affirmed the value of supporting roles (Romans 12:3–8). He began by saying that we should have a realistic opinion of ourselves (v. 3), and he concluded with a call to genuine, unselfish love: "Be kindly affectionate to one another with brotherly love, in honor giving preference to one another" (v. 10). Or, as J. B. Phillips translates it, "a willingness to let the other man have the credit."

Our gifts and abilities come to us by God's grace and are to be used, by faith, in love and service for Christ—not for personal recognition (vv. 3, 6).

May God grant us the ability to embrace with enthusiasm the supporting roles to which He calls us. The ultimate goal is His glory and not our own. —DM

The church works best when we see ourselves
as participants, not as spectators.

Avoid the Husks

READ: Luke 15:11–24

He would gladly have filled his stomach with the pods that the swine ate. —LUKE 15:16

Ah, the life of a pig! Each new day brings nothing but slopping through the mud and snorting happily at mealtime. And what meals they have! Crunchy corn husks—or whatever leftovers get tossed into the pen.

Sound good? No? It probably didn't sound good to the prodigal son either.

Before he started eating with pigs, he had a warm bed, a rich inheritance, a loving father, a secure future—and probably good food. But it wasn't enough. He wanted "fun." He wanted to run his own life and do whatever he desired. It resulted in a pig's dinner.

Whenever a young person ignores the guidance of godly parents and the instruction of God's Word, similar results occur. It always shocks me when someone who professes to know Jesus chooses a life that rejects God's clear teaching. Whether the choices include sexual sin, addictive substances, a lack of ambition, or something else, any action that leaves God out risks ending badly.

If we ignore clear biblical morals and neglect our relationship with God, we can expect trouble. Luke tells us that the young man turned things around after he came to his senses (Luke 15:17). Keep your senses about you. Live for God by the guidance of His Word—unless you have a hankering for the husks. —DB

If sin were not deceitful, it wouldn't seem delightful.

Hope in Him

READ: Isaiah 53

*The virgin shall conceive and bear a Son, and
shall call His name Immanuel.* —ISAIAH 7:14

As we drove home from a Christmas party one evening, my family and I approached a small country church nestled between glittering snowbanks. From a distance, I could see its holiday display. Strings of white lights formed the capital letters: H-O-P-E. The sight of that word shining in the darkness reminded me that Jesus is, and always has been, the hope of humankind.

Before Jesus was born, people hoped for the Messiah—the One who would shoulder their sin and intercede with God on their behalf (Isaiah 53:12). They expected the Messiah to arrive through a virgin who would bear a son in Bethlehem and would name Him Immanuel, "God with us" (7:14). The night Jesus was born, their hope was fulfilled (Luke 2:1–14).

Although we're no longer waiting for Jesus in the form of an infant, He is still the source of our hope. We watch for His second coming (Matthew 24:30); we anticipate the heavenly home He is preparing for us (John 14:2); and we dream of living with Him in His celestial city (1 Thessalonians 4:16). As Christians, we can look forward to the future because the baby in the manger was, and still is, "the Lord Jesus Christ, our hope" (1 Timothy 1:1). —JBS

> *That night so many years ago*
> *Which brought the Savior's birth,*
> *Gave promise of a brighter hope:*
> *Good will—and peace on earth.* —Anonymous

The key word of Christmas is "Immanuel"—God with us!

Christmas Journey

READ: Luke 2:1–7; Galatians 4:4–5

*When the fullness of the time had come,
God sent forth His Son.* —GALATIANS 4:4

How far is it from Nazareth to Bethlehem? If you're in Pennsylvania, it's about nine miles and takes about ten minutes by car. But if you're in Nazareth of Galilee, it's about eighty miles to Bethlehem. And if you were traveling on foot, along with your pregnant wife, as Joseph was, that journey probably took about a week, and they didn't stay in a nice hotel when they got there. All Joseph could find was a stall in a stable, and that's where Mary delivered "her firstborn Son" (Luke 2:7).

But the journey for the infant Jesus was much farther than eighty miles. He left His place in heaven at God's right hand, came to earth, and accepted our humanity. Eventually, He was stretched out on a cross to die, and He was buried in a borrowed tomb. But the journey was not over. He conquered death, left the tomb, walked again among men, and ascended to heaven. Even that is not the journey's end. Someday He will return as King of Kings and Lord of Lords.

As you take a Christmas journey this month, reflect on the journey Jesus made for us. He came from heaven to earth to die for us, making salvation available through His death on the cross and His glorious resurrection.

Praise God for that first Christmas journey! —DE

*When God stepped out of heaven above
And came down to this earth,
He clothed himself in human flesh—
A child of lowly birth.* —D. DeHaan

Jesus came to earth for us so we could go to heaven with Him.

All Is Well

READ: Psalm 46:1–3

I will never leave you nor forsake you. —HEBREWS 13:5

Recently, my husband and I were reacquainted with a young man we had known as a child many years ago. We fondly reminisced about a Christmas program when Matthew had sung—in a perfect boy soprano—the song "All Is Well" by Wayne Kirkpatrick and Michael W. Smith. It was a wonderful memory of a song beautifully sung.

To hear the words of that song at Christmastime is comforting to many. But some people are unable to absorb the message because their lives are in turmoil. They've experienced the loss of a loved one, persistent unemployment, a serious illness, or depression that will not go away. Their hearts loudly cry out, "All is not well—not for me!"

But for those of us who celebrate the birth of our Savior —despite the dark night of the soul we may experience—all is well because of Christ. We are not alone in our pain. God is beside us and promises never to leave (Hebrews 13:5). He promises that His grace will be sufficient (2 Corinthians 12:9). He promises to supply all our needs (Philippians 4:19). And He promises us the amazing gift of eternal life (John 10:27–28).

As we review God's promises, we can agree with the poet John Greenleaf Whittier, who wrote, "Before me, even as behind, God is, and all is well."   —CHK

God's peace pillows the head when God's promises calm the heart.

Always on Duty

READ: Acts 20:22–32

Obey those who rule over you, and be submissive, for they watch out for your souls, as those who must give account. —HEBREWS 13:17

As my kids were discarding their trash at the local mall food court, my oldest son was almost run into by a man who was clearly on a mission. My younger son jokingly remarked, "Maybe he stole something." Thinking I might be able to use this as a teachable moment, I said, "That's what the Bible calls judging." He then asked with a smile: "Why are you always 'pastoring' me?" After I finished laughing, I told my sons that I could never take a vacation from shepherding them.

The apostle Paul told the Ephesian elders that they too could never take a vacation from shepherding God's people (Acts 20). He was convinced that false teachers would try to ravage the church (v. 29), and the elders needed to protect the group from them. Caring for God's people includes feeding them spiritually, leading them gently, and warning them firmly. Leaders in the church are to be motivated by the incalculable price Christ paid on the cross (v. 28).

Church leaders have a big responsibility to watch over our souls, for one day they will give an account to the Lord for their work among us. Let's bring them joy now by responding to their faithful, godly leadership with obedience and submission (Hebrews 13:17).   —MW

We join our hearts and hands together
Faithful to the Lord's command:
We hold each other to God's standards—
All that truth and love demand. —D. DeHaan

After we hear the Word of God, we should then take up the work of God.

Rejected Light

READ: John 12:35–46

*I have come as a light into the world, that whoever believes
in Me should not abide in darkness.* —JOHN 12:46

In the early hours of December 21, 2010, I witnessed an event that last occurred in 1638—a total lunar eclipse on the winter solstice. Slowly the shadow of the earth slipped across the bright full moon and made it appear a dark red. It was a remarkable and beautiful event. Yet it reminded me that while physical darkness is part of God's created design, spiritual darkness is not.

Scottish pastor Alexander MacLaren said: "Rejected light is the parent of the densest darkness, and the man who, having the light, does not trust it, piles around himself thick clouds of obscurity and gloom." Jesus described this self-imposed spiritual eclipse of heart and mind when He said, "If therefore the light that is in you is darkness, how great is that darkness!" (Matthew 6:23).

The great invitation of Christmas is to open our hearts to the Savior who came to end our darkness. Jesus said, "While you have the light, believe in the light, that you may become sons of light . . . I have come as a light into the world, that whoever believes in Me should not abide in darkness" (John 12:36, 46).

The way out of our spiritual night is to walk in the light with Him.
—DM

*Come to the Light, 'tis shining for thee,
Sweetly the Light has dawned upon me;
Once I was blind, but now I can see—
The Light of the world is Jesus.* —Bliss

When we walk in the Light, we won't stumble in the darkness.

Hidden Treasure

READ: Colossians 1:27–2:3

*In [Christ] are hidden all the treasures of
wisdom and knowledge.* —COLOSSIANS 2:3

A British treasure hunter discovered a huge stash of Roman coins buried in a field in southwest England. Using a metal detector, Dave Crisp located a large pot holding 52,000 coins. These ancient silver and bronze coins, which date from the third century AD and weigh more than 350 pounds, are valued at $5 million.

While Crisp's treasure may cause us to dream about somehow finding similar riches, we as Christians should be on a different kind of treasure hunt. What we seek does not consist of silver and gold. Our quest is to gather the precious gems of insight so that we might gain the "full assurance of understanding . . . both of the Father and of Christ, in whom are hidden all the treasures of wisdom and knowledge" (Colossians 2:2–3). The hidden treasure of knowing the Lord more completely is found in the Bible. The psalmist said, "I rejoice at Your Word as one who finds great treasure" (Psalm 119:162).

If we read the Word of God hurriedly or carelessly, we will miss its deep insights. These truths must be sought earnestly with all the attention of someone seeking hidden treasure.

Are you eager to find the treasures stored in Scripture? Start digging! —DF

*When reading God's Word, take special care,
To find the rich treasures hidden there;
Give thought to each line, each precept hear,
Then practice it well with godly fear.* —Anonymous

The treasures of truth in God's Word are
best mined with the spade of meditation.

The Pursuing God

READ: Galatians 4:1–7

God sent forth His Son, born of a woman . . . to redeem those who were under the law. —GALATIANS 4:4-5

Pastor Tim Keller of Redeemer Presbyterian Church in Manhattan rightly observes that Christianity is unique among all religions for it is about God's pursuit of us to draw us to himself. In every other religious system, people pursue their god, hoping that through good behavior, keeping of rituals, good works, or other efforts they will be accepted by the god they pursue.

The British poet Francis Thompson catches the profound nature of this reality when he writes of the relentless pursuit of God in his life. In his work titled "The Hound of Heaven," he writes that as he fled from God he couldn't outrun "those strong feet that followed . . . with unhurrying chase and unperturbed pace." But God's untiring pursuit of the wayward is not just Thompson's story. At the heart of the Christmas message is the wonderful truth of God's pursuit of every one of us. As Paul affirms, "God sent forth His Son, born of a woman, born under the law, to redeem those who were under the law" (Galatians 4:4–5).

And it's not just the Christmas story. It's the story of God's pursuit of Adam and Eve after the fall. His pursuit of me! His pursuit of you! Where would we be today if God weren't the "Hound of Heaven"?   —JS

Died He for me, who caused His pain?
For me, who Him to death pursued?
Amazing love! How can it be
That Thou, my God, shouldst die for me? —Wesley

God's undying desire for you will never cease.

Death Destroyed!

READ: 1 Corinthians 15:50–58

O Death, where is your sting? O Hades, where is your victory? —1 CORINTHIANS 15:55

Medical researchers are working tirelessly to find a cure for cancer, a clue to the mystery of Alzheimer's, and ways to conquer a host of other debilitating diseases. But what if you awoke to headlines saying DEATH DESTROYED! Would you believe it? Could you believe it?

The New Testament proclaims that for the believer in Christ, death has been destroyed—reduced to inactivity—rendered incapable of doing what it once did. "So when this corruptible has put on incorruption, and this mortal has put on immortality, then shall be brought to pass the saying that is written: 'Death is swallowed up in victory'" (1 Corinthians 15:54).

This good news is for everyone who will receive it, just as the angel told the shepherds when Jesus was born, "Do not be afraid, for behold, I bring you good tidings of great joy which will be to all people. For there is born to you this day in the city of David a Savior, who is Christ the Lord" (Luke 2:10–11).

The birth of Jesus was the beginning of the end for death. "The sting of death is sin, and the strength of sin is the law. But thanks be to God, who gives us the victory through our Lord Jesus Christ" (1 Corinthians 15:56–57).

That is why we celebrate Christmas! —DM

Mild He lays His glory by,
Born that man no more may die.
Born to raise the sons of earth,
Born to give them second birth. —Wesley

The birth of Christ brought God to man;
the cross of Christ brings man to God.

Now Is the Time

READ: Luke 2:8–20

Glory to God in the highest! —LUKE 2:14

During our church's Christmas celebration, I watched the choir members assemble in front of the congregation while the music director rifled through papers on a slim black stand. The instruments began, and the singers launched into a well-known song that started with these words: "Come, now is the time to worship."

Although I had expected to hear a time-honored Christmas carol, I smiled at the appropriate choice of music. Earlier that week I had been reading Luke's account of Jesus' birth, and I noticed that the first Christmas lacked our modern-day parties, gifts, and feasting—but it did include worship.

After the angel announced Jesus' birth to some wide-eyed shepherds, a chorus of angels began "praising God and saying: 'Glory to God in the highest!'" (Luke 2:13–14). The shepherds responded by running to Bethlehem where they found the newborn King lying in a barnyard bassinet. They returned to their fields "glorifying and praising God for all the things that they had heard and seen" (v. 20). Coming face-to-face with the Son inspired the shepherds to worship the Father.

Today, consider your response to Jesus' arrival on earth. Is there room for worship in your heart on this day that celebrates His birth?　　—JBS

> *Grant us, Father, hearts of worship*
> *At this time of Jesus' birth;*
> *We would see anew His glory*
> *Shine throughout this sin-cursed earth.* —D. DeHaan

Heaven's choir came down to sing when heaven's King came down to save.

Wrong Worship

READ: Acts 19:23–41

This trade of ours [is] in danger of falling into disrepute. —ACTS 19:27

If you really want to get folks upset, threaten their economy. A bad economic picture gets politicians voted out of office, and the threat of a downturn nearly got the apostle Paul kicked out of Ephesus.

Here's what happened. Paul came to town and started "reasoning and persuading concerning . . . the kingdom of God" (Acts 19:8). For more than two years he shared the gospel, and many began following Jesus. Because Paul was so successful in getting people to see that there is only one true God, many Ephesians stopped worshiping the goddess Diana. This was bad news for the local silversmiths, who made their living creating and selling Diana statuettes. If enough people stopped believing in her, business would dry up. A commotion and an uproar broke out when the craftsmen figured this out.

This Ephesus incident can remind us to evaluate our reasons for worshiping God. The silversmiths wanted to protect their worship as a way of protecting their prosperity, but may that never be said of us. Don't ever let your worship of God become an avenue to good fortune.

We worship God because of His love for us and because of who He is, not because loving Him can help our bottom line. Let's worship God the right way. —DB

We worship God for who He is,
And not because of what we'll get;
When we acknowledge what we owe,
We'll thank Him that He paid our debt. —Sper

Don't worship God to gain His benefits—you already have them.

Grace-Filled Waiting

READ: 2 Corinthians 4:7–18

We do not lose heart. —2 CORINTHIANS 4:16

Roger lost his job due to the company being downsized. For months he searched, applied for jobs, prayed, asked others to pray, and trusted God. Roger and his wife Jerrie's emotions fluctuated though. They saw God provide for them in unexpected ways and experienced His grace, but sometimes they worried that a job would never come. For fifteen long months they waited.

Then Roger had three interviews with a company, and a week later the employment agency called and said, "Have you heard the saying, 'Sometimes clouds have a silver lining'? Well, you've got the job!"

Jerrie told me later, "We wouldn't trade this hard experience for anything. It brought us closer together and closer to the Lord." Friends who had prayed rejoiced and gave thanks to God.

Paul wanted the Corinthian church to see the grace of God at work in his life, which could cause "thanksgiving to abound to the glory of God" (2 Corinthians 4:15). His trials were so severe that he was "hard pressed on every side," "perplexed," "persecuted," and "struck down" (vv. 8–9). Yet he encouraged the people not to lose heart in troubles (v. 16) but to trust God.

During our difficulties we can be drawn nearer to God and others, as Roger and Jerrie experienced, and praise will go to the Lord for His grace. —AC

Thank the Lord when trouble comes,
His love and grace expressing;
Grateful praise releases faith,
Turns trials into blessing. —Egner

There's no better time to praise God than right now.

Choices and Consequences

READ: Galatians 6:1–10

Do not be deceived, God is not mocked; for whatever a
man sows, that he will also reap. —GALATIANS 6:7

In the International Slavery Museum in Liverpool, England, the devastation of generations of enslaved men, women, and children is remembered. The price innocent people have paid for the greed of others is horrific—but theirs is not the only cost. Engraved in a wall of the museum is a profound observation made by Frederick Douglass, former slave and crusader for human rights, which reads, "No man can put a chain about the ankle of his fellow man without at last finding the other end fastened about his own neck." In the act of dehumanizing others, we dehumanize ourselves.

The apostle Paul put it another way when he wrote, "Do not be deceived, God is not mocked; for whatever a man sows, that he will also reap" (Galatians 6:7). Paul's words form a stark reminder to us that our choices have consequences—and that includes how we choose to treat others. When we choose to hate, that hate can return to us in the form of terrible consequences—we can find ourselves alienated from others, angry with ourselves, and hamstrung in our ability to serve Christ effectively.

Instead, let's choose "not [to] grow weary while doing good, for in due season we shall reap . . . As we have opportunity, let us do good to all" (vv. 9–10). —BC

Sowing seeds of greed and hatred
Reaps corruption, loss, and pain;
But if we sow love and kindness,
We will reap eternal gain. —Sper

The seeds we sow today determine the kind of fruit we'll reap tomorrow.

Yet I Will Rejoice

READ: Habakkuk 3:11—19

*Yet I will rejoice in the Lord, I will joy in
the God of my salvation.* —HABAKKUK 3:18

Life can be difficult. At some point, most of us have wondered, *Where is God in my trouble?* And we may have thought, *It seems like injustice is winning and God is silent.* But we have a choice as to how we respond to our troubles. The prophet Habakkuk had an attitude worth following: He made the choice to rejoice.

Habakkuk saw the rapid increase in Judah's moral and spiritual failings, and this disturbed him deeply. But God's response troubled him even more. God would use the wicked nation of Babylon to punish Judah. Habakkuk did not fully understand this, but he could rejoice because he had learned to rely on the wisdom, justice, and sovereignty of God. He concluded his book with a wonderful affirmation: "Yet I will rejoice in the Lord, I will joy in the God of my salvation" (3:18). Though it was not clear how Judah would survive, Habakkuk had learned to trust God amid injustice, suffering, and loss. He would live by his faith in God alone. With this kind of faith came joy in God, despite the circumstances surrounding him.

We too can rejoice in our trials, have sure-footed confidence in God, and live on the heights of His sovereignty.   —MW

*Be this the purpose of my soul
My solemn, my determined choice:
To yield to God's supreme control,
And in my every trial rejoice. —Anonymous*

Praising God in our trials turns burdens into blessings.

Playing Your Part

READ: Romans 12:1–8

*We have many members in one body, but all the members
do not have the same function.* —ROMANS 12:4

For the past several years, my daughter Rosie has been the director of drama at a local middle school. Students come to audition, and a few are selected to play the lead roles. But there are still many other important supporting roles that must be cast—roles that are vital to the production.

There are other young people who want to be a part of the show but don't relish being in the spotlight. They are the ones who will change scenery, open and close the curtains, run the lights, and assist with makeup and costume changes. Then there are the parents from the community who provide pizza and cookies for rehearsals, donate goods, build sets, sew costumes, make signs, and hand out programs.

The successful performances are the culmination of an intense 4- to 5-month process that is dependent on the hard work of a wide range of dedicated volunteers.

Similarly, for the body of Christ to function fully, each of us must play a part. Every believer is uniquely gifted for service. When these gifts are combined in a cooperative relationship, "every part does its share" (Ephesians 4:16), and the separate parts make up the whole (Romans 12:5).

We need each other. What part are you playing in the life of the church? —CHK

> *For the church to function fully,*
> *We must all fulfill our role;*
> *While the Spirit's gifts are many,*
> *They combine to serve the whole.* —Sper

For a church to be healthy, its members must exercise their spiritual gifts.

Reflections

READ: Psalm 40:1–5

He also brought me up out of a horrible pit . . .
and set my feet upon a rock. —PSALM 40:2

Not long ago I passed a milestone marking twenty years since I began keeping a spiritual journal. As I reread my first few entries, I was amazed I ever kept it up. But now you couldn't pay me to stop!

Here are some benefits I have received from journaling: From life experiences, I see that progress and failure are both part of the journey. I'm reminded of God's grace when I read how He helped me to find a solution to a major problem. I gain insight from past struggles that help with issues I am currently facing. And, most important, journaling shows me how God has been faithfully working in my life.

Many of the psalms are like a spiritual journal. They often record how God has helped in times of testing. In Psalm 40, David writes: "I waited patiently for the Lord; and He inclined to me, and heard my cry. He also brought me up out of a horrible pit, out of the miry clay, and set my feet upon a rock, and established my steps" (vv. 1–2). Later, David needed only to read that psalm to be reminded of God's faithful deliverance.

Journaling may be useful to you too. It can help you see more clearly what God is teaching you on life's journey and cause you to reflect on God's faithfulness. —DF

To begin a journal: Record your struggles, reflect on
a verse that is especially comforting or challenging,
or write a prayer of thankfulness for God's faithfulness.

Reflecting on God's faithfulness in the past brings hope for the future.

Acknowledgments

February 5: Lines by Haldor Lillenas, © Renewal 1945, Haldor Lillenas. Assigned to Hope Publishing. Used by permission.

July 21: Lines by Avis B. Christiansen, © Renewal 1965. Assigned to Singspiration. Used by permission.

October 22: Lines by Virgil P. Brock, © Renewal 1964, The Rodeheaver Company.

October 23: Lines from the hymn "The Lord My Shepherd Guards Me Well," words by Carl P. Daw, Jr., © 1990 Hope Publishing Company, Carol Stream, Illinois. All rights reserved. Used by permission.

November 24: Lines from Thomas O. Chisholm, © Renewal 1951, Hope Publishing. Used by permission.

Contributors

DB – Dave Branon

AC – Anne Cetas

BC – Bill Crowder

DD – Dennis DeHaan

MD – Mart DeHaan

DE – Dave Egner

DF – Dennis Fisher

CPH – C. P. Hia

CHK – Cindy Hess Kasper

RK – Randy Kilgore

AL – Albert Lee

JAL – Julie Ackerman Link

DM – David McCasland

DR – David Roper

JBS – Jennifer Benson Schuldt

JS – Joe Stowell

JY – Joanie Yoder

MW – Marvin Williams